East Asian
Security
in the
Post-Co

East Asian Security in the Post-Cold War Era

Sheldon W. Simon, Editor

Paul H.B. Godwin
Paul Marantz
Edward A. Olsen
Robert A. Scalapino
William T. Tow
William S. Turley
Donald E. Weatherbee
Donald S. Zagoria

Copyright © 1993 by M. E. Sharpe, Inc.
80 Business Park Drive, Armonk, New York 10504

Library of Congress Cataloging-in-Publication Data

East Asian security in the post–Cold War era / edited by Sheldon W. Simon.
p. cm.
Based on papers from a March 1991 conference held at the
Monterey Institute of International Studies.
Includes bibliographical references and index.
ISBN 1-56324-058-0 (cloth). — ISBN 1-56324-238-9 (pbk.)
1. East Asia—National security—Congresses.
I. Simon, Sheldon W., 1937– .
UA832.5.E37 1993
355′.03′095—dc20
92-43961
CIP

Printed in the United States of America
The paper used in this publication meets the minimum
requirements of American National Standard for
Information Sciences—Permanence of Paper for
Printed Library Materials, ANSI Z 39.48-1084.

∞

MV   10 9 8 7 6 5 4 3 2 1

Contents

About the Contributors

PAUL H.B. GODWIN is professor of international affairs at the National War College, Washington, D.C., where he specializes in Chinese security policy. He has written extensively on the Chinese military and, in 1987, was a visiting professor at the Chinese People's Liberation Army National Defense University in Beijing.

PAUL MARANTZ is associate professor of political science at the University of British Columbia. He is the author or editor of three books on Soviet and Middle Eastern politics and a specialist in both Soviet foreign policy and foreign policy theory. Professor Marantz has been a National Fellow at the Hoover Institution.

EDWARD A. OLSEN is professor of national security affairs and Asian studies at the Naval Postgraduate School in Monterey. He is the author or editor of eleven books and monographs and numerous scholarly and newspaper articles on East Asian security with a particular emphasis on Japan and Korea. He began his career as an East Asia specialist in the U.S. Department of State.

ROBERT A. SCALAPINO is Robson Research Professor of Government Emeritus and former director of the Institute of East Asian Studies at the University of California, Berkeley. Frequently known as the "Dean of East Asian politics" in the United States, he is also an editor of *Asian Survey,* perhaps the best known scholarly monthly journal on Asian affairs. Author of countless books and articles, Professor Scalapino is equally well known on both sides of the Pacific.

SHELDON W. SIMON is professor of political science at Arizona State University. In 1991 he held the Gordon Paul Smith Visiting Chair at the Monterey Institute of International Studies. A specialist on Asian security, Professor Simon is author or editor of six books and seventy scholarly articles and book chapters, a member of the Advisory Board of The Asia Society, and a vice-president of the International Studies Association.

WILLIAM T. TOW is senior lecturer at the University of Queensland, Australia, and a specialist on East Asian security as well as NATO. He has written extensively on military issues in both areas of the world. In 1991 three of his books were published: one on NATO, one dealing with regional security organizations, and the third on extended deterrence in Asia.

WILLIAM S. TURLEY is professor of political science at Southern Illinois University, Carbondale. One of America's leading analysts on Vietnam, Professor Turley has published widely on both domestic and foreign affairs of that country as well as on its army and communist party. He has held visiting posts in both Thailand and Singapore.

DONALD E. WEATHERBEE is the Donald E. Russell Professor of Contemporary Foreign Policy at the University of South Carolina and a well-known specialist on both the domestic and international politics of Southeast Asia. A frequent visitor to the region, he has held visiting posts in several of the ASEAN countries. A member of the editorial board of several journals on Asian affairs as well as a member of both the Pacific Forum and Asia Society Councils, he publishes extensively on Southeast Asia in both scholarly journals and his own books.

DONALD S. ZAGORIA is professor of political science at Hunter College and a research professor at both the Graduate College of the City University of New York and Columbia University. One of the country's best known scholars on Sino-Soviet affairs, Professor Zagoria also writes extensively on the international politics of the Asian region. He is a member of numerous editorial boards of scholarly journals and is on the boards of the Council of Foreign Relations and the Asia Society, among other foreign policy organizations.

Preface and Acknowledgments

This volume emerged from a March 1991 conference cosponsored by the International Policy Studies Division of the Monterey Institute of International Studies and the Academic Research Support Program of the Defense Intelligence College. The Monterey gathering brought together some of North America's leading academic specialists on East Asian international politics and asked them to examine the region's future security prospects in light of the Cold War's end. Among the issues addressed in *East Asian Security in the Post–Cold War Era* are changes in Asian alignments of the post–World War II period attendant upon the removal of the Cold War overlay from the region; the growing prominence of important regional actors less dependent on great power mentors; opportunities for the great powers to establish new relations with yesterday's adversaries; and finally, prospects for the peaceful resolution of such Cold War legacies as the division of Korea, Japan's territorial dispute with the former Soviet Union, tensions between the ASEAN states and Indochina, and China's new security posture as it balances the need for foreign investment with more traditional great power aspirations in East Asia. All of the chapters were rewritten in 1992 to take into account the Soviet Union's demise, movement toward a new *modus vivendi* in Korea as well as the future of nuclear weapons on the peninsula, the prospect of peace in Cambodia, and rapprochement between Indochina and ASEAN.

Several individuals at both the Monterey Institute and the Defense Intelligence College deserve expressions of appreciation for financing and arranging the Monterey event. They include Robert Gard, Glynn Wood, and Steven Baker, respectively president, provost of MIIS, and dean of International Policy Studies. Their unstinting support for both the conference and book project was instrumental in its successful completion. From the Defense Intelligence College, special thanks is extended to Robert Slater, director of Academic Research Support, and his associate Steve Dorr for both financial support and planning assistance. The Monterey conference was the first in a set of such meetings planned by the Defense Intelligence College with civilian academic institutions.

Sheldon W. Simon
Summer 1992

East Asian Security in the Post-Cold War Era

Introduction

Sheldon W. Simon

The kaleidoscopic pace of global political change witnessed between the late 1980s and early 1990s has been somewhat blandly termed "the end of the Cold War." It is, indeed, the end of an era in international politics. In the Asian Pacific over the past forty years, virtually all conflicts incorporated an ideological overlay that placed the Soviets and Americans on opposite sides of a divided Korea, a divided Vietnam, a divided China, and in contention over the political orientation and socio-economic systems of the remainder of the region.

With the breakup of the Soviet Union and Russian abandonment of hegemonic aspirations in Asia, the security alignments of the post–World War II period seem increasingly irrelevant, and their costs—both political and financial—to great powers unjustified. Retrenchment by the latter has facilitated the emergence of Asian multipolarity and a broadening of the concept of security to include a larger economic dimension. Global military strategies are being decoupled from regional conflicts, and the old alignments are no longer assured. Although the United States as the remaining dominant great power believes it must stay an active Pacific player, it is still searching for a new role and justification. Russia, by contrast, appears to be in full retreat from previous alliances and forward deployments. As ascending powers, though on different dimensions, China and Japan also seek recognition and acceptance as regional players, while the two Koreas and the Indochinese and ASEAN groups concentrate on establishing their own autonomous subregional orders.

Explaining this volatile new environment is the task of this book. In addition to assessing how regional conflicts may evolve with diminished superpower participation, the authors also explore opportunities for tension reduction and, beyond that, reconciliation along the Asian-Pacific rim as the twenty-first century approaches.

* * *

This introduction reviews some of the major themes and debates developed by the authors in the following chapters. The review is designed to highlight the areas of both consensus and dissensus in expert assessments about the future of Pacific security.

Paul Marantz emphasizes the unpredictability of Russia's future. As Moscow turns inward, focusing on political and economic survival, Marantz sees the Russian leadership virtually abandoning Moscow's Vietnamese and North Korean allies, which have become economic albatrosses, and turning instead to South Korea, Japan, and other Asian capital surplus states in search of financial and technological assistance.

Conflicts between the Russian Federation and the former Soviet Central Asian Republics may occur over the role of Islam. And the Russian far eastern Sakhalin *oblast* staunchly opposes any effort by Moscow to return the southern Kurile Islands to Japan—a precondition for substantial financial assistance from Tokyo for Russian economic development.

Professor Marantz also believes that even though the Soviet military remains a powerful conservative political force in domestic politics, it is improbable that the armed forces will push a militaristic foreign policy. Not only was the Afghan intervention unpopular both inside the military and among the general population, but any new military action could strain the economy to the point of collapse. Russian support for the UN coalition during the 1991 Iraq war demonstrated that above all, the USSR would do nothing to jeopardize Western aid.

Therefore, Professor Marantz argues that the post-Soviet leadership is interested in moderating and resolving Asian conflicts in Korea and Cambodia and in reducing the expensive naval confrontation that developed over the past two decades in the western Pacific.

The American position in Asia since the Second Indochina War provided a military umbrella over noncommunist states, permitting them to focus on economic development and the control of domestic insurgencies. Because external challengers have withdrawn and economic growth has dramatically reduced internal threats, the United States is also bent on reducing its western Pacific military presence. Yet no other power is poised to take America's place. Instead, Donald Zagoria believes U.S. naval and air forces will remain in Asia, oriented less toward the old task of containing the former Soviet Union and more toward the role of balancer among a number of possible regional powers—akin to Great Britain in nineteenth-century Europe.

Unlike such analysts as Edward Olsen, Chalmers Johnson, Donald Hellman, Clyde Prestowitz, and James Fallows, who predict a falling-out between the United States and Japan over trade and investment concerns, Zagoria foresees a continued partnership, operating to promote political normalization in Korea and economic aid to vulnerable Southeast Asian states. While not at all sanguine about arms negotiations, Zagoria nevertheless avers that the great powers will reduce their military forces unilaterally as threats decline and budgets shrink. He warns, however, that a precipitous reduction in U.S. Asian deployments could have the paradoxical effect of encouraging a new arms race as Asian states act to provide for their own security following an American exit.

Sheldon Simon expects a general reduction in the size of Asian armed forces over the next decade even as their lethality increases. This will be particularly apparent in Southeast Asia as militaries shift from counterinsurgency concerns to higher-technology conventional capabilities designed to defend their own air and sea spaces. Simon agrees with Zagoria that an American military presence will generally remain welcome in this new environment, though nationalist sensitivities will prefer that this presence be located over the horizon rather than permanently based in the region. In effect, U.S. Pacific forces may develop limited access arrangements with several states, including Singapore, Malaysia, Thailand, Brunei, and the Philippines, while further reducing their permanent base deployments in Japan and Korea. Should the latter experience a *modus vivendi* between North and South, a complete American withdrawal is conceivable.

Professor Simon believes U.S. forces will remain in Japan, however, to reassure Asian neighbors that Tokyo will not be tempted to create an independent military capacity for controlling sea routes to the Persian Gulf. Simon also points out that possibilities exist for closer Japanese defense cooperation with the ASEAN states, not necessarily through joint exercises but rather by providing dual-use technological assistance for the creation of sophisticated command and control networks required in modern navies and air forces.

Professors Edward Olsen and William Tow agree that the most dangerous area in Asia is the highly militarized Korean peninsula where the end of the Cold War has had little impact on conflict resolution and none on arms reductions. The regimes on both sides of the 38th parallel spent the majority of the Cold War years having to please their superpower mentors. Yet, over time, each gained increasing autonomy over internal, if not, external policy. In the aftermath of the Vietnam War, Olsen argues that Seoul developed a more mature relationship with the United States, concluding that Washington had become a less reliable guarantor. The Republic of Korea (ROK) developed an ability to fend for itself politically and economically in the 1980s. By contrast, the North stagnated under the deadening influence of Kim Il-song's Stalinism. Despite internal political turmoil in the South, the world saw the ROK as a vibrant stable society and the Democratic People's Republic of Korea (DPRK) as an isolate whose only international actions were support of terrorism and smuggling by North Korean diplomats.

Olsen states that the South has won the Cold War on the peninsula. Not only has Seoul become a major player in Asia's political economy but it has also become more important to its former adversaries—Russia and China—than their formal North Korean ally. In effect, North Korea has now become truly isolated. The combination of the ROK's economic success, Soviet and Chinese pressure on the DPRK to open its economy to the international market, and apprehension about the German model prevailing in Korea have resulted in some tantalizing changes in North Korean policy in the early 1990s. These include dual membership in the United Nations and the prospect of diplomatic recognition by both Japan and the United States, a development that could open foreign aid prospects to the North from capitalist states for the first time since 1945. As for the ROK, Olsen foresees it becoming a major aid donor and investor in the 1990s for Eastern Europe, Southeast Asia, the Middle East, and perhaps even its northern counterpart.

President Bush's October 1991 decision unilaterally to remove land- and sea-based tactical nuclear warheads from U.S. forces worldwide may have profound effects on the Korean peninsula. Because North Korea has insisted that it would only permit international inspection of its nuclear power facilities in the context of a peninsulawide agreement, the new American policy has removed the major stumbling block to a denuclearized Korea. By mid-1992, the two Koreas seemed to be moving toward a nuclear inspection arrangement for the peninsula that would permit each side to examine suspected facilities of the other on a challenge basis. If such a regime is created, the path is open for North Korean diplomatic relations with both the United States and Japan, which, in turn, could open western coffers for economic aid to the virtually bankrupt DPRK.

Tow foresees a significant military issue in the 1990s centering on how the two Koreas would respond to fewer American ground forces on the peninsula as well as a reduction in American air and naval forces in the northwest Pacific. This would be a particularly sensitive development if it were accompanied by a growing Japanese military capability. Professor Olsen emphasizes Korean-Japanese mutual suspicions in concluding that bilateral security cooperation is improbable. Tow, on the other hand, believes that Tokyo still sees the ROK as a buffer against potentially hostile continental forces, though he agrees with Olsen that the ROK would not want Japanese protection as a substitute for the Americans.

Professor Tow sees the challenge to the United States to be one of finessing economic tensions with the ROK while simultaneously removing American ground forces from the peninsula. By the end of the decade, he sees a self-sufficient ROK army protecting the South with American naval and air forces performing essentially a backup role. Growing anti-American sentiment in the South could accelerate the U.S. withdrawal. But a combination of the ROK's own military strength and its economic prowess should prove to be a sufficient deterrent to the North as the 1990s progress.

Professors Paul Godwin and Robert Scalapino address the remarkable changes that have occurred in the Sino-Russian relationship and assess the effects of the current rapprochement on regional security. They note that the strategic triangle (China–Russia–United States) for the first time since World War II is characterized by mutual cordiality. In the aftermath of Desert Storm, Godwin comments that PRC analysts display some concern that the United States is now the only superpower and may use that status to try to undermine communism within China. In defending Chinese Communist Party internal hardline policies, these analysts believe the United States is attempting to lead China into the same political revisionism that resulted in the USSR's demise.

Godwin credits astute Chinese diplomacy for Gorbachev's policy shifts in the 1980s, leading to rapprochement. These included Soviet withdrawal from Afghanistan, reduction of forces along the Sino-Soviet border, and pressure on Vietnam to remove its military from Cambodia. Particularly significant was Gorbachev's agreement to withdraw larger numbers from their common border region than he required from China's People's Liberation Army, acknowledging the Red Army's offensive potential and the PLA's defensive posture.

The PRC seeks to resolve the festering conflicts on its peripheries with Russia, Indochina, and India, since they all interfere with long-term modernization plans requiring a peaceful environment. Nevertheless, Beijing fears that too complete a détente could alter the balance of power in East Asia by accelerating an American exit, thus leaving Japan as the dominant political and economic power on the Pacific rim. Therefore, Godwin argues, the PRC opposes any total American military withdrawal and supports the continuation of the Japan–United States security relationship.

Overall, Professor Godwin predicts the 1990s will see China in a conciliatory mood, willing to resolve the Cambodian conflict through international conciliation and even prepared to postpone sovereignty claims in the South China Sea in order to effect a joint development arrangement among the claimants to the Spratly Islands. Because China no longer perceives itself to be surrounded by Soviet-linked adversaries, regional problems can be addressed on their own merits rather than as elements in a global struggle.

Professor Scalapino explains first Brezhnev's and then Gorbachev's decisions to seek better relations with China in the 1980s as recognition that earlier policies had left the USSR friendless among the dynamic Asian states, with communist allies who served only to drain their resources.

While Sino-Soviet rapprochement led to political relaxation, Scalapino underlines the inherent limits in the new relationship, which are primarily economic. Neither country has the capital or technology needed by the other for modernization. Both are essentially competitors alongside other Third World states and Eastern Europe for Western capital and technology.

Concurring with Godwin, Scalapino foresees China and Russia drifting apart politically if the hardliners remain in power in Beijing and the reformers succeed in Moscow. Scalapino argues, moreover, that even if a hardline regime emerged in the former USSR, Sino-Russian relations could be jeopardized. A conservative neonationalist Russian leadership might attempt to reassert itself as an Asian power, raising old Chinese apprehensions.

The preceding concerns notwithstanding, the Gorbachev–Yeltsin military policies are welcomed by the PRC. The reduction of forces along the border, reduced Pacific Fleet exercises, and the impending withdrawal from Vietnam's Cam Ranh Bay all portend a greatly reduced military presence in China's vicinity and thus the end for the old encirclement policy. Although China and Russia will not become allies again—no common enemy—they benefit from détente, mutual trade, and reduced regional tension.

While Korea remains the most dangerous potential flashpoint in East Asia, the region's most intractable continuous hot war is found in Southeast Asia: the Cambodian war, which entered its thirteenth year in 1991. As William Turley avers, the Cambodian war was not directed by Vietnam against ASEAN. Rather, its two main protagonists have been Vietnam and China in a struggle over hegemony in Indochina. For Hanoi, security has always meant friendly governments in Laos and Cambodia. For China, similarly, border regions such as Indochina must not be governed by hostile regimes, particularly if they are aligned with even more powerful adversaries. Hanoi's security relationship with the Soviet Union, sealed by a 1978 treaty, ensured that the PRC and SRV would be on opposite sides in determining Cambodia's future. China's support for the Khmer Rouge, then, was not an endorsement of that pariah regime, but based rather on the calculation that it was the only credible opponent of Vietnamese hegemony.

The Cambodian stalemate of the early 1990s, according to Turley, reflects both Hanoi's and its Phnom Penh client's fear that any UN-administered interim arrangement prior to elections would undermine the Cambodian government's position and permit the Khmer Rouge a legitimate role in a successor regime from which it could launch a politico-military campaign to regain control of the country. Nevertheless, the Socialist Republic of Vietnam believes that, in time, it can build new ties to ASEAN based on economic development needs and even improve its relations with China since the Russian alliance is virtually moot. Moreover, Professor Turley holds, support for the contending sides during the 1980s was deeply entwined with the Asian dimension of the Cold War. The Cambodian war cemented the Sino-U.S. relationship, aligned ASEAN with China, bled Vietnam, and provided both the PRC and the Soviet Union with access to Southeast Asia.

In the 1990s, that array of alignments has unraveled. Even Beijing has agreed through the United Nations Perm Five peace plan that the Khmer Rouge should not become the dominant political element in a postwar Cambodia. By late 1991, a major political breakthrough occurred through which China and Vietnam pressured their respective Cambodian clients to accept the Perm Five plan. The four Cambodian factions established separate offices in Phnom Penh and agreed to a United Nations military and administrative presence as a prelude to national elections tentatively scheduled for 1993. The agreement, hammered out with the aid of Thailand, Indonesia, and France, also provides for each Cambodian contender to demobilize 70 percent of its armed forces and locate the remaining 30 percent in separate cantonments under UN supervision, although this provision has been abandoned.

Meanwhile, Turley sees Hanoi transcending the Cambodian impasse. Vietnam is seeking aid and technology to replace the drastic reduction in Soviet assistance that began in 1991, when the USSR cut its transfers to the SRV from approximately $U.S. 1 billion annually to $U.S. 110 million. Hanoi has even raised the prospect of Western navies using Cam Ranh Bay on a fee basis.

Donald Weatherbee is optimistic about prospects for a rapprochement between Indochina and ASEAN in the 1990s. Both parties agree that the Khmer Rouge should be excluded from power in Cambodia, and both accept some role in a successor regime for all other Cambodian factions. Hanoi's exit from Cambodia, Weatherbee believes, has permitted ASEAN to make political peace with Vietnam, thus finally closing the Southeast Asian chapter of the Cold War.

Vietnam's economic reconstruction will also restore an important buffer against PRC ambitions in Southeast Asia and remove the rationale for any continuation of a Sino-Thai alliance. Thailand's new commercial orientation toward Indochina has presaged these trends, although Bangkok must take care that its plans to exploit Indochinese natural resources do not generate a whole new set of resentments.

For Indochina, normalization with ASEAN opens the door to investment from Japan, Europe, and ultimately the United States. Weatherbee does not foresee any integration of Indochina into a greater ASEAN. Rather, he believes that the Indochinese governments will attempt to maintain communist regimes while liberalizing their economies. Linking capitalist and socialist systems into a greater ASEAN does not seem feasible.

Projecting to the end of the decade, Weatherbee believes that ASEAN could well become obsolete. Future economic and security ties among the six members may be reconstituted at a subregional level with maritime and mainland divisions. In the wider Asian setting, he sees Southeast Asia becoming more integrated into a larger Pacific enterprise such as the Asia–Pacific Economic Cooperation forum (APEC). Weatherbee concludes that ASEAN faces a new series of challenges that could erode its fragile security consensus once the Cambodian war is settled. These include differences between mainland and insular members, overlapping maritime exclusive economic zones (EEZs), the Spratly Islands, and the future presence of the United States as an external guarantor.

In sum, while the Cold War era in Asian politics has ended, the millennium has not yet arrived. New maritime conflicts inherent in exclusive economic zones' claims over islands and seabed resources, and potential new subregional political arrangements all portend the continuation of security dilemmas in Asia's future.

1

Regional Security Structures in Asia: The Question of Relevance*

Sheldon W. Simon

Introduction

During the Cold War era, U.S. alliance goals in Asia were straightforward: to create a series of primarily bilateral security agreements that would serve as a *cordon sanitaire* around the Soviet Union and People's Republic of China as well as their allies in North Korea and Indochina. It was hoped that these alliances would deter any expansionist designs on the parts of Moscow, Beijing, Pyongyang, and Hanoi. When deterrence failed, the United States fought its only protracted wars since 1945 in Korea and Vietnam with mixed results for Washington's future alliance commitments. The Nixon Doctrine (1969), formulated to cope with the disappointments and trauma of the Second Indochina War (1965–75), underlay America's Asian strategy through the 1980s. Briefly, it promised military aid to friendly and allied states to assist in the creation of their own capacities to defend against potential communist aggressors; but it no longer guaranteed direct U.S. military involvement in the event of hostilities. Both the decision to go to war and its prosecution became the responsibility of Asian leaders, not American.

The single-minded focus on anticommunism from the 1950s well into the 1980s created other problems for U.S. foreign policy. In order to construct the largest possible coalition against the USSR and its clients, Washington fre-

* This chapter first appeared in Gary Guertner, ed., *Collective Security in Europe and Asia* (Carlisle Barracks: Strategic Studies Institute, 1992).

quently subordinated and sometimes ignored other policy values such as human rights and democratic development. Repressive and habitually corrupt regimes were supported from Korea through Southeast Asia as long as they professed anticommunism. Additionally, the United States subsidized the early industrialization of its Asian allies' economies by providing preferential access for their products in the American market and permitting protectionism against U.S. goods and services in Asian markets. These policies encouraged U.S., Japanese, and European multinational corporations to establish export industries throughout East Asia whose primary consumers were in the United States. Indeed, during the 1980s, exports to the United States generated by these MNCs contributed substantially to the current U.S. balance-of-payments deficit. In short, America's Asian allies have also become important economic competitors, complicating the security relationships that have been established over the past thirty to forty years. In addition to military capabilities and intentions, then, security arrangements for the 1990s must take economic linkages into account. The key issue for U.S. strategic planners dealing with Asia will be whether alliances and economic rivalry can coexist. In other words, can U.S. political leaders continue to underwrite the defense of states for whom that subsidization enhances commercial competitiveness?

Throughout the twentieth century, U.S. interests in East Asia have been remarkably consistent through two world wars as well as the Cold War. As a trading nation, the United States has sought stability, opposition to hegemony by any regional power, and political and economic access for all to the region's goods and services. Since the end of the Second Indochina War, the United States has pursued these goals through a balance-of-power policy, endorsing the China–ASEAN Cambodian resistance coalition against a USSR–Vietnam backed rival; bolstering South Korea against North Korea; urging increased military spending and more regional defense responsibilities upon Tokyo; fostering ASEAN's development; and offsetting Soviet naval activities by maintaining forward deployed U.S. forces along the western Pacific littoral.[1]

By the 1990s, however, the underlying rationale for this strategy was unraveling. The Soviet Union had disintegrated. China was focusing inward on its own economic development and political stability. The ASEAN states and Vietnam were moving toward a new rapprochement as the latter abandoned its plan for Indochina hegemony and agreed to a United Nations Perm Five plan for resolution of the protracted Cambodian imbroglio; and the two Koreas finally seemed to agree on a program of peaceful coexistence, possibly leading to some form of confederation by the end of the century. In effect, the Cold War had ended with what appears to be a major Western triumph.

However, the dismantling of one international political structure does not mean the cessation of international politics. On the contrary, the transition through which the world now moves is potentially more unstable than its Cold War predecessor. Clear lines between old allies and enemies fade as the former become commercial competitors and the latter new trade, aid, and investment partners.

The reduced East Asian military threat environment has been acknowledged by the Defense Department's April 1990 East Asia Strategy Initiative (EASI). While claiming to sustain all previous alliance commitments to Japan, the ROK, Thailand, the Philippines, and Australia, the Defense Department (DoD) announced a 10 percent personnel cut of the 143,000 forward deployed U.S. forces in East Asia by 1993. Two subsequent phased reductions would draw down U.S. forces in the western Pacific to less than 100,000.

EASI logically follows the end of the Cold War and U.S. budgetary constraints. However, it also introduces new uncertainties into East Asian security considerations. First and foremost is the possible dissolution of the U.S.–Japan alliance, no longer buttressed by a common Soviet threat. This prospect is particularly unnerving to other Asian states, which fear that Japan will increase its own air and naval deployments to compensate for the loss of U.S. protection for its trade routes. The addition of a dominant Japanese military presence to its imposing regional economic position as major aid and investment partner could recreate the old "Greater East Asia Coprosperity Sphere" so prized by Japanese planners during the Pacific War (1937–45).

To assuage these concerns, Assistant Secretary of State Richard Solomon has insisted that the United States will maintain alliance commitments and that even reduced U.S. forces are sufficient to help sustain stability in a less threatening international environment. Moreover, since the number of American military personnel in East Asia constitutes such a small portion of the total U.S. defense budget, it will not be further reduced.[2]

Tokyo is particularly concerned that its bilateral security ties with the United States remain a prominent regional security emblem despite (or perhaps partly because of) severe economic frictions. Japan remains virtually the only noncommunist Asian state that still sees Russia as a security threat. While the formidable former Soviet Pacific fleet and air force are stationed in the Sea of Okhotskh and northern Sea of Japan, these forces no longer present an imminent threat of invasion. Indeed, they apparently lack resources for even normal exercises. Rather, Japan's emphasis on a continued threat from the north may best be understood as a means of sustaining the U.S. alliance. That alliance still serves as the linchpin in Japan's foreign policy. It reassures the rest of Asia that Japan's commercial dominance will not also expand into political and military hegemony. The U.S. alliance legitimates Japan's foreign economic policy for it ensures that Japan will remain an incomplete superpower.[3]

The end of superpower confrontation has removed a layer of antagonism from other Asian regional disputes that has facilitated their resolution—this time with major power cooperation. The Perm Five plan for Cambodia's future and prospects for détente between the two Koreas could not have transpired without the concurrence of the United States, the former Soviet Union, and China. Vietnam's desire for rapprochement with the PRC and its plans for some kind of association with ASEAN also emerged after Soviet abandonment. China, meanwhile, had completed its new relationship with the ASEAN states in 1990–91 when diplomatic relations were established with Brunei, Indonesia, and Singapore. The common element in all these political changes is the search for prosperity through trade, aid, and investment rather than political and military dominance.

While the United States insists on retaining a western Pacific military presence, which, in turn, is welcomed within the region, these forward deployed forces will increasingly depend on part-time access arrangements in Southeast Asia and direct financial payments from Japan and the ROK in the north. Japanese and Korean subsidies for American forces in their countries permit the U.S. government to make the case to Congress that it costs less to maintain these forces forward deployed in the western Pacific than to repatriate them. (In 1992, Tokyo paid almost 50 percent—$3.5 billion—of the maintenance costs of U.S. forces in Japan. By 1995, Japan will cover 75 percent.)

Through the early 1990s, Washington has rebuffed Australian, Canadian, and Soviet proposals for new Asian security institutions that would replace the bilateral alliances of the Cold War era. U.S. officials have argued that differing security challenges in Northeast and Southeast Asia do not lend themselves to regionwide resolution. Proven bilateral mechanisms should continue to be used to meet specific challenges. Underlying these agreements are Japanese and American concerns that multilateral arrangements will accelerate the departure of U.S. forces from the region.[4] Nevertheless, if Washington follows its EASI timetable, by the end of the decade there may be no more than 60,000 U.S. troops in East Asia. Indigenous regional arrangements may then become a necessity.

The Northeast Asian Security Environment

A volatile mix is brewing in Northeast Asia's security future. The combination of U.S. trade frictions with Japan and South Korea and increased demands for burden sharing, growing ROK anti-American sentiment, and the collapse of the Soviet threat all portend a breakdown in the parallel bilateral security arrangements of the past forty years. Tokyo and Seoul have relied exclusively on the United States for their defense, though not on each other. Although South Korea and Japan both feared expansionist communist neighbors, each felt almost equal antipathy toward the other, going back to Japan's brutal occupation of Korea from 1905 to 1945. If the United States were to disengage militarily from the western Pacific, Korean-Japanese relations might well deteriorate as the former foresaw the latter's hegemony. Indeed, the prospect of a militarily ascendant Japan might conceivably lead to a PRC-Korean mainland coalition to balance Japan's maritime position. The point of these ruminations is to demonstrate that there is no consensus on a revamped security network for the region because there is no commonly perceived threat. Although the United States remains generally welcome—particularly if it foots most of the bill for its own presence—it is unlikely that the region's members are willing to go much beyond their current level of financial contributions to maintain U.S. forces. At some point, using those resources to build their own defense capacities may become more cost-effective, especially since regional defense decisions in a post–Cold War setting will be made locally rather than by a global power.

Despite regional anxieties over a dominant Japanese military role sometime in the future, there is little evidence to suggest that Japanese political leaders are moving in that direction. An expansionist policy requires the ability to seize and maintain control of territory on, over, and under the sea, more than 1,000 nautical miles from Japan for an extended period. The Japanese Self Defense Forces (JSDF) would also have to transport a significant military force, undertake an opposed landing, and support that force during subsequent action and occupation. In fact, the JSDF is not equipped for any of these tasks. Nor are there plans to build or acquire the equipment to effect them.

Rather, aircraft acquisition plans for the 1990s are designed to enhance Japan's capability for successfully fulfilling its 1980s commitment: to defend the sea and air lanes within 1,000 nm of the home islands. New fighters (FSX), AEW, and ASW aircraft, as well as tankers for inflight refueling will all add to sea patrol and attack capabilities. Neither bombers nor fixed wing aircraft carriers nor amphibious forces are in Japan's future—all of which would be required for a power projection capability. The Japanese navy's mission continues to be sea lane protection in collaboration with the U.S. Seventh Fleet.[5]

U.S. forces in Japan, meanwhile, no longer serve to protect Japan from attack but rather as the primary location for America's forward deployment in the western Pacific, particularly with the closure of facilities in the Philippines. In the immediate future, these forces provide for contingencies that could grow out of turmoil in the Russian Far East or the possibility of war on the Korean peninsula. Yet, internal Japanese politics could accelerate the reduction of some of these forces. It is unlikely that 20,000 U.S. marines will remain much longer in Okinawa. A source of tension between Okinawa and Japan's main islands for years, the new governor of the Ryukyus has demanded for the first time an American withdrawal. If effected, a base would be eliminated from which the marines traveled to the Persian Gulf during Desert Storm.[6] Japanese officials more generally, however, continue to insist that the Japan–U.S. security arrangement is "the mainstay" of the relationship and "the anchor of peace and stability" in the Asia-Pacific region.[7]

To demonstrate its commitment to America's regional interests, Japan has also downplayed the prospect of an Asian economic grouping under Tokyo's auspices. After months of hesitation, Tokyo rejected Malaysia's offer of membership in a proposed East Asian Economic Group (EAEG) because it excluded the United States. By this action, Japan demonstrated its continued willingness to subordinate its relations with other Asian countries to its predominant U.S. ties.

As Chief Cabinet Secretary Koichi Kato explained, the United States should not be excluded from any regionwide economic arrangement because of its important regional security role.[8] In effect, America's role as a security guarantor should entitle it to participate in any Asian economic group it desires.

Nor has Japan displayed any interest in incorporating Soviet successor authorities into a new regional security regime. Russian president Boris Yeltsin has been no more forthcoming on the southern Kurile Islands' return than was President Gorbachev. Undoubtedly constrained by the negative views toward reversion of Sakhalin *oblast* officials who include the Kuriles within their jurisdiction, Yeltsin has devised a complex, drawn out, five-stage negotiating plan. The pace of its implementation may depend on how much aid Japan is prepared to provide Russia. Even if some agreement can be reached on the islands' return, the future of some 30,000 Russian residents would also have to be resolved.[9]

Assuming Russian continuation of Soviet East Asian policy, Moscow will probably persevere in suggesting Asian collective security accords along the lines of the Conference on Security and Cooperation in Europe (CSCE). A regionwide gathering of states, including Russia, would reassert the latter's legitimacy as an Asian actor and serve as a forum to bring pressure on both the United States and Japan for a new understanding on the deployments of naval and air assets around Russia's Asian coast.[10] An understanding that could lead to a reduction of U.S. and Japanese ASW deployments in the northern Sea of Japan would, in turn, permit Russia to continue to lower its military budget and deployments while ensuring the safety of its reduced SSBN second strike capability in the Sea of Okhotsk.

As the former Soviet Union recedes from the position of adversary, Japan–ROK relations may become more tense. Thomas Wilborn of the U.S. Army War College's Strategic Studies Institute found in recent interviews with PRC and South Korean defense intellectuals that Japan was now perceived as a potential new threat to their nations' security.[11] Seoul has gone so far as to identify Japan officially in the ROK 1991–92 National Defense White Paper as bent on developing offensive forces. While Tokyo has tried to reassure the Koreans that the JSDF possesses neither offensive capabilities nor intentions, the ROK, nevertheless, expressed concern over the prospect of Japanese forces participating in UN peace-keeping operations. The ROK Defense Ministry also claimed that by the end of the 1990s, Japan's defense capacity at its present rate of growth will exceed force levels necessary merely to defend the home islands.[12]

The Korean Peninsula as a Nexus for Northeast Asian Security

The security concerns of the United States, China, Japan, and the former Soviet Union all converge on Korea's future. Moscow has virtually ceased military and economic aid to Pyongyang and since 1989 has been busily promoting economic and/or political ties with Seoul, Taipei, and the ASEAN states. While Russia has not yet articulated its own East Asia policy, one of Gorbachev's last major proposals for the region was delivered during his April 1991 visit to Japan. At that time, he suggested a five-power collective security system in Asia composed of the United States, the Soviet Union, China, Japan, and India—presumably to replace the bilateral treaty arrangements of the Cold War. Gorbachev offered an additional suggestion—the creation of a Northeast Asian economic development arrangement among the countries bordering the Sea of Japan that could marry Japanese and South Korean capital, management, and technology to North Korean and Chinese labor, and Russian industrial capabilities.[13] While the latter has elicited some interest from South Korea as a means of further committing Beijing and Moscow to Seoul's continued political progress, none of the other putative members has responded.

The arms control issue that has most concentrated the minds of those states adjacent to Korea has, of course, been the future of nuclear weapons on the peninsula. The threat of an autonomous North Korean nuclear weapon capability has been the focus of concern by Pyongyang's friends and foes alike.[14] The development of these facilities was accelerated in the last half of the 1980s, possibly because of a belief that neither the USSR nor China were reliable backers any longer of the North's unification hopes. Kim Il-song's regime may have concluded that only its own nuclear weapon would be both a sufficient deterrent against an attack from the South—when the latter achieved military superiority sometime early in the next century—as well as a bargaining lever to exact concessions from all its neighbors to improve its economy and sustain its political independence.

Both China and Russia have more to gain from access to South Korean capital and trade than by backing an anachronistic Stalinist ideologue in the North. Korea's future could become the basis for a multilateral collaborative arrangement through which the peninsula's neighbors and the United States underwrite a series of confidence-building measures that lead to arms reductions and, in time, reunification.[15] The initiative must, however, come from the two Koreas. And, indeed, North Korea's apparent compromises during the 1991–92 Korean prime ministerial negotiations demonstrated that the Korean impasse could be broken before most analysts had thought possible.

The reasons for Pyongyang's sudden flexibility are complex. They may have included an assessment of the performance of U.S. air power and precision-guided munitions in the Persian Gulf that could also be employed against North Korean forces from offshore locations. They may also have grown from the realization that the North's economy could collapse with cataclysmic political results unless outside assistance is obtained. In any event, the December 1991 draft treaty of reconciliation and nonaggression was a precedent-setting event on the peninsula. It will reopen telephone and postal communications between the two states and provide some economic interaction as well. Railroad and road links are also to be constructed across the border. Perhaps most significant of all,

Pyongyang and Seoul agree to forswear all acts of terrorism or any effort to overthrow the other.[16]

Undoubtedly, Kim Il-song would prefer to accelerate an American military exit from South Korea along with the abrogation of U.S. extended deterrence. Significantly, neither of these stipulations is found in the DPRK–ROK draft treaty. Successful implementation of the accord may well accelerate the time-table for withdrawal of U.S. forces from Korea, however, as well as the transfer of command from American to ROK officers.[17]

Interestingly, Washington has pressured the North to accept International Atomic Energy Agency (IAEA) inspection of its nuclear power facilities by threatening to postpone the drawdown of U.S. forces from the South and by increasing the potential lethality of such joint ROK–U.S. exercises as the annual *Team Spirit*. With respect to the latter, Washington had offered to sell Seoul several Patriot missile batteries and to add F-117 Stealth fighters and AWACs aircraft to the 1991 exercise. As a carrot to the North, the United States has agreed to open U.S. bases in Korea to international inspection, though it should be noted that North Korea would still be in easy range of American nuclear submarines.[18]

In effect, the North has few strategic options: the Gorbachev–Deng summit of May 1989 combined with Soviet-U.S. rapprochement has removed whatever leverage Pyongyang may have had with its backers. Indicative of the North's weak position are reports that the USSR has not exercised with North Korean forces nor supplied additional modern aircraft (Mig-29s and Su-25s) since 1989 and that Moscow is now demanding immediate payment in hard currency for any new weapons sales.[19] Moreover, without Soviet logistics assistance, there is some question about whether these modern systems will remain workable.

Arms control makes sense for North Korea. Abandoned by the former Soviet Union, the cost of maintaining an army of one million in one of the world's poorest economies has exhausted the DPRK, which faces external debts esti-mated to be $5 billion, stagnant foreign trade, and has a GNP of only $47 billion. The South's economic, population, and technological superiority will prevail over time if the current confrontation continues. The North needs a respite if its regime is to survive.

The autumn 1991 decision by the United States and ROK to withdraw Ameri-can tactical nuclear weapons from the South offered the DPRK a way to reciprocate through IAEA inspections without losing face. When President Roh Tae-wu promised the North that the ROK would never develop nuclear weapons on its own, a path was opened for both governments to permit international inspection of their respective nuclear facilities. As an additional incentive, Presi-dent Bush, in his January 1992 visit to Seoul, offered to cancel *Team Spirit* for that year if the North opened its nuclear plants to international scrutiny.[20] The only caveats to these promising developments are the possibility that the North has already produced and hidden enough plutonium to produce one or more bombs and that the IAEA experience in Iraq provides little assurance that international inspectors can locate all the facilities designed for the production of nuclear weapons materials if the host government chooses to hide them.

Defense ties between the United States and South Korea have expanded into burden sharing and joint production over the past decade. By 1995, Seoul has agreed to provide about one-third of the won-based (ROK currency) costs of maintaining approximately 31,000 American forces on the peninsula. That would amount to about $300 million annually.[21] Nevertheless, there are both political and economic limits to this relationship.

Given an increasingly open democracy in the South and declining tension with the North, political priorities will change. Resources will be shifted from the defense budget to welfare expenditures. The termination of the National Defense Tax in 1990 may be the harbinger of a new age.[22] While the United States has agreed to coproduction in the $4 billion General Dynamics F-16C/D contract, the U.S. aerospace industry is beginning to have the same kinds of concerns about future Korean competition that it has had for some time about Japan. ROK officials have complained that the United States has been reluctant to transfer defense technology despite a memorandum of understanding signed in 1988. The ROK has posited a turn to Europe or Russia as an alternative if Washington continues to hold back on coproduction arrangements and technology transfer. In military trade for 1990, the ROK ran a $1.6 billion deficit with the United States.[23]

In sum, the end of the Cold War, the prospect of détente on the Korean peninsula, growing democracy and anti-American sentiment in the South, as well as bilateral trade frictions, do not portend a continued smooth U.S.–ROK relationship. South Korea lacks an obvious resource asset such as oil. Under these conditions, Korean political leaders may reasonably ask what long-term stake America has in their country's future for the post–Cold War era other than strategic denial and the protection of Japan—both increasingly outdated objectives.

Transitional Arrangements for Southeast Asia

Southeast Asia's strategic importance to the United States during the Cold War was based on its location astride the sea lanes between the Indian Ocean/Persian Gulf and the northwest Pacific. The Philippine bases provided U.S. naval and air forces with a surge capability in either direction. As in Northeast Asia, American defense relationships have been bilateral with the Philippines and Thailand, though the Five Power Defense Arrangement (FPDA) incorporates Malaysia and Singapore with Great Britain, Australia, and New Zealand in a parallel security structure.

The future of these arrangements is increasingly problematic, however, as the former Soviet naval and air forces withdraw from the region and Vietnamese troops leave Cambodia. In a more relaxed security environment, U.S. forces will serve less as primary defender of the region and more to reassure and share in the burden of promoting its defense. Equally important, Southeast Asian states want to ensure that the United States remains involved economically, as an important trade and investment partner.

Indicative of this new, reduced role has been Washington's acquiescence to the closure of the Philippine bases in 1992. Although hoping to keep the bases open until 1994, the United States preferred a rapid phaseout to the prospect of Philippine control over the exit. Without the bases' superb location and repair facilities, there is no doubt that the size and duration of U.S. deployments in Southeast Asia will be reduced as forces are relocated to the mid- Pacific, Japan, and Alaska. Nevertheless, in all probability these forces would have been diminished even if the Philippine bases had remained in operation because of the altered threat environment and defense budget cutbacks.

The United States is searching for facilities to replace Subic Bay's ship repair and Crow Valley's air–ground training range. Their loss not only affects U.S. forward deployed forces but also those of a number of Southeast Asian states that trained at the Philippine facilities. Navy officials have been negotiating with Malaysia, Indonesia, and Brunei for training, repair, and access arrangements. These prospects include ship and aircraft maintenance on a commercial basis in Surabaya in Indonesia and Lumut on Malaysia's peninsular west coast. Indonesia and Singapore have proposed the construction of a new air combat range on Sumatra that could be ready by 1995 and available to other regional air forces.[24] Malaysian authorities, meanwhile, have stated that repair arrangements at Lumut could provide employment for Subic Bay's skilled Filipino workers if Malaysians lack sufficient expertise.[25]

As the United States reduces its regional presence, ASEAN militaries are increasing their own capabilities for external defense, expanding beyond their traditional counterinsurgency orientation. Least able to undertake this new task is the Philippines. Its armed forces had estimated it would take $7 billion in new appropriations for modernization over a ten-year period that would cover the gamut from fast patrol craft to interdict smuggling to armed helicopters for counterinsurgency and combat aircraft and airlift capacity to defend the islands' air and sea space as well as its claims in the Spratly chain. With the U.S. exit, however, the resource base for these modernization plans also disappears.[26]

Other more affluent ASEAN states fare better in their modernization plans. Tiny Singapore is acquiring new missile corvettes to better defend adjacent sea lanes. Its air force includes eight F-16s and a much larger number of A-4 Super Skyhawks, which have been upgraded with new engines and avionics. Particularly significant are Singaporean plans to acquire new radars for an enhanced Command, Control, Communication, Intelligence (C^3I) capability. When integrated with command and control centers, Singapore will be able to monitor traffic all along the Malacca Strait and into the South China Sea.[27]

Thailand, too, is seeking to develop a greater maritime capability along both its Gulf and Andaman Sea coasts. To enhance its coastal patrol and oil rig defense, the Thai navy is acquiring four Chinese frigates, which although equipped with only 1950s technology, should be adequate for surveillance. (The four Chinese ships cost the equivalent of one modern European vessel.)[28] Thailand is also buying P-3 aircraft through the U.S. Foreign Military Sales program for EEZ patrol. This naval upgrade will enhance Thailand's ability to operate along both its coasts while still leaving outer Gulf and South China Sea SLOC defense to the U.S. Seventh Fleet.[29] Thailand's continued security cooperation with the United States was revealed when former prime minister Chatichai Choonhaven acknowledged that his government permitted U.S. planes to use U-Tapao air base as a staging point in the Gulf War.[30]

Malaysia plans to allocate $2.2 billion to defense between 1991 and 1995, 11 percent of its budget. This is a 400 percent increase over its previous five-year plan. Under a 1988 agreement with Great Britain, most of these funds will go for 28 Hawk aircraft, two missile corvettes, the construction of new bases, and possibly the purchase of two submarines.[31]

Enhanced regional defense cooperation is also planned. The FPDA is expanding its integrated air defense system to include east as well as west Malaysia. Brunei has been asked to join. Malaysia and Indonesia have begun joint surveillance of the Malacca Strait. And U.S. officials have proposed greater access for their ships and aircraft on a temporary basis to increase joint training exercises.[32] None of this portends a precipitous U.S. withdrawal from the western Pacific even without the Philippine bases, though plans do suggest more intermittent deployments.

Why No ASEAN Defense Community?

A number of ASEAN leaders in recent years have speculated about the prospects for regionwide defense cooperation. Interest in expanding bilateral defense exercises has grown as ASEAN states acquire more power projection capabilities and as the former Soviet Union and United States reduce their forces in the area. While ASEAN may be a *security community* in the sense that no member would seriously consider the use of force against another to settle disputes, it has not and will not become a *defense community*. Common cultural, ideological, and historical experiences are absent; and most importantly, there is no common threat. The benefits ASEAN has achieved—relative peace, stability, and security—do not form the base for wider military collaboration. Rather, they allow each state to pursue an independent path.

Despite parallel efforts to increase their external defense capabilities, ASEAN leaderships continue to define their security futures through economic development and cooperation rather than through a military pact. In the 1970s and 1980s, a common defense arrangement was rejected for fear that it would only encourage countermeasures by Vietnam and the Soviet Union and that external defense was irrelevant for addressing internal threats of insurgency, ethnic separatism, and political dissent. Moreover, the overall military weakness of the ASEAN states made them dependent on Western security guarantees. A mutual defense pact would have had little deterrent value.

In recent years, although the security environment has changed radically, interest in a defense pact has not increased. Communist insurgencies have collapsed in Southeast Asia (with the partial exception of the Philippines). Joint exercises and training on a bilateral basis emphasizing conventional military threats have increased. However, there is little impetus from the regional environment to move beyond these modest informal arrangements. The naval and air forces of the former Soviet Union are moving back to the North Pacific. Moscow's alliance with Vietnam has all but ended, with Hanoi now seeking political and economic cooperation with ASEAN rather than confronting the region militarily. China, too, has normalized relations with both the ASEAN states and Indochina. In sum, Southeast Asia's security environment has never seemed more benign.

Small wonder, then, that there is scant interest among the ASEAN states to remedy the lack of interoperability in their armed forces because of differences in doctrine, language, training procedures, and logistics systems. Divergent strategic priorities between, for example, Singapore's forward defense out to the South China Sea and Indonesia's defense in depth or Thailand's primary orientation toward land-based threats versus Malaysia's maritime focus render multilateral cooperation problematic at best.[33]

Under these conditions, no ASEAN state perceives indigenous cooperative defense arrangements as preferable to the maintenance of external ties through the FPDA, the Manila Pact, and in the case of Thailand, continued links to China. Malaysia's defense minister has noted that his country and Singapore have been able to exercise effectively and develop common procedures through the FPDA. That capability might not have emerged in the absence of outside arrangements. On the other hand, a trilateral straits defense regime among Singapore, Malaysia, and Indonesia could have the negative effect of dividing ASEAN into maritime and land-oriented subgroups. Minister Mohammed Abdul Rajak also foresaw the prospects of greater Chinese, Japanese, and Indian naval activity in Southeast Asia as reasons why the ASEAN states should retain their own linkages to external guarantors.[34] Moreover, should Vietnam and the other Indochina states affiliate with ASEAN by the end of the decade, associationwide defense collaboration would seem even more unwieldy.

Although defense collaboration with Vietnam would appear out of the question, its contribution to ASEAN's economic diplomacy could be considerable. Vietnam's membership could also facilitate a peaceful resolution to overlapping EEZs in the South China Sea. Continental shelf disputes could be settled comprehensively, not just bilaterally. And, an ASEAN that included Vietnam could enhance Southeast Asia's bargaining position in dealing with the regionalization of the global economy.

Finally, it should be noted that even in a post–Cold War world, new regional tensions arise. China's involvement in supporting the repressive military regime in Burma is a case in point. Burma's army is entirely dependent for its equipment on Beijing; and northern Burma's economy is reportedly under China's domination. PRC aid to Rangoon's military leaders could add to Southeast Asian security problems by exacerbating refugee flows into Thailand and Bangladesh.[35]

Conclusion

Forecasting regional security arrangements in Asia is a speculative enterprise indeed. On the one hand, political inertia and past sunk costs in military investment, represented, for example, by U.S. carrier battle groups, suggest the continuation of forward deployed American naval and air forces. These forces would be assisted through access arrangements with a number of friendly states along the Asian littoral. On the other hand, modern-day elements of power are increasingly based on economic performance, technological know-how, and capacity for innovation. Military capabilities play a secondary role in this new environment. In fact, high levels of military investment may actually slow a country's general economic growth and harm its competitive performance. The irony of these conditions for America's Asian policy is that while most members of the region will continue to welcome a U.S. presence that contributes to stability by dampening indigenous arms races, the United States itself has concluded that its deployments must be reduced as part of an overall revitalization of the U.S. economy.

The Soviet Union's collapse has meant that the ideological basis for U.S. commitments in Asia has evaporated. While regional conflicts remain in Korea, between Japan and Russia, China and Taiwan, and among the Southeast Asian states over boundaries and maritime development zones, these disputes are endemic and do not require the intervention of external powers for resolution. Nor do they threaten vital American interests. Regardless of their outcomes, no new regional hegemon will emerge to threaten international commerce or block U.S. investments.[36]

This is not to deny that residual U.S. commitments to Korea should be abrogated while the Stalinist Kim Il-song regime survives. By the end of the decade, however, rapprochement between the two Koreas and/or drastic political changes in the North attendant upon a successor regime or economic collapse could lead to new arms control measures that would greatly alter the need for U.S. forces. Should Korea be unified by the century's end, it may still desire a U.S. presence to protect against a rearmed Japan. The same reasoning suggests that both China and Korea would prefer the continuation of American bases in Japan rather than the latter's development of an autonomous naval and air power projection capability.

In Southeast Asia, even though the Spratly Islands remain a potential flashpoint, resolution through armed hostilities seems improbable. A joint development regime involving all claimants may be on the horizon or, at minimum, separate national consolidations of each country's holdings. Even were China to decide to acquire the Spratly Islands through naval and air attacks—an unlikely prospect—the ASEAN states possess neither the capability nor training to repulse them. While collective military action would not occur, collective diplomacy, based on the Cambodian experience, probably would. ASEAN's past diplomatic successes will sustain its political cohesion for some purposes, while security cooperation operates at a lower level—between and among contiguous states.

Vietnam could affiliate with a loose ASEAN political group, adding to regional reconciliation. It is improbable, however, that Vietnam will become a full member of ASEAN while the SRV remains a Leninist state with a centrally planned economy. Compatible political and economic values would simply be lacking. More probable will be Vietnam's participation in a Southeast Asian balance of power which would place it as the northern continental pole opposite Indonesia at the southern flank.[37] Moreover, with the cessation of Soviet military aid to Vietnam, its military's deterioration will degrade Hanoi's threat potential in the region over time.

In sum, ASEAN defense cooperation will remain at the level of regular consultations and the exchange of intelligence and some training among its members; joint exercises among neighbors primarily for border control, antipiracy and antismuggling purposes; notification of national exercises particularly in border regions; and the development of border agreements to cope with both land- and sea-based illegal labor movements and contraband. Southeast Asian defense, then, will remain at the state rather than regional level. In an environment no longer dominated by Cold War ideological conflicts and extraregional alliances, the impetus for *regional* defense collaboration atrophies. While ASEAN will continue to function as a regional political and economic consultative mechanism, it should not be expected to become Southeast Asia's NATO or even its Conference on Security Cooperation.

The foregoing assessment of regional security for Asia in a post–Cold War environment yields several conclusions about the future of collective security and U.S. forward presence:

1. No collective security pact for either Northeast or Southeast Asia is on the horizon, much less an Asiawide organization. For the foreseeable future, no single Asian state or combination of actors is perceived to threaten either the territorial integrity of others or international sea lanes. The absence of any clear threat, then, precludes the necessity for new, multilateral defense arrangements.

2. Nevertheless, security problems will persist in overlapping EEZs, competitive claims to the Spratly Islands, illegal migration, and maritime resource disputes, as well as in the uncertainty over Korea's political future, and the

prospect of nuclear weapons development on the peninsula. Most of these issues are exclusively local and can only be resolved by the affected states. Outside powers have little substantive interest in them—with the exception of Korea—unless an outbreak of hostilities would threaten international commerce. A continued U.S. naval and air presence, then, can no longer be justified by reference to an overarching great power menace.

3. The maintenance of reduced U.S. air, naval, and army deployments in Asia will depend on a series of mutually beneficial bilateral agreements that also have the concurrence of neighboring states. Periodic access, prepositioned supplies, and regular joint exercises will probably characterize U.S. arrangements in Southeast Asia, initially with Singapore, Thailand, and Brunei. Over time, similar agreements might be reached with Malaysia and Indonesia—incentives for Kuala Lumpur and Jakarta being additional business for some of their shipyards. These exercises should focus on assisting regional armed services in developing their own capacities to monitor and defend their maritime and airspaces. The broader U.S. role would be one of patrolling the international waters and airspaces along the western Pacific littoral in collaboration with the region's members.

4. Finally, a sustained, though reduced, U.S. presence in Japan, Korea (for the time being), and along the sea and air routes of Southeast Asia probably inhibits efforts by Japan, China, or India to move their forces into the region to meet their own extended security needs. That is, reliance on an American presence dampens the prospect of a regional arms race and reduces the probability that Japan might add a military dimension to its economic dominance in Asia.

A nagging question remains: Can the United States afford this new *constabulary* role? In all probability, only if those states involved in these relationships are willing to share some of the burdens. Both Korea and Japan already provide direct financial subsidation for U.S. forces in their countries. While the Southeast Asian states are less affluent, if they are willing to provide access arrangements without rental costs, that, too, would be a form of burden sharing and would assist the United States in helping the Asian littoral promote international stability through this transitional era in world politics.

The era of Pax Americana has ended in Asia. New collaborative arrangements can, however, foster an international environment conducive to trade, investment, and economic growth. As a dominant trading state, the United States should be an integral part of these new arrangements, though it may no longer dominate them.

Notes

1. For a discussion of the components of U.S. Asian strategy during the Cold War, see Lawrence E. Grinter, *East Asia and the United States into the 21st Century*, Maxwell Air Force Base (AL: Air University Press, 1991).

2. Quoted in Susuma Awanohara, "Double Standards," *Far Eastern Economic Review*, October 24, 1991, p. 26.

3. See the statement by Yukio Satoh, an official of Japan's *Gaimusho* (Ministry of Foreign Affairs) quoted in Michael Richardson, "Mixed Views on 'Pax Americana,' " *Asia-Pacific Defence Reporter*, September 1991, p. 33.

4. Michael Richardson, "Quest for Cooperative Effort," *Asia-Pacific Defence Reporter*, September 1991, p. 32.

5. A.W. Grazebrook makes a persuasive argument for the JSDF's continued defensive orientation in "Maritime Potential No Cause for Concern," *Asia-Pacific Defence Reporter*, September 1991, pp. 27–28.

6. "Japanese and Americans Struggling to Overcome Their Mutual Resentment," *New York Times*, December 3, 1991.

7. Statement by Vice Foreign Minister Hisashi Owada carried by Kyodo, November 18, 1991, in *Foreign Broadcast Information Service (FBIS)*, Daily Report—East Asia, November 18, 1991, p. 2.

8. Kyodo, November 12, 1991, in *FBIS*, Daily Report—East Asia, November 12, 1991, p. 3.

9. *New Times* (Moscow), November 5–11, 1991, in *FBIS*, Daily Report—Soviet Union, December 5, 1991, p. 54. For a Japanese view, see Hiroshi Kimura, "Gorbachev's Japan Policy: The Northern Territories Issue," *Asian Survey* (31,9) July 1991, pp. 646–661.

10. For a discussion of Gorbachev's East Asian strategy some of which may be adopted by Yeltsin, see Stephen Blank, "Soviet Perspectives on Asian Security," *Asian Survey* (31, 7) July 1991, pp. 646–661.

11. Thomas L. Wilborn, *How Northeast Asians View Their Security* (Carlisle Barracks: U.S. Army War College Strategic Studies Institute, 1991). Especially chapters 2, 4, and 5.

12. *Yonhap* (Seoul) October 28 and December 3, 1991, in *FBIS*, Daily Report—East Asia, October 28 and December 3, 1991, pp. 32 and 18 respectively. Japan's response is carried by Kyodo, October 29, 1991, in *FBIS*, Daily Report—East Asia, October 29, 1991, p. 1.

13. Soviet policy toward Korea is analyzed by Byung-joon Ahn in "South Korean–Soviet Relations: Contemporary Issues and Prospects," *Asian Survey* (31,9) September 1991, pp. 816–825.

14. For a thorough discussion of arms control issues on the Korean peninsula, see the special issue on arms control of the *Korean Journal of Defense Analysis* (3,1) Summer 1991.

15. William T. Tow, "Post–Cold War Security in East Asia," *The Pacific Review* (4,2) 1991, pp. 97–108.

16. The draft treaty's provisions may be found in the *New York Times*, December 13, 1991.

17. A good brief review of South Korea's foreign policy is found in Byung-joon Ahn, *South Korea's International Relations: Quest for Security, Prosperity, and Unification* (New York: The Asia Society, September 1991), passim.

18. David E. Sanger, "Cheney Calls Halt to Korea Pullout," *New York Times*, November 21, 1991. Also see *Yonhap* (Seoul), December 12, 1991, in *FBIS*, Daily Report—East Asia, December 12, 1991, p. 23.

19. *Chungang Ilbo* (Seoul), October 30, 1991, in *FBIS*, Daily Report—East Asia, October 30, 1991, p. 18. Also see the articles by Gary Klintworth, "Arms Control and Great Power Interests in the Korean Peninsula," *The Korean Journal of Defense Analysis* (3,1) Summer 1991, pp. 155–219; and William T. Tow, "Reassessing Deterrence on the Korean Peninsula," in the same issue.

20. *New York Times*, January 6, 1992.

21. *Korea Herald*, November 23, 1991, in *FBIS*, Daily Report—East Asia, November 25, 1991, p. 17.

22. Chung-in Moon, "The Political Economy of Defense Industrialization in South Korea," *Journal of East Asian Affairs* (5,2) Summer/Fall 1991, especially pp. 462–465. Also see *Janes Defence Weekly*, December 7, 1991, p. 1120.

23. *Yonhap*, November 18, 1991, in *FBIS*, Daily Report—East Asia, November 18, 1991, p. 16.

24. Michael Vatikiotis, "Spreading the Load," *Far Eastern Economic Review*, November 7, 1991, p. 35; and Michael Richardson, "Asia Adjusts to U.S.-Philippine Bases Deal," *Asia-Pacific Defence Reporter*, September 1991, p. 10.

25. *New Straits Times* (Kuala Lumpur), November 1, 1991, in *FBIS*, Daily Report—East Asia, November 4, 1991, p. 27.

26. Quezon City, GMA 7 Radio–Television Arts Network, December 11, 1991, interview with PAF Chief-of-Staff General Lisandro Abadia, in *FBIS*, Daily Report—East Asia, December 11, 1991, p. 43.

27. Interviews with the commanders of the Singapore Air Force and Navy, *Jane's Defence Weekly*, October 12, 1991, p. 684, and November 9, 1991, p. 926.

28. Robert Karniol, "Thais Defend Frigate Buy," *Jane's Defence Weekly*, October 19, 1991, pp. 724–725.

29. Interview with Thai Navy Commander-in-Chief Admiral Vichet Karunyawanit, *Bangkok Post*, October 11, 1991.

30. *Bangkok Post*, December 16, 1991.

31. *Far Eastern Economic Review*, November 7, 1991, p. 53.

32. Michael Richardson "Filling the U.S. Gap," *Asia-Pacific Defence Reporter*, July 1991, p. 8.

33. See the discussion in Amitav Acharya, "The Association of Southeast Asian Nations: 'Security Community' or 'Defense Community'?" *Pacific Affairs* (64,2) Summer 1991, pp. 159–178.

34. Michael Richardson, "Tightening Security Bonds: A Malaysian View," *Asia-Pacific Defence Reporter*, August 1991, pp. 18–19.

35. Muthiah Alagappa, "Confronting the SLORC," *Far Eastern Economic Review*, November 29, 1991, p. 28.

36. This argument is persuasively made by Edward Olsen in *The Evolution of U.S. Maritime Power in the Pacific*, Monterey: Naval Postgraduate School, October 1991.

37. Donald Weatherbee, "ASEAN and Indochina: The ASEANization of Vietnam," chapter 10, this volume.

2

Moscow and East Asia: New Realities and New Policies

Paul Marantz

This chapter examines the evolution of Moscow's policy toward the Asia-Pacific region, focusing primarily upon relations with China, South Korea, and Japan. It is divided into three sections, which deal with Gorbachev's reorientation of Soviet policy in 1985–91, the attempts of Yeltsin's new government to improve further relations with the countries of East Asia, and the prospects for Russian foreign policy toward Asia in the years ahead.

The Soviet Union and East Asia

Although Gorbachev began to articulate the central premises of the "new thinking" toward international politics within a year of becoming general secretary in March 1985, not surprisingly, there was a significant lag between the articulation of new perspectives and the translation of this new outlook into concrete policy initiatives. This was especially true in the case of Soviet policy toward Asia, since Asian concerns were less critical than other matters pressing upon the Soviet leadership. Gorbachev was far more concerned with establishing better relations with the United States and Western Europe and grappling with the Soviet Union's growing domestic problems than he was with trying to improve Soviet-Asian relations.

Brezhnev's central foreign policy goal was to expand the Soviet Union's power and influence as one of the world's only two superpowers. He relied heavily upon military strength and intimidation, and he actively attempted to supplant Western influence in the Third World. In contrast, Gorbachev recognized the need to reorganize and reorient the Soviet Union's international activities. His initial goal, before domestic chaos fatally eroded the foundations of Soviet power, was not to expand Moscow's power but to do what he could to maintain it. He sought to preserve the Soviet Union's superpower status by making timely adjustments to the new international realities that had been ignored by his immediate predecessors.[1]

The phrase "normalization" effectively encapsulates the central thrust of Gorbachev's policy toward the Asia-Pacific region. In a very real sense, the Soviet position in Asia in the mid-1980s was an abnormal one crying out for redress. Despite the expenditure of vast resources (primarily on military hardware and manpower), Moscow lacked significant influence in East Asia. It was alienated from the key states in the region and was without a close ally other than Vietnam. The Soviet Union benefited little from the economic dynamism of this rapidly developing region, and its relations with Japan, the major powerhouse of East Asia, were paralyzed by the territorial dispute over the islands north of Hokkaido.[2]

Normalization meant, in the first instance, overcoming the barriers to stable and business-like relations, so that diplomatic, economic, cultural, and political interchange could be expanded. Gorbachev was highly successful in achieving this goal. By the time he was forced from office in December 1991, Moscow had fundamentally transformed its relations with the key actors in East Asia—China, South Korea, and Japan. Moscow's innovative diplomacy in 1987–90, combined with the collapse of Soviet power in 1990–91, produced a far-reaching diplomatic realignment throughout Asia.

As early as the autumn of 1982, shortly before Brezhnev's death, there were indications that the Soviet leadership recognized the need to improve relations with China. However, in the absence of fresh ideas and concrete initiatives, there was little tangible progress in improving Sino-Soviet relations. When Gorbachev assumed the leadership of the Soviet Union, Sino-Soviet relations were burdened by a quarter of a century of conflict, mistrust, and rivalry. The territorial dispute between the two communist giants remained unresolved, and a vast array of military equipment and troops was deployed along their long border. The Soviet Union and China competed bitterly for influence in Indochina and the Korean peninsula. Their long-standing ideological dispute continued to simmer, and there was an absence of direct personal contact between the Soviet and Chinese leaders for more than two decades.

China unequivocally declared that there would be no thaw in Sino-Soviet relations until Moscow addressed three major obstacles to improved relations: the Soviet military buildup along their mutual border, the Soviet military presence in Afghanistan, and Moscow's support for the Vietnamese occupation of Cambodia. Whereas Gorbachev's predecessors had hoped to ease Sino-Soviet tensions "on the cheap," through symbolic gestures, the toning down of public polemics, and cosmetic changes, Gorbachev soon accepted that more tangible concessions would have to be made.[3] He announced substantial troop cuts in Mongolia and the Far East. Soviet troops were withdrawn from Afghanistan. The Soviet Union sharply reduced its military presence in Cam Ranh Bay and pressured Vietnam to withdraw from Cambodia.[4]

In May 1989, Gorbachev and Deng Xiaoping held their historic summit in the Chinese capital, the first such meeting between the leaders of these countries in thirty years. Recognizing their common interest in economic reform, they minimized their ideological differences, treated one another with civility and respect, and held constructive discussions on Cambodia and other issues. Subsequently, the Soviet leadership reacted to the repression in Tiananmen Square with great circumspection so as to avoid damage to the fragile sprouts of Sino-Soviet friendship.

Two years later, in May 1991, the Chinese general secretary, Jiang Zemin, traveled to Moscow to meet Gorbachev, thereby becoming the highest Chinese official to visit the Soviet capital since Mao Zedong's trip in 1957. This continued process of reconciliation resulted in the signing of an agreement that resolved most of the territorial disagreements along the long eastern stretch of the Sino-Soviet border. In his six years as Soviet leader, Gorbachev accomplished a great deal to heal the rift with China. Sino-Soviet relations were put on new footing, and a genuine normalization was achieved.

Notable success was also achieved in transforming Soviet relations with South Korea. Gorbachev had inherited a highly abnormal situation. Diplomatic relations did not exist between Moscow and Seoul; the Soviet Union's shooting down of a Korean airliner in 1983 deepened Korean animosity toward Moscow; the two Koreas were not members of the United Nations; the Korean border bristled with armaments; Soviet support for North Korea engendered mistrust toward Moscow throughout East Asia; and the Soviet Union was tied to an unpredictable, Stalinist regime that was an economic burden, at the same time that Moscow was deprived of the benefits that economic links with the fast-growing South Korean economy would bring.

In an effort to unfreeze relations with South Korea, the Soviet Union undertook a number of small steps. In 1987, Moscow announced that it would participate in the 1988 Seoul Olympics despite Pyongyang's boycott of the event. In 1988, the Soviet Union and South Korea agreed to establish trade representation in each other's capitals. Annual trade between the two countries increased rapidly from $85 million in 1985 to $1 billion in 1990.[5]

In June 1990, following the completion of a Soviet-American summit meeting, Gorbachev met with South Korean President Roh Tae-wu in San Francisco. On September 30, 1990, much sooner than most people had expected, the establishment of full diplomatic relations between the Soviet Union and South Korea was announced. In December of that year, President Roh traveled to Moscow and announced that South Korea would provide extensive credits to the Soviet Union.

In April 1991, Gorbachev and Roh met for the third time in less than ten months, this time in Korea. During their meeting, Gorbachev indicated that Moscow would support South Korea's entry into the United Nations. The two countries agreed to make further efforts to increase their trade, and Gorbachev proposed working out a formal treaty of friendship between the Soviet Union and South Korea. Soviet policymakers hoped that improved ties with South Korea, Seoul's granting of large-scale credits to Moscow, and Korean investment in the Soviet Union would exert pressure on Japan to be more forthcoming in its dealings with Moscow so as to avoid being left out of the expanding Soviet market.[6] As a consequence of the full normalization of relations between Moscow and Seoul, North Korea was forced to take steps to lessen its international isolation. The diplomatic chessboard in the Asia-Pacific region was fundamentally altered. In the present situation of unusual fluidity, new opportunities exist for constructive relations between Moscow and her Asian neighbors.

Gorbachev was far less successful in unblocking Soviet relations with Japan, but even here there was significant movement. After years of insisting that the territorial settlements of World War II must not be reopened, the Soviet Union finally accepted the fact that there would be no formal peace treaty with Japan and no real normalization of relations until some accommodation was reached over the disputed islands north of Hokkaido.

In April 1991, Gorbachev became the first Soviet leader ever to travel to Japan. Although he did not have anything dramatic to offer, a number of small constructive steps were taken. Moscow formally acknowledged that there was an unresolved territorial dispute, and it pledged to reduce some of its military forces on the disputed islands. More than a dozen agreements and memoranda resulted from the summit meeting between the Soviet and Japanese leaders. These included agreements dealing with trade, the environment, the establishment of a Japanese study center in Moscow, the exchange of students and cultural exhibits, and the provision of modest amounts of Japanese technical assistance.[7] As a result of Gorbachev's trip to Japan, the atmospherics of Soviet-Japanese relations were improved, even though the territorial dispute—which stands as a solid barrier to any further progress in their relations—remained unresolved.

On the whole, Gorbachev's diplomacy toward the key actors in the Asia-Pacific region can be considered a success. While he failed disastrously in his domestic policy, wrecking the Soviet economy and destroying the communist system that he set out to reform and strengthen, his foreign policy was vastly more productive. In part through constructive initiatives and vision, and in part by accepting the inexorable decline of Soviet power with good grace, he succeeded in breaking the fetters of earlier policies, improving Moscow's ties with its Asian neighbors, and opening up unprecedented opportunities for even better economic and political relations in the future. Russian diplomacy now has the opportunity to build upon these past successes and to take advantage of the new fluidity that has replaced the frozen positions of the past.

Russia and the Asia-Pacific Region

With the breakup of the Soviet Union into fifteen separate sovereign states by the end of 1991, Yeltsin and his foreign policy advisers have discarded any lingering illusions about Moscow's international might and power. Russian foreign policy is now based upon a frank acceptance of the fact that Russia will play a much diminished role in world affairs for many years to come. Whatever Russia's long-term capabilities and aspirations may be, for now that country's urgent domestic needs have become the foundation for its posture to the outside world.[8]

Throughout most of the Soviet period, the well-being of the population and the basic national interests of the country counted for little in the formulation of Moscow's foreign policy. Ideology, the quest for empire, the dynamics of super-power rivalry, the striving for influence in the Third World, and the parochial interests of the party elite and the military-industrial complex were the driving forces behind Soviet foreign policy. Domestic needs were ruthlessly subordinated to external ambitions.

Breaking with this legacy, Moscow's current leaders recognize that international threats to Russian security and well-being are minimal when compared to the acute domestic sources of instability. Unless the economy can be reformed and a stable democratic political system created, catastrophe looms. There is an acute threat of political paralysis, hyperinflation, economic collapse, civil disorder, civil war, and even the breakup of the fragile Russian Federation, which is composed of more than thirty separate ethnic and political entities. The present, moderate, westward-oriented government of Yeltsin could easily be swept away by demagogic ultra-nationalistic forces. To avoid these very real dangers, Russian foreign policy must aim not for an expansion of foreign power but to do everything possible to create the external conditions that will facilitate the domestic transformations that are so urgently needed.

More specifically, Russian foreign policy is directed at securing the economic assistance from the outside world that the country so desperately needs. It seeks an expansion of Russia's foreign trade, foreign investment, the integration of Russia into the world economy, loans, credits, technical assistance, and the creation of a benign international situation so that sharp reductions in military spending can be made safely. Since Russia is currently without any serious external enemies, and no state or coalition of states looms as an immediate threat, the Russian government has much scope for constructing a foreign policy based upon the primacy of domestic needs.

In regard to the Asia-Pacific region, this orientation translates into the following goals: the sharp expansion of trade; the obtaining of credits, technology, and investment, especially from South Korea and Japan; the use of trade and foreign investment to develop the Russian Far East so that separatist tendencies will not grow in this key region and so that the Russian Far East will contribute to the process of economic rebirth throughout the country; the elimination of perceptions in the region that Russian military might is a threat to other states; the establishment of stable, cordial relations so that Russia will not become the target of hostile coalitions (e.g., a Sino-Japanese alliance); and the preventing of North Korea from obtaining nuclear weapons, since this would encourage nuclear proliferation and might lead to extensive Japanese militarization.

The unceasing Soviet military buildup under Brezhnev engendered fear and mistrust throughout much of East Asia. The aged Politburo was unable to take a fresh look at its actions and extricate itself from this counterproductive policy. The Soviet Union was feared as a serious military threat. Japan and China were driven closer together, and American influence was strengthened as Beijing, Tokyo, and Seoul sought a counterweight to Moscow's massive military might.

Far from being a liability, the recent collapse of Russia's once mighty military machine facilitates the attainment of Moscow's new political and economic objectives. Fears of armed conflict have been sharply reduced, and now, after many years of anxious concern about the Soviet military threat, Russia's neighbors are presently far more worried about that country's instability and weakness. The possibility that North Korea might acquire a few nuclear weapons is much more unsettling than the dwindling military strength of Russia.

According to American intelligence estimates, in 1991 the Soviet government's procurement of weapons for its ground forces was 40 percent below the level of 1988, while purchases for the air force were reduced by 50 percent and those for naval forces were down by one-third. It was expected that there would be an additional decline in weapons procurement in 1992 of some 60 percent.[9] Naval exercises have been sharply cut because of the shortage of fuel. The reduction in regular maintenance is taking its toll on military equipment, and the effectiveness and cohesion of Russian military forces have been sapped by the deterioration of military morale due to the sharp drop in the living standard of troops and officers. This withering away of the Soviet military threat has opened up new possibilities and incentives for cordial relations in Asia that were largely absent in the past.

The prospects for closer Sino-Russian cooperation are quite good. There are a number of strong factors promoting improved relations between these two countries, and the potential sources of disagreement are now far less significant than they have been for several decades.

Russia and China are both preoccupied with the critical process of economic reform and transformation. Given the fragility of their political systems, they share a strong interest in defusing tension and reducing the level of military confrontation. The salience of ideological differences is lower than it has been at any time since the early 1950s. Even though China continues to define itself as a communist country, while Russia is stridently post-communist, both countries are committed to pragmatic market-based economic reform. While the Chinese bitterly criticized Gorbachev for abandoning communism within the Soviet Union and for destroying the communist regimes of Eastern Europe, his departure from the political scene has robbed these polemics of political significance, and continued differences in perspective between Russia and China have little weight compared to the concrete interests that they share.

There is a high degree of complementarity between the Chinese and Russian economies. China can supply consumer goods and agricultural products to Russia in return for industrial equipment and military hardware. Both countries are short of hard currency, so that barter trade, which they are experienced in, has a mutual appeal. Geographical proximity, their long shared border, and the difficulty that the Russian Far East has in obtaining goods from the European part of Russia also facilitate trade. It is a sign of their complementary needs and the dramatically improved state of their relations that Russia is willing to sell advanced military equipment, including SU-27 aircraft, to China, a country that only a few years ago was regarded as a direct military threat.[10]

On the level of geopolitics, China and Russia are both mindful of their diminished international power and leverage. Good mutual relations strengthen their hand in dealing with other countries, and Sino-Russian cooperation can serve as a partial counterweight to the continued superpower predominance of the United States or the potential growth of Japanese power.

The rise of Muslim consciousness in the new states of Central Asia is a shared concern of China and Russia. China is nervous about the effect this might have on its minority Muslim population, while Russia is concerned that increased ethnic tensions would adversely affect the millions of Russians still living in Central Asia and would create problems along its lengthy border—the longest of any European nation—with the Muslim world. Moscow and Beijing are also concerned about the inroads that other states—such as Iran, Saudi Arabia, and Turkey—might make in the region.

These strong shared interests draw China and Russia together. In comparison, the areas of contention between them are fewer and less powerful.

Their border dispute has lessened in severity, but it has not been fully resolved. The treaty that was ratified by China and Russia in early 1992 covered most of the border that China shares with Russia and Mongolia. The status of some small islands near Khabarovsk still has to be decided upon, and the western Chinese border with Kazakhstan, Kyrgyzstan, and Tajikistan is still under discussion. However, these issues should be susceptible to pragmatic resolution.[11]

Other potential areas of dispute include Russia's future ties with Taiwan, competition between China and Russia for influence in the new states of Central Asia, and friction over Russia's stand on human rights in China. Given Taiwan's vast currency reserves and its rapidly expanding economy, Russia is desirous of strengthening commercial links between the two countries. Although this will tread on Beijing's sensitivities, pragmatic compromises are readily available along the lines that China has worked out with the United States and Japan.

Competition for influence in Central Asia is unavoidable, as the recently created states of that region search for economic assistance, political support, and a new independent identity. However, the common interest that Moscow and Beijing have in seeing the emergence of stable, secular societies that are not dominated by other regional powers should moderate their rivalry.

The strong stand that Yeltsin's government has taken on human rights has created some strain in Sino-Russian relations, and this is likely to be a continuing area of disagreement between the two countries. However, Moscow has already demonstrated that it is willing to temper its support for human rights with a realistic appreciation of its own national interests. Russian policymakers are under no illusions about their ability to shape Chinese political practice. The main reason for their strong stand on human rights is to decisively break with their own communist past, to win support in the West by demonstrating how much Russia has changed, and to meet domestic demands that something be done to defend the interests of the Russians who now find themselves living as a vulnerable minority in the Baltic states, Ukraine, and other former Soviet lands.

Most Russians are weary of ideological crusades and tired of telling other nations how to conduct their affairs. Whatever their personal views of the Chinese communist regime, they are prepared to accept reasonable compromises that will enable Russia to benefit from an expansion of commercial relations with China. Hence, the prospects for a continued improvement in Sino-Russian relations are very good.

Much the same can be said about Russia's relations with South Korea. South Korea has already become an important source of credits, investment capital, and trade. Moscow is keenly interested in the economic benefits of expanded commercial relations with South Korea and would like to use South Korea as a means of prodding Japan to become more involved in the Russian market.

Russia and South Korea have a common interest in preventing North Korea from acquiring nuclear weapons. Neither country would like to see this unstable and unpredictable dictatorial regime in possession of nuclear capabilities. Such a prospect would increase the danger of war by accident or miscalculation, and might provoke Japan to upgrade its military capabilities sharply to meet this new threat. Unlike the past, when the Soviet Union tried to curtail American influence in East Asia, Moscow now shares Seoul's interest in preventing a precipitous departure of the U.S. from this region. The U.S. presence provides an important degree of stability, deters North Korean adventurism, lessens the likelihood of Japanese militarization, and serves as a counterweight to China.

North Korea now has very little to offer Moscow. A democratic Russia—unlike a communist Soviet Union—sees no ideological value in links with an unreformed Stalinist regime, which it regards as a lingering relic from its own tragic past. Now that Russian trade in oil and other commodities is being conducted for hard currency at world prices, North Korea can buy little. In 1991, Soviet trade with North Korea dropped by approximately 75 percent.[12]

When the Soviet Union had a strong military presence in Vietnam's Cam Ranh Bay, North Korea could offer valuable overflight rights connecting Vietnam to the Russian Far East. But since Russia's military presence in Cam Ranh Bay has been sharply reduced, and Russia is no longer trying to project its naval power into the Pacific and Indian oceans, this is of greatly diminished value. Moscow's withdrawal of political, military, and economic support from Pyongyang has heightened North Korea's international isolation and has been an important factor compelling North Korea to enter into a dialogue with Japan and South Korea, to accept the membership of the two Koreas in the United Nations, and to sign the Safeguards Agreement with the International Atomic Energy Agency in January 1992.

When Andrei Kozyrev, the Russian foreign minister, visited South Korea in March 1992, he indicated that Moscow was reexamining the Treaty on Friendship, Cooperation, and Mutual Assistance with Pyongyang that Russia had inherited from the former Soviet Union, and he stated that Russia was desirous of concluding a treaty with South Korea that would recognize the two countries' vastly improved relations. In response to a question at a news conference about the possibility of military cooperation between Russia and South Korea, he indicated that "in principle we are ready to develop cooperation in the military sphere."[13]

Should Korean unification by peaceful means become possible at some point in the future, Moscow would have little difficulty accepting this. The disappearance of the Stalinist regime in the North would not be mourned, and a united Korea might well be seen by Moscow as a useful counterweight to Japan and China.

Although Moscow's relations with China and South Korea are developing well, and smooth sailing appears to lie ahead, Russo-Japanese relations remain relatively immobile due to the intractable legacy of their unresolved territorial dispute. The disintegration of the Soviet Union and the emergence of Yeltsin's reformist government in Russia have created new opportunities for the improvement of relations between Moscow and Tokyo, but thus far the potential of these opportunities has not been realized.

There are a number of potent factors standing in the way of a negotiated compromise of their territorial dispute. First of all, Yeltsin's government is in a weak and vulnerable position, despite his continued personal popularity. There is galloping inflation, the general standard of living has dropped sharply, and the economy continues to deteriorate. In the eyes of many people, the nation has been humiliated by its loss of superpower status, by the separation of lands traditionally associated with Russia (especially Ukraine and the Crimea), and by the precarious position in which the 25 million Russians living outside Russia in other states of the Commonwealth of Independent Nations now find themselves. Opposition to Yeltsin's economic reforms is growing, and he already has had to soften key elements in his program. He cannot afford to give his opponents a powerful emotional issue to use against him.

A second factor is the nature and strength of the opposition to a territorial compromise. This opposition springs from several sources. Ultra-nationalists see concessions to Japan as constituting a further debasing of the great Russian nation. For example, Sergei Baburin, a conservative member of the Russian Parliament, has denounced negotiations with Japan as constituting a "path to the destruction of the Russian state."[14] The Russian Parliament, which was elected in early 1990, while the Communist Party was still in power, has a large number of conservatives who feel strongly about this matter and are delighted to have an issue to use against the current government.

Many military officers are also unwilling to give up the islands due to their conception of national prestige and their continued belief in the importance of the islands in protecting Russia's nuclear submarines in the Sea of Okhotsk. In addition, the inhabitants of the disputed islands are fearful of living under Japanese authority and have overwhelmingly opposed a change in the islands' status. A referendum conducted in March 1991 indicated that less than one out of five of the 27,000 inhabitants of the islands supported their separation from the Soviet Union.[15]

Moscow is fearful of fanning the separatist sentiment that is growing in the Russian Far East and threatening the dismemberment of the fragile Russian Federation. Many people in the Russian Far East would regard the surrender of the islands as a crass selling off of Russian territory for Japanese money and as constituting further evidence that far-away Moscow has little concern for their interests. The governor of Sakhalin Island, Valentin Fedorov, has been especially vociferous in rallying the nationalist opposition. He has charged: "Once again we are bowing to Japan, contrary to common sense, spitting on our own national dignity—in the hope of transitory benefits."[16]

A third factor diminishing the prospects for the resolution of this troublesome issue is that the Russian government no longer expects a very great economic return from territorial concessions. Past expectations that Japan might pump tens of billions of dollars into Russia if the islands were returned no longer seem realistic. Japanese businessmen are not very interested in investing in Russia. They are wary of the political instability, the economic chaos, the difficulty of repatriating profits, the absence of a developed infrastructure, the corruption, and the unresolved questions of property rights and resource ownership.[17] They see far more attractive investment opportunities throughout Asia and the United States. The recent slowing of the Japanese economy also limits the credits and aid that the Japanese government is willing to offer Russia.

Another complicating factor is the inflexibility of the Japanese government concerning the islands. Moscow is groping for a compromise, one that would see the two smallest island groups returned to Japan, while the fate of the other two islands would continue to be discussed. Thus far, Japan has said that at a minimum it wants Russia to acknowledge its sovereignty over all the islands now, something that Russia has not been prepared to do.[18] Domestic constraints on the Japanese government limit its freedom to maneuver.

Despite intensive diplomatic contact and continued discussions, a compromise solution has proved elusive. Nonetheless, some movement has taken place, and the two sides are not as far apart as they were a couple of years ago. A number of conditions are now more favorable to a deal. With the end of the Cold War, the military significance of the islands is greatly diminished. Even if the economic payoff from a territorial settlement were to be limited, Russia is in desperate need of all the assistance it can obtain.

Russian officials have floated the idea of a compromise based upon the Soviet-Japanese declaration signed in 1956. This declaration, which was never implemented, provided for the return of the two small islands, Shikotan and the Habomais, once a peace treaty between the USSR and Japan was signed, while leaving open the subsequent fate of the other two islands.[19] Russian spokesmen are attempting to use this earlier declaration as a way of legitimizing a new compromise and as a means of refuting charges of national humiliation, since the earlier agreement was voluntarily entered into by the Soviet Union in 1956, at a time when the country was clearly a formidable superpower. Advocates of a deal based upon the 1956 declaration defend it as representing a fulfillment of past commitments, as constituting a necessary repudiation of the Stalinist past, and as being a reasonable compromise that balances the conflicting interests of Russia and Japan.[20] Many in the Russian government seem to feel that this is something they could sell to the people.

The outline of a comprehensive agreement between Russia and Japan is now emerging. It would involve a settlement in discrete stages stretching over a number of years. All the islands would not be returned at the same time. A joint economic zone encompassing the islands would be created, and pending their final disposition, there might be some form of joint administration. Russians living on the islands would be offered guarantees of permanent resident rights, and financial assistance would be provided for those who chose to resettle in Russia. An interesting straw in the wind is that a spokesman for the Russian Foreign Ministry was recently reported by the Japanese news agency KYODO as having said on a radio program that one way of ending the present stalemate would be to ask the International Court of Justice to rule on the legal ownership of the islands.[21]

For the present time, however, Russia and Japan remain far apart, as was graphically demonstrated by Yeltsin's sudden decision to cancel his trip to Tokyo in September 1992. The abrupt cancellation of this trip indicates how unlikely a breakthrough on the territorial dispute is and how vulnerable the Yeltsin government is feeling to pressure from nationalist forces within Russia.

Until the territorial issue is resolved, Russo-Japanese relations will remain cool, and the Japanese government will refrain from providing any large-scale financial assistance to Moscow. However, with the collapse of the Soviet regime, Japan has already become more forthcoming financially than it was previously, and it is now willing to provide limited amounts of assistance for specific projects, such as developing oil and gas wells off the coast of Sakhalin, upgrading the safety of Russia's nuclear power stations, and distributing medical supplies and humanitarian assistance.[22]

Tokyo has decided that its interests are better served by providing limited amounts of aid than by a complete refusal to assist Russia. Japan is attempting to use this aid to improve its image among the inhabitants of the disputed islands and the Russian Far East; to keep a foot in the door, so that it is not foreclosed from taking advantage of subsequent economic opportunities in Russia; to shore up Yeltsin so that he is not replaced by hostile, ultra-nationalistic forces; and to avoid being totally out of step with the policies of the other members of the Group of Seven (G-7) industrial nations. Until a territorial settlement is reached, this policy of limited and selective aid is unlikely to change.

The Uncertain Future

Thus far, there has been a high degree of continuity linking Soviet foreign policy toward the Asia-Pacific region under Gorbachev with the policy of the Russian government led by Yeltsin. However, there is no guarantee that this line of policy will continue in the future. In the wake of communism's sudden demise, the search for a new Russian identity and for a new orientation toward the outside world has just begun. Stable, democratic political structures have not been built, and ultra-nationalism and xenophobia have not been vanquished. The present moderate and conciliatory foreign policy may not last.

Already, there has been a clash between two different schools of thought in Russia, "Atlanticism" and "Eurasianism," regarding that country's foreign policy.[23] The Atlanticists, led by Boris Yeltsin and Russian foreign minister Andrei Kozyrev, currently hold the upper hand, but there has been repeated criticism of their policy from the Eurasians.[24] The Atlanticists see the new Russia as being an integral part of the highly developed Western world. They want to build a modern democratic state that fully respects fundamental human rights and is based upon a market economy that is closely integrated with the international economic system. Their eyes are directed westward, and they see Russia as sharing the basic interests of the developed North and as aspiring to eventual membership in the G-7 and some kind of affiliation with the European Community and perhaps even with NATO. Their foreign policy is built upon the primacy of good relations with the United States and Western Europe. They favor a sharp reduction in nuclear weapons and have given their support to Western policy in Iraq and Yugoslavia.

In contrast, the Eurasians are more focused on Russia's regional interests. They stress the importance of establishing sound relations with the members of the Commonwealth of Independent States, with Russia's neighbors in the Middle East, and with China. They are concerned that too close an identification with the developed North will alienate the less developed South and, in particular, strain relations with the Muslim world which are so important given rising Muslim consciousness in Central Asia.

Echoing the nineteenth century controversy between the Slavophiles and the Westerners, these two schools of thought have very different conceptions of Russia's identity and how it should relate to the West. However, it is striking that thus far they have not differed that much on policy toward the Asian-Pacific region. The Atlanticists, such as Yeltsin and Kozyrev, have not neglected Asia and, as we have seen, have made a major effort to improve relations with China, South Korea, and Japan. The Eurasianists fully support this policy. The Eurasianists are not so much critical of present actions as they are anxious about what may lie ahead. They are fearful that in the quest for closer ties with the West, Asia will be neglected, the Muslim world will be alienated, and that too much emphasis on universal standards of human rights might lead to conflict with China over its domestic political system, its domination over Tibet, or even its population control policies.[25] Thus, despite significant differences over how Russia should relate to the United States and Western Europe, there is at present a good deal of agreement between the Atlanticists and the Eurasians on Russian policy toward Asia.

There is, however, a third group—the ultra-nationalists—who must be taken into account as well. Although they presently have only a limited impact upon Russian foreign policy, their strength is growing. They have already succeeded in bringing about the cancellation of Yeltsin's scheduled September 1992 visit to Japan. If Yeltsin's economic reforms fail, and political paralysis or chaos results, they may well come to power, by peaceful or not so peaceful means.

The ultra-nationalist camp draws upon the forces of the far Right, who yearn for the Russian Empire, and those of the far Left, who have not reconciled themselves to the break-up of the Soviet Union and its loss of superpower status. Many in the military support it as well. If people become disillusioned with Yeltsin, despair of seeing an improvement in their standard of living, and are unwilling to tolerate the increased crime and corruption, they may look to the ultra-nationalists to restore law and order and to prevent a further deterioration in their living conditions. A coup by a "red–brown" alliance (i.e., a union of communists and fascists) can by no means be ruled out, as Andrei Kozyrev warned in early July 1992.[26]

The ultra-nationalists have been vocal critics of Russia's foreign policy. They are deeply suspicious of the West and believe that Russia should stop kowtowing to the United States. They decry the selling off of Russian natural resources to foreigners and are fearful of the penetration of alien ideas into Russian life. They argue that Moscow has not adequately defended the interests of Russians in the Baltic states, Moldova, and Ukraine, and they advocate strong measures on their behalf.[27]

If the ultra-nationalists were to come to power, this development would quickly bring a sharp deterioration in relations with the West. Western aid would dry up, foreign investment would drop, East–West trade would decline, and efforts to integrate Russia into the world economy would be retarded. The ultra-nationalists, who draw much of their support from the armed forces, would attempt to strengthen Russia's military might and would be hostile to arms control. Russia would once again view the outside world with suspicion and mistrust. It would become truculent, well-armed, and inward-looking.

Under such circumstances, Moscow's search for broad accommodation in the Asia-Pacific region would probably be suspended. Territorial concessions to Japan would certainly be ruled out, relations with China would become more tense, and the interest in attracting South Korean investment would diminish.

Nonetheless, it is clear that the ability of the ultra-nationalists to alter the new realities in Asia is quite limited. They can prevent the further warming of relations, but they cannot turn the clock back to the days when the Soviet Union was an awesome and intimidating military power. The Russian economy is in shambles, and it cannot even feed the people adequately, let alone support a strong military. The days when military expenditures constituted 15 percent and more of a steadily growing GNP are over.

In addition, there is no longer an overarching ideology to rally the population against foreign adversaries. Ethnic tension and separatist sentiment are very acute, and Moscow must make concessions to the demands for local autonomy. People are no longer cowed by the government. They are restive and will take to the street if their aspirations for a decent standard of living are not satisfied. The huge sums of money needed to support a bloated military can no longer be extracted from the population. The morale of the armed forces is at rock bottom. The military are consumed by anxieties over housing, food, and their uncertain future. While they would like to see more money spent on defense and more status accorded their profession, they have little faith in communist ideology and little enthusiasm about risking their lives for the glory of the fatherland.

If the ultra-nationalists were to come to power, they would soon have their hands full dealing with separatist movements within Russia and coping with rising tensions in Ukraine, Moldova, and the Baltic states. This would leave few resources for adventures further afield. Thus, the direct military consequences for Asia of even the worst-case scenario of an ultra-nationalist coup are likely to be limited. Russia will influence Asia in the years ahead more through its weakness and potential for instability than through its strength.

Internal conditions are the key to the future of Russian foreign policy. Economic collapse may well bring the ultra-nationalists to power, while successful economic and political reform will allow the present government to continue the gradual improvement of its relations with its Asian neighbors.

Notes

1. Soviet policy toward East Asia is examined in: Peggy Levine Falkenheim, "Moscow and Tokyo," *World Policy Journal*, vol. 8, no. 1 (Winter 1990–91), pp. 159–179; Vladimir I. Ivanov, "The USSR Breakup: New Strategic Realities in the Pacific Basin?" presented at the 1992 Pacific Symposium, Washington, D.C., February 1992; Robert Legvold, "Soviet Policy in East Asia," *Washington Quarterly*, vol. 14, no. 2 (Spring 1991), pp. 129–142; Rajan Menon, "New Thinking and Northeast Asian Security," *Problems of Communism*, vol. 38, nos. 2–3 (March–June 1989), pp. 1–29; Donald S. Zagoria, "Soviet Policy in East Asia," in Robert Jervis and Seweryn Bialer, eds., *Soviet-American Relations after the Cold War* (Durham: Duke University Press, 1991), pp. 164–182; Alexei V. Zagorsky, "Soviet-Japanese Relations in the Perestroika Era," in Tsuneo Akaha and Frank Langdon, eds., *Japan in the Post-Hegemonic World* (Boulder: Lynne Rienner, forthcoming).

2. Legvold, "Soviet Policy in East Asia," p. 131.

3. Ibid., p. 134.

4. Zagoria, "Soviet Policy in East Asia," pp. 166–171.

5. Legvold, "Soviet Policy in East Asia," p. 139.

6. Suzanne Crow, "The Soviet-Japanese Summit: Expectations Unfulfilled," *Report on the USSR*, vol. 3, no. 17 (April 26, 1991), pp. 4–5.

7. Ibid., p. 4.

8. Vladislav Zubok, "Tyranny of the Weak: Russia's New Foreign Policy," *World Policy Journal*, vol. 9, no. 2 (Spring 1992), pp. 191–217.

9. See the congressional testimony of analysts from the Central Intelligence Agency and the Defense Intelligence Agency reported in the *New York Times*, June 9, 1992.

10. *Izvestiya*, March 4, 1992, in Foreign Broadcast Information Service, *Daily Report: Soviet Union* (hereafter *FBIS*), March 5, 1992, p. 8.

11. Suzanne Crow, et al., "Weekly Review," *RFE/RL Research Report*, vol. 1, no. 14 (April 3, 1992), p. 66.

12. Ivanov, "The USSR Breakup," p. 8.

13. TASS, March 19, 1992, in *FBIS*, March 20, 1992, p. 30.

14. Interfax June 11, 1992, in *FBIS*, June 12, 1992, p. 23.

15. Gennady Chufrin, "The USSR and Asia in 1991: Domestic Priorities Prevail," *Asian Survey*, vol. 32, no. 1 (January 1992), pp. 14–15.

16. *Rabochaya Tribuna*, May 15, 1992, in *FBIS*, May 20, 1992, p. 19.

17. *Nikkei Weekly*, July 4, 1992.

18. ITAR-TASS, April 18, 1992, in *FBIS*, April 20, 1992, p. 19; *Izvestiya*, April 21, 1992, in *FBIS*, April 24, 1992, p. 15.

19. Crow, "The Soviet-Japanese Summit," p. 2.

20. *Nezavisimaya gazeta*, May 6, 1992; and *Izvestiya*, May 5, 1992, in *Current Digest of the Post-Soviet Press*, vol. 44, no. 18 (June 3, 1992), pp. 14–15.

21. KYODO, May 30, 1992, in *FBIS*, June 1, 1992, p. 22. This proposal was also offered in an earlier article by a Russian international lawyer. See *Nezavisimaya gazeta*, April 4, 1992, in *FBIS*, April 14, 1992, p. 20.

22. Interfax, May 7, 1992, in *FBIS*, May 13, 1992, p. 25; Interfax, May 20, 1992, in *FBIS*, May 21, 1992, p. 43.

23. This terminology has been suggested by Sergei Stankevich, an influential adviser to Yeltsin in an article in *Nezavisimaya Gazeta*, March 28, 1992. It is reprinted in as "Russia in Search of Itself," *National Interest*, no. 28 (Summer 1992), pp. 47–51.

24. Alexander Rahr, " 'Atlanticists' versus 'Eurasians' in Russian Foreign Policy," *RFE/RL Research Report*, vol. 1, no. 22 (May 29, 1992), pp. 17–22.

25. *Izvestiya*, February 25, 1992, in *Current Digest of the Post-Soviet Press*, vol. 44, no. 8 (March 25, 1992) pp. 9–10; Sergei Solodovnik, "Stability in Asia: A Priority for Russia," *International Affairs* (Moscow), February 1992, pp. 65–68.

26. *New York Times*, July 3, 1992.

27. *Pravda*, February 24, 1992, and *Sovetskaya Rossiya*, January 23, 1992, in *Current Digest of the Post-Soviet Press*, vol. 44, no. 8 (March 25, 1992), pp. 8–9, 16, 27.

3

The Changing U.S. Role in Asian Security in the 1990s

Donald S. Zagoria

The world has changed since 1989 and strategic analysts will be debating a new array of questions in the decade ahead. The collapse of communism in Eastern Europe, the termination of the Warsaw Pact, the reunification of Germany, the entry of a unified Germany into NATO, the disintegration of the Soviet Union, Russia's retreat from the Third World, and unprecedented cooperation between Moscow and Washington on arms control and regional conflict resolution, including the crisis in the Persian Gulf, all signal the end of the Cold War.

But there is a good deal of disagreement about the nature of the post–Cold War world. What will be the main dividing lines? What role will America's Cold War alliances play in a post–Cold War era? What forms of power will be important? What is America's role in this new world? What are America's interests and what are the primary threats to those interests? What policies should the United States adopt in order to protect its interests? What military forces and strategy will be required to carry out those policies?[1]

The end of the Cold War and the collapse of the Soviet Union is bound to have an enormous impact on the U.S. role in the Asia-Pacific region. With the decline of the Soviet threat, some analysts are already suggesting that we focus more attention on the new economic challenge from Japan. Others are calling for even more substantial reductions in our military forces in Asia and a new emphasis on reviving the American economy.

In addition to the end of the Cold War, the decisive U.S. and allied military victory in the Persian Gulf is also bound to have an enormous impact on future U.S. strategy and to raise fundamental new questions. Does the allied victory in the Gulf mean that we are now in reach of President Bush's avowed goal of building a new world order "where the rule of law . . . governs the conduct of nations" and "in which a credible United Nations can use its peacekeeping role to fulfill the promise and the vision of the UN's founders"? Or was the U.S.-led coalition in the Gulf crisis the product of an unusual set of circumstances that are unlikely to be duplicated in the future?[2]

The purpose of this chapter is to provide a possible prologue to dealing with these issues, particularly as they affect U.S. policy in Asia, by: (1) identifying some of the basic reasons why international relations in the Pacific have remained peaceful and relatively stable during the past two decades; (2) inquiring how the end of the Cold War and the victory in the Gulf are likely to influence these factors; (3) considering some of the likely threats to Asian stability in the decade ahead; and (4) analyzing some of the implications of these considerations for U.S. policy in Asia in the 1990s.

The Five Pillars of Asian Security

Eighteen years ago, after the fall of Saigon, there was pervasive pessimism throughout Asia. The failure of the United States in Vietnam did great damage to the American will and to American prestige. The trust in the United States held by Asian friends and allies was badly shaken. Many predicted that the fall of Saigon would soon be followed by the collapse of other Asian "dominos." Meanwhile, the Soviet Union began to profit from America's misfortune by rushing in to fill the vacuum created by America's withdrawal. Moscow accelerated its buildup of forces in the Pacific, deployed SS-20s, and assisted the invasion of Cambodia by its client state, Vietnam.

Yet despite these and other challenges, international relations in the Pacific region have remained generally peaceful during the past two decades. What accounts for this?

Asian regional stability since 1975 has, I believe, rested on five pillars. First, the region has benefited from a Pax Americana. The United States has been the central unifying hub of a network of bilateral security relationships that have helped to deter potential aggressors and to reassure American friends and allies. The U.S. security umbrella in East Asia has also allowed the friendly governments of the region to maintain relatively low defense budgets while concentrating on economic development.

The United States will remain the preeminent power in the Asia-Pacific region during the 1990s for at least two basic reasons. First, no other power, nor any likely combination of powers, can replace it. China, Japan, India, and a weakened Russia will all play more active roles in Asia, and the United States, to be sure, will have to take these great powers much more into account in its future dealings in the region. But none of these powers can replace the United States. Although Russia still possesses several elements of power—military, diplomatic, economic, and political—all are in rapid decline. Japan is an economic dynamo but a political and military midget. It has neither the ability nor the desire to challenge U.S. leadership in the region. China is still a poor, Third World country struggling to modernize its economy.

The second reason why the United States will remain preeminent in the Pacific is that almost all of the countries in the region prefer the Pax Americana to any conceivable alternative. As Charles Krauthammer has pointed out: "no country in East Asia—from South Korea to China to Thailand to Australia—fears the deployment of American forces. What they do fear is American withdrawal. In the absence of Pax Americana there would be enough nervousness about ultimate Japanese intentions and capabilities to spark a local arms race and create instability of a kind that has not been seen in Asia for decades."[3] Even the Soviet Union came to realize that the U.S.–Japan alliance may be preferable to an autonomous and heavily rearmed Japan that is cut loose from the American connection.

The Asian states want a continued U.S. presence not only because many of them fear a resurgent Japan but also because they all fear other "close-in powers" much more than they fear a distant United States with no territorial ambitions in the region. China and Japan continue to look to American power as a necessary counterweight to the still considerable land-based military power of Russia. South Korea fears the heavily armed and volatile North Korea. And the Southeast Asian countries, including Vietnam, fear either a resurgent Japan or a more powerful China, or both.

In short, the United States has performed and will continue to perform the indispensable balancing role in Asia, much as Great Britain performed that role in Europe after the defeat of Napoleon. In one of the most heavily armed regions of the world, this balancing role is crucial. Many Asian countries are heavily armed. China maintains an armed force of some three million men; North Korea has forces of more than one million, 75 percent of which are forward deployed alongside invasion corridors leading to Seoul; and Vietnam, even after cutting its armed forces of one million in half, still has by far the largest army in Southeast Asia.[4]

To help maintain the military balance in the Pacific, the United States has a relatively modest force structure. The United States has 135,000 forward deployed forces in the theater, including 50,000 in Japan, 44,400 in Korea, 14,800 in the Philippines, and 25,000 afloat. These forces will be reduced by 14–15,000 by mid-decade. Such a force structure hardly seems excessive under existing circumstances.[5]

Moreover, it is nonsense to suggest, as some analysts have, that the United States could save lots of money and rejuvenate its economy by drastically cutting its forces in the Pacific.[6] The United States is now spending about 5.4 percent of its GNP on defense and, by 1995, will be spending only 4 percent, the lowest since Pearl Harbor. Of this amount, some $50 billion, or about 15 percent of the defense budget, goes to maintain the U.S. forward deployment in Asia. The

United States surely does have serious domestic problems to address and certainly does need to become more competitive, to save more, to cut its budget deficit, and to improve its educational system. But America's domestic problems have not been caused by "imperial overstretch" in Asia. Rather they have been caused by "social overstretch"—an unwillingness of the American political system to do what is necessary, either by raising taxes or cutting spending or both, to pay for the country's vast system of domestic entitlements.

The second pillar of Asian stability during the past several decades has been the U.S.–Japan alliance. This alliance has helped to contain Soviet and communist expansion and it has contributed to political stability and economic prosperity throughout the region. Had Japan been allied with Russia or China, or had it been pursuing an independent or neutral policy during the past several decades, the whole history of East Asia would have been quite different.

The U.S.–Japan partnership has, moreover, been indispensable for both countries. Without American protection, Japan would have had to spend huge sums on its own defense while frightening and alienating its neighbors. For its part, without a strong Japanese ally in the region, the United States would soon see its influence sharply diminish.

Despite continuing—and to some extent justified—dissatisfaction in the United States about Japan's unwillingness to bear a fair share of the "burdens" of defense in the Pacific, Tokyo has taken a number of important steps during the past decade to help the United States maintain global and Asian stability. In the security realm, particularly during the Reagan–Nakasone era, Japan was steadily integrated into the Western alliance. It accepted responsibility for defense of its sea lanes to a distance of 1,000 miles. At the Williamsburg summit in 1983, Nakasone joined the Western powers in calling for a coordinated response to the deployment of Soviet SS-20 missiles; and he accepted for the first time the principle of the indivisibility of Western security. In the 1980s, Japan began joint military exercises with the United States and with other Pacific allies. In more recent years, Japan has substantially increased its support of U.S. forces stationed in Japan. And, during Desert Storm, Japan contributed some $13 billion to support the allied forces in the Persian Gulf and sent transport planes to the Gulf in order to assist the removal of refugees. After the Gulf War, Japan sent minesweepers to assist in reopening Persian Gulf sea lanes. And, in a historical watershed decision in the summer of 1992, the Japanese Diet approved Prime Minister Miyazawa's new policy of earmarking up to 2,000 Japanese military personnel for service in United Nations peace-keeping operations. This policy authorizes Japanese armed forces to serve abroad for the first time since World War II, though exclusively under UN auspices.

In the political realm, Japan has also been playing a more constructive diplomatic role in Asia. The Japanese hosted peace talks on Cambodia that were instrumental in keeping alive the UN peace process; Japanese prime minister Kaifu visited New Delhi in an effort to alleviate tensions between India and

Pakistan over Kashmir; and Tokyo has engaged in a dialogue with North Korea designed to improve North–South Korean relations and eventually to normalize relations between Tokyo and Pyongyang. Perhaps even more important, Japan's interests and those of the United States are virtually identical in Asia, as in other parts of the world.

In the economic sphere, Japan has become the largest worldwide donor of development aid and is providing this aid to a number of strategically important but vulnerable countries in Asia such as Pakistan, the Philippines, and Indonesia. In addition, Japan has become the principal investor and trade partner for most countries in Asia.

A third pillar of Asian stability during the past two decades has been the increasing trend toward regional integration. Despite strong initial skepticism, the Association of Southeast Asian Nations, or ASEAN, has become a remarkably cohesive and effective political organization that brings together Indonesia, Singapore, Thailand, Malaysia, the Philippines, and Brunei in a pattern of regional cooperation. Although ASEAN has been careful not to turn itself into a military alliance, patterns of bilateral security cooperation have emerged and will almost certainly be strengthened in the 1990s.

In the political realm, an arrangement called the Six-Plus-Five brings together the six ASEAN foreign ministers annually with their counterparts from the five developed countries of the Pacific (the United States, Canada, Japan, Australia, and New Zealand) to explore political and economic problems in the region.

In the economic arena, a new government organization, the Asia-Pacific Economic Cooperation or APEC, has been created to facilitate economic cooperation in the region. Within APEC, which now consists of the United States and eleven other nations of the Pacific basin, efforts are now under way to enhance regional integration in telecommunications and transport, to remove impediments to investment flows, and to develop a shared sense of the future through, for example, analysis of future energy needs. At the July 1990 APEC meeting in Singapore, U.S. secretary of state James Baker proposed an education initiative that would expand linkages between U.S. and Asian education institutions.

In sum, although the forces of regional integration in Asia are still much more fragile than those in Europe, because of great cultural, political, and economic differences, a process of what Robert Scalapino calls "soft regionalism" is already well advanced.

A fourth factor that has contributed to regional stability is the failure of communism and the increasing preoccupation of China, Vietnam, and other Asian communist states with modernization and reform at home. This process has had a profound impact on the foreign policies of the Leninist states. In the 1970s, China abandoned its revolutionary foreign policy and its radical domestic agenda and instead adopted the four modernizations as its main objective. To achieve its new goal, China has required a calm international environment, peace with its neighbors, and access to foreign capital and technology, which could best be provided by the West. As a result of these imperatives, China began to enter the regional family of nations instead of trying to subvert it. Just in the past year, China has entered into normal diplomatic relations with Indonesia and Singapore and has established a trade office in South Korea.

When Gorbachev came to power in 1985, the Soviet Union also adopted modernization as its main objective. To achieve this goal, the Soviet Union, too, required stable relations with all the Asian powers and increasing economic integration into the dynamic Pacific economy. Gorbachev therefore placed a high priority on improving relations with all the Pacific states. He normalized relations with China, extended diplomatic recognition to South Korea, courted Japan, and stepped up the pace of Soviet diplomatic activity throughout Southeast Asia. Boris Yeltsin, as president of the Soviet successor state (Russia), continues to solicit Asian aid and investment for Moscow's development plans.

Since 1988, Vietnam has also embarked on a reform program at home, withdrawn its forces from Cambodia, and begun to improve its economic and political relations with all of its neighbors. Indonesia's President Suharto visited Hanoi in September 1990 and agreed to hold annual meetings and to spur joint efforts to create a new framework of cooperation in Southeast Asia. Suharto also signed a science and technology agreement with Vietnam. The Vietnamese have also begun to improve relations with Thailand. Meanwhile, Singapore's trade with Vietnam rose to over $300 million in 1991, making it Hanoi's largest trading partner.

In sum, the Asian Leninist states are looking outward in an effort to revive stagnant economies; and the military and ideological threat they once posed to the region has been substantially reduced.

The fifth and final factor that has contributed to Asian stability during the past two decades has been the impressive economic performance of the region. The region now accounts for nearly a quarter of world gross product; its share of this product has grown by 30 percent or more each of the last three decades; and its volume of exports has increased annually by nearly 20 percent for the last twenty years. By the end of the century, the Pacific region will account for almost as much of the world's GNP as Europe and North America. This economic growth has greatly contributed to a moderation of politics in the region and to political and social stability in several countries. It has also helped make several countries militarily stronger. South Korea, for example, is now becoming a major arms manufacturer.

The Impact of the End of the Cold War

The end of the Cold War has had both positive and adverse impacts on the region but, on balance, its impact is likely to be quite beneficial. First, there will now be growing opportunities for "confidence-building measures," as well as for arms control and arms reductions, even though a good deal of this process is likely to remain unilateral and informal. Second, there will be new opportunities to re-solve the regional conflicts in Korea and Indochina and to bring about a solution of the Russian-Japanese territorial dispute. I will have more to say about these issues in the conclusion.

To be sure, the end of the Cold War could also have an adverse impact on the strategic environment in Asia. First, it may create strong pressures within the United States to bring about larger reductions in the U.S. military presence in Asia than are warranted, and this could easily stir a new and dangerous arms race in the region. Second, the end of the Soviet threat will increase the pressures in the United States to concentrate on the economic challenge from Japan. This is a desirable objective provided it is handled in a constructive manner. But if the emphasis is placed on blaming Japan for America's lack of competitiveness, the effect could be to further erode the U.S.–Japan alliance.

The end of the Cold War will also have a substantial impact on U.S. military strategy in Asia. For several decades, this strategy was predicated to a consider-able extent on the notion of "horizontal escalation" as a form of deterrence. The idea was that the United States could best deter a Soviet attack in Europe—where the Russians had conventional military superiority—by threatening to escalate in Asia—where the Americans had conventional military superiority. But now that the Russians have left Eastern Europe and the Warsaw Pact is no more, and there are huge cuts in both American and Russian forces, the strategy of "horizontal escalation" has become obsolete. In the future, the United States will need to develop a new military strategy for Asia no longer focused on Russia but rather on dealing with a diffuse and multiple threat environment.

In this connection, the Persian Gulf crisis underscored an essential factor emerging from the new global security environment: U.S. forces should be de-ployable between different theaters. U.S. marines on Okinawa were redeployed to the Gulf along with a significant proportion of the U.S. naval forces in the Pacific, as were ground and air forces from the NATO command area and ships and supplies from the Mediterranean and Atlantic as well as the continental United States. This greater maneuverability of forces is bound to open new opportunities for deployment and basing and it is also likely to have a substantial impact on future U.S. defense strategy.[7]

There is one final point to be made. The post–Cold War era will require that the United States share power and responsibilities with its allies and friends to a much greater extent than was necessary or desirable during the bipolar era. This will require not only more diplomatic consultation and coalition building. It will necessitate fundamental institutional changes. For example, the United Nations Security Council should be expanded to include both Germany and Japan.

The Impact of the Victory in the Gulf

The decisive U.S. victory in the Gulf War highlights an important development in the history of warfare. For the first time, airpower employing precision-guided bombs and missiles played a decisive role in war, paving the way for the invasion of Kuwait and Iraq. With these weapons, the United States and its allies critically weakened the fourth largest army in the world while suffering surprisingly light casualties during the month of air war. Even small, armored targets like tanks and personnel carriers, previously almost impossible to destroy with bombs, have now fallen victim to the new bombs' accuracy. This same accuracy has substantially reduced the accidental damage that would otherwise have befallen civilian buildings.[8] This revolution in warfare is bound to have a sobering impact on a variety of Third World dictators from Kaddafi in Libya to Kim Il song in North Korea.

Equally important, the victory in the Gulf is likely at long last to end the "Vietnam syndrome" in the United States and to demonstrate that America can use military power to achieve political ends, particularly when the use of that military power has the overwhelming support of the American people. As a result, the United States is likely to gain new respect throughout the world, including Asia.

Potential Threats to Asian Stability

Potential threats to Asian stability in the next decade can be divided into several categories. First, there are classic threats from adventurist and unpredictable regimes such as the one in North Korea. The North Korean dictator, Kim Il-song, and a few associates rule over this isolated, totalitarian, Stalinist system with few constraints on their power. They preside over a huge army with more than a million men. Despite on-again off-again negotiations with South Korea, Pyongyang has yet to accept the very legitimacy of the South Korean government, which it continues to denounce in its propaganda as a puppet of U.S. "imperialism." Meanwhile, North Korea continues to acquire weapons of mass destruction.

A second category of threat in Asia comes from a variety of unresolved territorial disputes, including the Russian-Japanese conflict over what Japan calls its "northern territories," and the Chinese-Vietnamese dispute over the Spratly Islands. China continues to develop a power projection capability focused on the Spratlys.

A third more diffuse category of threat emanates from the danger of domestic instability in many, if not most, of the Leninist states in Asia. There is enormous uncertainty surrounding the efforts by the Soviet Union, China, and Vietnam to move from state-controlled to market economies and from totalitarian to more pluralistic political systems. In China, since the Tiananmen tragedy, an octogenarian leadership has steered the country on a more conservative path. In Vietnam, too, the aging party leaders, frightened by the collapse of communism in Eastern Europe, have made clear their opposition to political liberalization and tightened their reins on power. The official media darkly suggest that the West is seeking to subvert the "socialist" system through a conspiracy of "peaceful evolution." The West has a strong interest in steady democratization in the Leninist world not only because of its interest in advancing human rights. Perhaps just as important, the West sees a connection between liberalization in China on the one hand and Western security on the other. A political system with few constraints on the power of its leaders is clearly more dangerous to Western security than one in which there are a variety of such limits.

There is a danger of instability not only in the Leninist states but also in a number of other countries that are modernizing rapidly. Economic modernization, even when it goes smoothly, requires difficult societal and cultural adjustments, the failure of which may result in serious political crisis. South Korea and Taiwan are now facing problems associated with the transition from authoritarian to democratic regimes in a context of rapid modernization. South Korea is troubled by labor and student unrest. Taiwan has named a military leader as prime minister and is gearing up for a long battle over constitutional reform. Instability in both South Korea and Taiwan have serious foreign policy implications. To the extent that South Korea is perceived as unstable by North Korea, this will encourage the North to continue both to meddle in Southern politics and to adopt obstructionist policies. In the Taiwan case, greater democratization is bound to strengthen the forces of the local independence movement and this, in turn, is bound to cause growing anxieties in Peking.

Yet another major threat to Pacific stability in the decade ahead is the potential for gradual erosion of the U.S.–Japan alliance as economic squabbles become increasingly intense. The deterioration in civil discourse about mutual problems is already evident. Its impact on public opinion in the United States is reflected in the recent increase in the number of Americans who, though still a minority, express negative attitudes about Japan. Should this erosion in the tenor of the relationship continue over the longer term, it is bound to have adverse policy consequences. A related danger is that neither the United States nor Japan will take the steps necessary to put their own economic houses in order and that both will find it more convenient to blame the other for growing economic tensions.

Finally, there is the danger that if the U.S. reduces its forces in Asia too much and too soon, other "rising" powers will move to fill the vacuum. This would lead to a new arms race in Asia. Much in Asia will therefore depend on America's willingness to remain a strong and credible Asia-Pacific power, even while it reduces its military presence in accordance with changed circumstances. This willingness is by no means assured. America is suffering from severe fiscal constraints. At a time when the Cold War ends and substantial numbers of troops will be withdrawn from Europe, there are bound to be increasing calls for greater reductions in Asia.

A Security Agenda for the Pacific

In light of the foregoing analysis, what should be the security agenda for the United States in the Pacific during the 1990s? I see the following U.S. interests in the region: first, maintaining the United States as the premier power in the Pacific, which in the coming decade means countering the Japanese economic challenge; second, preventing the emergence of a hegemonic power in Eurasia by promoting a stable equilibrium of power; third, encouraging regional economic cooperation; fourth, encouraging arms control and confidence-building measures and developing a crisis-prevention regime; and finally, dampening down regional hot spots such as the Korean peninsula.

Meeting the Japanese economic challenge should be the primary U.S. goal in the Pacific during the 1990s for several reasons. First, with the end of the Cold War, economics will move much closer to the top of the global agenda. The international position of individual countries will derive increasingly from their economic prowess. Although the United States will be the only true superpower in both military and economic terms, that status will be of declining utility as global military tensions are reduced and international competition becomes largely economic. In this new context, Americans inevitably will see Japan as a major threat to U.S. primacy in a crucial arena of power. The concern will be not missile vulnerability but semiconductor vulnerability.[9]

As C. Fred Bergsten and Samuel Huntington both indicate, a central question for the world of the 1990s and beyond is whether the new international framework will produce conflict over economic issues or a healthy combination of competition and cooperation. History suggests that there is considerable risk of conflict that could spill over from the economic to the political arena. The emergence of regional trade blocs, or the development of a tripolar economic system, with the United States, Europe, and Japan each fearing an alliance of the other two against it, would be particularly destabilizing.

Fortunately, there are good reasons why the Big Three may avoid such an outcome. Chief among these reasons is that they enter the 1990s as political allies with strong security ties, democratic governments, and a strong sense of common interest throughout the world, a sense that has been fortified by their common stand in the Persian Gulf.

Nevertheless, as Huntington argues, an economic cold war is developing between the United States and Japan, and Americans have good reason to be concerned about doing poorly in that competition. American national security could be threatened if the Japanese expand their lead in a variety of important military technologies. The loss of American markets to Japan means the loss of jobs and profits. And the increase in Japanese economic power means an increase in Japanese influence and a relative decline in American influence.[10] In the Pacific, Japan is already the dominant economic power in terms of trade, aid, and investment, and Japanese influence in the region is growing.

In order to meet the Japanese economic challenge, the United States must develop a new strategy. "Japan-bashing" and protectionism are counterproductive. What is required is a positive American strategy that is designed to correct the weaknesses that have made possible the relative growth of Japanese economic power. Such a strategy would require an emphasis on: trimming the budget deficit, increasing America's savings rate, spending more on research and development, particularly in nonmilitary areas, and correcting the catastrophic decline in the education and training of American youth.[11]

Maintaining a stable equilibrium of power in Eurasia should be another U.S. priority in the 1990s. In the short term, this should not be a difficult problem simply because no single power now, or in the foreseeable future, appears able to dominate Europe and Asia. Russia is a declining military power, and the reunification of Germany, the liberation of Eastern Europe, and Moscow's desperate need to restructure mark the disappearance of any hegemonic threat. Japan and/or China could become hegemonic threats in the future, and many Asian countries are worried about such a possibility. But there is little possibility of such a development in the next decade.

It should therefore be possible for the United States to maintain a stable equilibrium in the Pacific, albeit at lower force levels, by continuing its bilateral alliances, especially with Japan, and by diversifying its system of forward deployment to countries such as Singapore and Brunei, both of which now appear to welcome an American military presence.

A third U.S. goal in the Pacific should be to encourage regional economic cooperation. By forming APEC, the United States and the market economies of the region have taken a major step forward in this direction. Moreover, by joining the World Bank and the International Monetary Fund, and by seeking to join the General Agreement on Tariffs and Trade (GATT), China has indicated clearly its own intention to participate in this regional cooperation. And China's membership in these "keystone international economic organizations" has already had a profound impact on its economic development strategy and foreign policy.[12] Russia has also indicated its desire to join these international and regional economic organizations and has already become an observer at Pacific Economic Cooperation Council (PECC) meetings and at meetings of the Asian Development Bank. And although the IMF has not yet resumed lending to Vietnam, IMF technical teams have visited Hanoi and helped Vietnam to develop a new economic strategy that relies much more on the market and much less on state planning.

A fourth U.S. objective in Asia should be to enhance the prospects for arms reductions, confidence-building measures, and crisis prevention. Confidence-building measures should be chosen with care so that they do not benefit one side more than the other. Many of the confidence-building measures previously proposed by the former Soviet Union are likely to be counterproductive because they are considered by many Western analysts to be self-serving and to hamper the access of the United States Navy to the Pacific. As a maritime nation, dependent on the seas for its economic health, and with critical alliances across both oceans, the United States will be reluctant to enter into any agreements that interfere with the freedom of its navy. Nevertheless, modest steps such as encouraging the exchange of data on defense budgets and defense plans, encouraging meetings of naval officials to discuss naval doctrines and future shipbuilding programs, and pre-notification of some exercises should be feasible.

With regard to arms reductions and arms control, there may be no need for formal arms control negotiations. But a good deal of "arms control" can be accomplished unilaterally and informally. Russia, China, the United States, and Vietnam have already announced substantial reductions in their forces in the region. Some of this reduction of Russian and U.S. forces in the Pacific is being brought about by defense budget constraints on both sides and some is taking place as a result of the strategic arms negotiations.

Another possibility may be to encourage crisis-prevention regimes. The Indonesians have proposed establishing a multiparty dialogue on how to prevent a crisis in the Spratly Islands. Finally, the United States has a substantial interest in trying to dampen down and resolve, if possible, outstanding regional conflicts. The most potentially dangerous such conflict in Asia remains the tense situation on the Korean peninsula.

There has been a series of encouraging new developments in the Korean peninsula during the past year or two: The Soviet Union extended diplomatic recognition to South Korea, and there has been a substantial increase in Russian–South Korean trade. China established diplomatic relations with Seoul in 1992, and Japan has begun negotiations to normalize relations with North Korea. The United States is engaging in a dialogue with North Korea in China; South and North Korea have held several meetings at the prime minister level; and Russia is seeking to cooperate with the United States to reduce tension in Korea. An increasingly confident South Korea is more open to contacts with North Korea; and the two Koreas joined the United Nations as separate states in 1991. In sum, the East–West dimension of the Korean problem has narrowed considerably.

But while all these are positive developments, uncertainty about the future of North Korea and of North Korea's intentions cloud the horizon. If there is to be any real progress in the North–South dialogue, North Korea must abandon its insistence on unification on its own terms and must end its self-isolating policy of autarchy. Above all, North Korea must acknowledge the legitimacy of the South Korean government and stop playing "united front" politics. Yet for North Korea to do all of this would require a radical change in the policies of its preeminent leader, Kim Il-song. Such a miraculous change might yet occur, but miracles seldom happen in international relations. So far, the North Korean dictator has changed his tactics toward South Korea because of a loss of Russian and Chinese support for his harder line and because of worsening economic conditions at home. But there is still little solid evidence of any substantial strategic change in North Korean policy.

There may be more hope for resolving the conflict in Cambodia. The Vietnamese have withdrawn their forces from Cambodia. Moreover, all the major powers and Vietnam have agreed to a United Nations Peace Plan for

Cambodia that would involve an end to the civil war and a new election for a legitimate Cambodian government. There are as of this writing many potential snags in this process, however, chief among which is the continuing suspicions and rivalries among the four Cambodian factions vying for power. Still, even if the UN Peace Plan does not work, there are good prospects for insulating the Cambodian civil war from the relations among the major powers and for preventing any escalation of the conflict.

Yet another important regional conflict in Asia is the territorial dispute between Russia and Japan over the four islands north of Hokkaido claimed by Japan and occupied by the Soviets. There are some encouraging developments. Gorbachev visited Japan for four days in April 1991, thereby becoming the first (and last) Soviet leader ever to visit Japan. Gorbachev and Japanese prime minister Kaifu signed fifteen documents dealing with trade, culture, nuclear power, fisheries, and aviation, and the Japanese resumed $100 million of humanitarian aid for Chernobyl victims that had been suspended in January, following the Soviet crackdown on the Baltic states. Japan also agreed to a large-scale program of advice to improve the Soviet economy. Gorbachev, for his part, agreed that a dispute over the territorial issue exists—something his predecessors had refused to concede. The Soviets also agreed to reduce their forces on the disputed islands, estimated at about 10,000 troops.

There were, however, no major breakthroughs either on the territorial dispute or on Japanese economic assistance to the beleaguered Soviet economy. In two speeches, Gorbachev failed to convince Japanese business groups to invest in the problem-plagued Soviet Union without investment insurance from the Japanese government, which will come only after a settlement of the territorial issue. Japanese business executives say that Moscow must restore political stability in Russia and pay overdue bills—the former Soviet Union owes $400 million in arrears to Japanese trading companies—if it wants Japanese aid.

In sum, Gorbachev's visit to Japan, and then Yeltsin's in early 1992, produced no new breakthroughs on the territorial issue, and both sides agreed that they would have to go a long way before they were able to sign a peace treaty ending World War II or contemplate major Japanese economic aid and investment. On the other hand, the visit did contribute to a lessening of the historic animosity between the two countries, and there was promise of more high-level talks.

Moreover, there are some signs of a Japanese softening of its earlier hard-line position. Japan has expanded cultural and personnel exchanges with Moscow and has softened its stand on Russian participation in regional and international economic organizations. In the Japanese Defense White Paper issued in September 1990, the Japanese no longer designate Russian forces in Siberia as a threat. And the Japanese have recently agreed to discuss with Russia a number of bilateral confidence-building measures proposed by then Soviet foreign minister Shevardnadze in September 1990. The Japanese clearly do not want to be left out of the global détente with Moscow.

Still, the Japanese-Russian accommodation will be limited. It will be constrained by the continuing primacy placed by Tokyo on its alliance with Washington, by a century of conflict which had led to considerable mutual mistrust, and by the fact that there is now scant Japanese interest in large private investment in Siberia at a time when Japan has no urgent need for Siberian oil, gas, and minerals.

In addition to the military tension still existing in the Korean peninsula and Cambodia, and the territorial dispute between Russia and Japan, there are several other potentially volatile regional conflicts in Asia. There are territorial conflicts in the South China Sea involving China, Vietnam, Taiwan, Malaysia, and the Philippines; and there are continuing tensions between China and Taiwan that are likely to increase as Taiwan moves further down the road of democracy and toward de facto independence.

American policy toward these regional disputes will vary with differing circumstances. In the case of Korea, the swift development of Russian–South Korean relations and increasing trade between China and South Korea have left some mid-level U.S. State Department officials urging the establishment of an official U.S. presence in Pyongyang. This would parallel the Soviet opening of an embassy in Seoul during 1990 and the establishment by Beijing of a trade office in the South Korean capital before establishing diplomatic relations. It would also be consistent with U.S. and South Korean support for "cross-recognition" of the two Korean governments and it could open a much needed U.S. window on Pyongyang.[1] In fact, it is hard to see what, if anything, the U.S. has to lose by making such a gesture.

On the other hand, it is unlikely that such a gesture will lead to any spectacular changes in North Korean policy. Such changes will remain improbable as long as North Korean dictator Kim Il-song is alive. Still, over the next decade, it is unlikely that North Korea will remain immune from the reformist pressures now at work throughout the communist world. At the very least, an American presence in North Korea would assist in making more informed U.S. judgments about Pyongyang's policies.

In the case of U.S. policy toward Cambodia and Vietnam, some adjustment seems also to be in order. The Vietnamese have withdrawn their forces from Cambodia; they have accepted the UN peace proposal for Cambodia; they have cut their armed forces in half; they have adopted market reforms; they have improved relations with almost all of their neighbors in Southeast Asia; and they have virtually eliminated their dependence on Russia. Under these circumstances, Vietnam is no longer a threat to its neighbors; and the United States should begin to pursue more flexible policies toward Hanoi, including the encouragement of Vietnamese participation in the IMF and the World Bank.

With regard to the territorial disputes in the South China Sea, the United States should welcome the Indonesian proposal for multilateral talks designed to defuse this issue and should encourage a regional initiative to develop the oil resources of that maritime region.

In sum, the end of the Cold War, although it has proceeded more slowly in Asia than in Europe, has brought a number of promising developments. Relations between all the major powers are improving, arms are being cut, and there are new prospects for taming the regional conflicts. The decisive U.S. victory over Iraq in the Persian Gulf has added to this optimistic scenario by increasing U.S. prestige in Asia as well as in the rest of the world and by promising an end to the Vietnam syndrome that has plagued American foreign policy for the past two decades.

There is, to be sure, still much uncertainty. And there are many dangers, particularly the rise of trading blocs that could erode the U.S.-Japanese alliance. Still, it is possible to look to the 1990s with cautious optimism.

Notes

1. See Samuel Huntington, "America's Changing Strategic Interests," *Survival,* January/February, 1991.
2. See Henry Kissinger, "Back to the Balance of Power," *New York Post,* February 26, 1991, p. 27.
3. Charles Krauthammer, "Universal Dominion: Toward a Unipolar World," *National Interest,* Winter 1989–90.
4. For the numbers, see the International Institute for Strategic Studies, *The Military Balance, 1990–91* (New York: Brassey's, 1990).
5. For the figures, see Department of Defense, *A Strategic Framework for the Asian Pacific Rim: Looking Toward the 21st Century,* 1990.
6. See Selig Harrison and Clyde Prestowitz, "Pacific Agenda: Defense or Economics?" *Foreign Policy,* Summer 1990.
7. See Paul Kreisberg, "The U.S. and Asia in 1990," *Asian Survey,* January 1991.
8. See Malcolm W. Browne, "Inventions that Shaped the Gulf War: The Laser-Guided Bomb," *New York Times,* February 26, 1991, p. C1.
9. See C. Fred Bergsten, "The World Economy after the Cold War," *Foreign Affairs,* Summer 1990; and Samuel P. Huntington, "America's Changing Strategic Interests," *Survival,* January/February, 1991.
10. Huntington, "America's Changing Strategic Interests."
11. Ibid.
12. See Harold Jacobsen and Michel Oksenberg, *China's Participation in the IMF, the World Bank and GATT* (Ann Arbor: University of Michigan Press, 1990).
13. See Kreisberg, "The U.S. and Asia in 1990."

4

The Military Dimensions of the Korean Confrontation

William T. Tow

Over forty years after the Korean War's eruption, the specter of conflict on the Korean peninsula remains one of the few vestiges of the Cold War. In 1971, in 1984, and again in 1991–92, the two Korean states—the Democratic People's Republic of Korea (DPRK) in the north and the Republic of Korea (ROK) in the south—initiated a series of negotiations designed to achieve reconciliation and eventual unification. The first two attempts were overwhelmed by each side's ideological hostilities and military threats toward the other; it remains to be seen to what extent the latest effort will succeed in bringing the Korean conflict to a close.

The involvement of outside powers in the Korean dispute has complicated the process of conflict resolution. In 1950, the United States led a United Nations coalition against North Korea following the latter's invasion of the South and after emitting misleading signals to Pyongyang and its allies that South Korea was beyond Washington's strategic purview. Recent emergence of previously classified Chinese documentation has revealed that Joseph Stalin and Mao Zedong were divided over the need to support Kim Il-song's military efforts to fill the apparent power vacuum created in the Korean peninsula in response to the ambiguity of the American commitment. While evidence of China's fore-knowledge about Kim's intentions to precipitate conflict with the South is still inconclusive, recently declassified Chinese documents point to Mao's support for the North Korean war effort as early as October 1950 and to Stalin's simultaneous reluctance to provide air support for PLA troops that might intervene in the war.[1] In early 1992, the Bush administration's East Asia Strategy Initiative (EASI) and the decision announced in September of the previous year to remove all U.S. land-based tactical nuclear weapons from allied territories have once more led to uncertainty in Seoul and in Tokyo.[2] Without a prevailing Soviet threat providing the rationale for continued U.S. bilateral defense alliances in Northeast Asia, it seems increasingly possible that China, Japan, and one or both of the two Koreas could be destined to engage in a regional power struggle if projected withdrawal of U.S. military power proceeds on course. If so, the Korean peninsula may well continue to fill the unwanted role as a catalyst for competition and conflict that it has played for centuries.

Debate still rages among postwar American historians and various South Korean political factions over whether U.S. military strategy applied to the Korean peninsula during the Cold War intensified or alleviated confrontation between the two Koreas.[3] Some opponents of that strategy have recently argued that Seoul's excessive strategic dependence on the Americans eroded South Korean political institutions and jettisoned any chance for Koreans on both sides of the 38th parallel to define their common sovereign identity before the end of the Cold War. Supporters of the U.S. extended deterrence posture counter that enduring North Korean bellicosity has left the South Koreans and their American allies little choice but to opt for confrontation over negotiation.

Understanding the relationship of Korea and great power military postures directed toward the Korean peninsula can provide a basis for discussing the still outstanding threat perceptions and force configurations that accompany continued division of North and South Korea. The dissolution of the USSR in late 1991 and concurrent American disarmament initiatives have somewhat modified the importance of these military postures. Moreover, economic constraints have combined with diplomatic progress to alter gradually the willingness and capacity of traditionally hostile powers to maintain a confrontational posture in this area of the world. Nonmilitary issues are clearly assuming more primacy in South Korea–U.S. relations, while Pyongyang's strategic importance to China, its only remaining important ally, is now measured relative to Beijing's desire to attract South Korean investment and trade. At present, however, the potential for military confrontation between the Koreas still underscores the reality that this sector of Northeast Asia represents the most explosive crisis point in the Asia-Pacific theater.

Origins and Parameters of the Conflict

From the outset of the postwar era, Korea's future emerged as a key point of disagreement between Washington and Moscow for managing the new world order. While the Korean peninsula was contiguous to Soviet territory, American strategic planners had come to view it by 1943 as critical to imposing an American "strategic denial" policy in Northeast Asia against postwar Soviet power.[4] The 38th parallel was demarcated as the line of division between Soviet and U.S. forces primarily to facilitate the management of Japanese surrender on the peninsula and, from the American vantage point, to guarantee at least a modest U.S. force presence in Korea at a time when American military planners were preoccupied with the surrender of Japan.[5] The December 1945 Moscow Conference produced agreement that a provisional Korean government should be established, with a trusteeship over Korea jointly managed by the USSR and the United States. Widening divisions between Korean political rivals, most notably Kim Il-song's communist North Korean Worker's Party and Syngman Rhee's pro-American Korean Democratic Party (KDP) based in South Korea, complicated the task of managing a postwar transition to a unified Korean state.

With the advent of Washington's containment policy against the USSR, and the Cold War, any prospects for Soviet-American collaboration in preparing South Korea's rancorous and deeply split internal political factions for unified government were dashed. The rising influence of Dean Acheson, George Kennan, Dean Rusk, and other containment advocates in the United States converged with American tactics to legitimize autonomous South Korean elections under UN auspices. By doing so, the United States was able to abrogate the Moscow accords and end any prospect for Soviet involvement in the postwar political evolution of South Korean politics. After two unsuccessful rounds of negotiations conducted by the U.S.-Soviet Joint Commission, the Soviets left Seoul for good in October 1947.[6]

In a strategic context, however, neither the United States nor the USSR was inclined to deploy substantial military resources in Korea prior to the outbreak of the Korean War. Both Soviet and American forces occupying the respective sectors of the peninsula in August–September 1945 were originally earmarked to contest Japanese forces, but President Truman's decision to use the atomic bomb against Hiroshima and Nagasaki produced an unexpected rapid Japanese surrender. Elements of the Soviet 25th Army were diverted from the USSR's invasion of Manchuria to occupy ports in northern Korea. General Douglas MacArthur, commander in chief, U.S. Army Forces, Pacific, issued General Order No. 1 directing the 24th Army Corps to link up with Soviet troops at the 38th parallel. Military historians estimate that no more than 3,000 Soviet personnel were pinned down along Korea's northeastern coast against still formidable units of Japan's Kwantung Army when Japan surrendered and the war ended in mid-August, and that American forces could have advanced on and seized control of territory far north of Seoul if MacArthur had not been so preoccupied with Japan.[7] Soviet force strength increased rapidly soon thereafter, however, and reached approximately a quarter-million personnel by late 1946, outnumbering the American deployment of around 45,000 troops.[8]

More significant than comparative Soviet-American occupation force strengths was the growing disparity between North and South Korean military capabilities. Prior to 1947, U.S. policy planners were hesitant to build up a military force in the South because rival extremists could use it to perpetuate their bids for power, destabilizing the political environment and complicating

Korean unification negotiations with Moscow. Furthermore, any South Korean effort to match Soviet and North Korean military power would inevitably involve more extensive American strategic commitments to the peninsula than Washington was prepared to extend. The U.S. War Department was on the defensive concerning Korea throughout much of 1946–47, experiencing serious divisions within its own agencies and frequent criticism from the U.S. Department of State over the utility of sustaining an American military occupation in South Korea. While Korea was viewed as strategic inasmuch as Soviet forces deployed there could put themselves within "easy striking distance" of the Japanese islands, defending Chiang Kai-shek's nationalist government in China was a higher priority in the eyes of Congress and of many within the Truman administration.[9]

The Soviets, by contrast, encouraged a rapid buildup of Kim Il-song's "people's militia" with both captured Japanese weapons and a formidable Soviet military assistance program. By September 1947, U.S. military officials were estimating that the strength of the North Korean People's Army (KPA) was approaching 125,000 troops, compared to 16,000 personnel in South Korea's constabulary or national police force.[10] While these initial estimates may have been high (later accounts give 60,000 as the operative figure, not counting the border constabulary and railroad guards), it was clear that North Korea was embarking on a major effort to achieve a preponderance of military power over the South.[11] Less than two years later (March 1949), the Soviet Union signed a military assistance agreement with the North Korean regime committing Moscow to the transfer of equipment sufficient for arming six divisions, twenty reconnaissance planes, 100 fighters, thirty bombers; to the deployment of over 100 military advisers; and to a 2.5 million ruble loan for North Korean use in further modernizing its defense forces.[12] During the Korean People's Army's "formulative years," 10,000 KPA technicians were reportedly trained in the USSR. While South Korean forces increased to over 65,000 by early 1949 when the constabulary was converted to a regular army, the KPA outpaced it; by the outbreak of the Korean War, North Korea could deploy 150,000 troops while South Korea could counter with only around 90,000.

Such force disparities, however, failed to prevent the almost complete withdrawal of American troops from the ROK by June 30, 1949. Only a 500-man military assistance group remained to advise South Korean forces. Given North Korean force superiority over the South, and Soviet expectations that the country could be unified under communist rule by tactics of politico-military infiltration and coercion, the Soviets had decreased their own occupation force to two divisions by the end of 1947, and had pulled out completely by the end of 1948. Concerned about what he viewed as an increasingly serious military imbalance between North and South Korea, U.S. Army Chief of Staff Omar Bradley had submitted a study to the U.S. Joint Chiefs of Staff arguing that the Truman Doctrine and U.S. containment strategy should be applied to the ROK more vigorously and that the strategic value of the peninsula should not be underrated. His remained the minority opinion, however, until the outbreak of the Korean War a year later.[13] Instead, the Truman administration opted to follow the recommendations of the National Security Council as exposited in NSC 48/1 (December 1949): that Korea was less important to the United States' strategic interests than other commitments, and that to station U.S. land forces on the peninsula could invite future American involvement in an Asian ground war that was to be avoided at all costs.[14]

The Korean War and Revised U.S. Strategy

North Korea's June 1950 invasion of the ROK propelled this small Northeast Asian peninsula that the Americans formerly regarded as a strategic backwater into the center of U.S. global strategic planning. A key State and Defense Department planning document, NSC 68, had already anticipated that U.S. military power would be required to meet a Soviet threat to various peripheries of the American sphere of influence, and the Korean War appeared to confirm this view.[15] With the Soviet Union boycotting the Security Council, the Truman administration managed to win UN support for an international police action against the North Koreans. Truman moved quickly to upgrade the American force presence in Taiwan, the Philippines, and throughout the Asia-Pacific theater. Underlying Washington's decision to project a higher strategic profile in Asia was its fear that Moscow was orchestrating Kim Il song's attack in Korea as a diversion for conducting its own military strike against Western Europe.[16] Korea became an important American security interest not on the basis of its local security environment but as a symbol of Washington's intensified determination to adopt an extended deterrence strategy throughout the Eurasian peripheries.

In retrospect, contemporary analysts are skeptical on just how effective was Washington's initial effort to project a credible nuclear deterrence posture in Northeast Asia. Secretary of State Acheson's speech to the Press Club in Washington, D.C., on January 12, 1950, appeared to exclude South Korea from U.S. deterrence commitments and has since been cited as a major failure of that strategy early in the Cold War.[17] Nor is it clear that deterrence played any real part in bringing that conflict to an end three years later. McGeorge Bundy and Roger Dingman have both argued that other factors apart from the Eisenhower administration's nuclear posturing in early 1953 were responsible for Chinese and North Korean acquiescence to a cease-fire. They attribute the softening of Beijing's and Pyongyang's attitudes to such factors as the death of Joseph Stalin in early March 1953, American peace overtures to the new Soviet government, and President Eisenhower's support for policy adjustments of the U.S. stance on the prisoners of war repatriation issue to a more flexible bargaining position. Contrary to earlier and predominant impressions, atomic coercion does not emerge from relevant and recently declassified documents as having been the key to ending the Korean War.[18]

Following the 1953 armistice, which effectively halted large-scale fighting on the peninsula, American conventional force strength dropped from eight to two divisions even while "Chinese People's Volunteers" remained deployed in the DPRK until 1958.[19] To compensate for the second large-scale American military pullout from South Korea within the decade, and to convince a skeptical Syngman Rhee to leave South Korean troops under the control of the United Nations Command (UNC), Washington promised to extend the military assistance needed to build up the ROK to twenty divisions. At the time of the June 1953 armistice, South Korea deployed fourteen divisions with a strength of 450,000 troops. Soviet military assistance programs to Kim Il-song, already extensive before and during the Korean War, were also accelerated immediately following the armistice to compensate for several hundred thousand North Korean casualties during that conflict. The size of North Korea's armed forces lagged behind South Korea's military manpower base until at least the early 1960s and perhaps even into the early 1970s (the DPRK's population is only half as large as the ROK's). Yet Soviet weapons and equipment (particularly jet aircraft) and a residual Chinese troop presence in North Korea were sufficient to deter the United States from exploiting its nuclear superiority by resorting to more aggressive military strategies against communism in the Far East.[20] This was particularly important during late 1953 when Syngman Rhee rebelled against U.S. wishes and refused to sign the armistice, insisting that the war once more be carried to the North, driving Chinese troops from the Korean peninsula, and unifying Korea under his own political rule.[21]

The United States' implementation of extended deterrence through the signing and ratification of a mutual defense treaty with South Korea following the war underscored the Eisenhower administration's determination to apply its "New Look" nuclear strategy in Northeast Asia as part of its overall global nuclear posture. The rapid expansion of the United States' nuclear stockpile during 1952–53 allowed the United States to contemplate, albeit briefly, the rationality of "preventive war" and nuclear escalation against North Korean, Chinese, and even Soviet targets to end the Korean War and to confront the Soviet military challenge once and for all. The adoption of NSC 162/2, however, signaled a more moderate American approach to Asia-Pacific and global security problems: the use of nuclear firepower as an asset for protecting the status quo of Japan, South Korea, and other allies rather than for deliberately precipitating conflicts against the Soviets and Chinese.[22]

By early 1954, American military officials in Washington and Seoul were speculating that future limited wars in Northeast Asia could be fought at the nuclear level without inevitable escalation to superpower confrontation. Eighth Army Commander Maxwell Taylor concluded, for example, that with the increased flexibility of the United States tactical nuclear arsenal, opposing field armies in close proximity could be neutralized by local nuclear strikes.[23] Although neither confirming nor denying their actual deployment on South Korean soil, Joint Chiefs of Staff chairman Arthur W. Radford answered "yes" to a press inquiry as to whether U.S. force modernization efforts about to be implemented in South Korea during late summer 1956 *could* include atomic weapons.[24] In early 1958, the UNC was acknowledging "unofficially" that it had reserved the right to equip its forces with nuclear artillery and nuclear-capable Honest John rockets in response to a steady, if unspectacular, growth of North Korean military strength and to the recent U.S. ground force withdrawals creating a conventional force imbalance that favored the communist powers in the Northeast Asian theater of operations.[25] The formalization of Soviet and Chinese defense commitments, signing mutual defense pacts with Pyongyang, appeared to confirm Washington's concerns about this military threat. Nuclear deterrence against Chinese forces stationed just beyond the Yalu River was deemed critical to both South Korea's survival and American global strategy.

The Nixon Doctrine and Deterrence Credibility

South Korea's contribution of combat forces to the American war effort in South Vietnam generated controversy within Korean decision-making circles about the degree to which any such contribution would detract from the UNC deterrent against a North Korean attack. A number of South Korean political opposition leaders argued that the reduction of South Korea's force strength along the 38th parallel could send precisely the wrong signal to Kim Il-song regarding Seoul's military resolve; that the North Koreans could be prompted to invade South Korea to ease the pressure of a combined U.S.-allied attack launched against North Vietnam from South Vietnamese positions.[26] The Americans did agree to upgrade the equipment of three South Korean reserve divisions and to upgrade its military assistance programs to the ROK as a quid pro quo for initially one and later two South Korean combat divisions' presence in Vietnam (approximately 52,000 troops). Seoul was, however, unsuccessful in its efforts to renegotiate the U.S.–ROK Mutual Defense Treaty along NATO lines—to replace a commitment to "consult" with each other about a proper response to another North Korean attack with a commitment for an automatic U.S. military response. Washington's position was that the two U.S. divisions stationed in the ROK provided a de facto trip wire and constituted sufficient credibility of U.S. commitment to South Korea's defense.[27]

The intensification of the Sino-Soviet rift and the potential softening of Chinese hostility against Washington's Asian allies led the Nixon administration to seek ways to decrease U.S. security commitments along the Asia-Pacific peripheries. Moreover, the United States' military stalemate in Vietnam reinforced the political unpopularity of Asian ground wars in the eyes of the American public and led President Nixon to seek ways to minimize any such future involvement.

Under the Nixon Doctrine, the United States moved between 1969 and 1971 to further reduce its land force strength on the Korean peninsula from 62,000 to approximately 42,000 personnel. The United States compensated the South Koreans for its smaller force presence by upgrading its conventional arms transfers programs to the ROK—particularly its airpower through the sales of F-4 and F-5 jet fighter aircraft, which were far more capable than any warplanes the Soviets had previously given to North Korea.

President Nixon postulated a strategic approach of "flexible commitment" and "realistic deterrence": "a sufficient degree of self reliance on the part of the allies as a precondition of effective American commitment."[28] Its implementation was predicated on an analysis of what effect a direct threat to an ally's security had on the United States' own security. Assuming that their preoccupation with each other would preclude Moscow and Beijing from supporting another North Korean invasion of the ROK, and that South Korea's military was far stronger in the early 1970s than in 1950, U.S. policy planners believed that the timing and political conditions justified a gradual American military retrenchment from the peninsula.

Certainly South Korea's rapid economic growth combined with wartime memories to preclude any significant inroads by Kim Il-song's revolutionary brand of politics. As important, however, was North Korea's own confrontationalist posture as reflected in a series of impressive military buildups undertaken during the 1960s and 1970s. Having rebuilt a large part of the economic infrastructure devastated by American attacks during the Korean War, Kim commenced a substantial force procurement program between 1961 and 1966, bringing the DPRK's military spending level up to 10–15 percent of the total national budget. The ensuing five-year program doubled military spending to near 30 percent of the budget between 1967 and 1972. Throughout the remainder of the 1970s, North Korean military outlays stayed between 15 and 16 percent and one-quarter of national expenditures.[29]

The nuclear weapons dimension remained an important one in South Korean military affairs during the Nixon/Ford presidencies. According to the Center for Defense Information and various Japanese sources, the American nuclear stockpile in Korea had grown by 1975 to 700 land and air tactical nuclear weapons, deployed in various missile and artillery systems.[30] These forces were designed to deter or to defend against a combined North Korean–Chinese or North Korean–Soviet threat against the South rather than against North Korea, per se.

The "rationality" of the North Koreans in the areas of threat perception and risk calculus was less evident. They still tended to engage in highly provocative acts against UNC forces. North Korea's seizing of the USS *Pueblo* in January 1968 and the shooting down of an American EC-121 reconnaissance aircraft in April 1969 are cases in point.

Given the DPRK's perceived bellicosity and the American desire to avoid becoming involved in a second Asian conflict while disengaging from Vietnam,

Washington was especially concerned about the continued credibility of its deterrence posture in the ROK in the eyes of Seoul. Pressures intensified by the mid-1970s in some South Korean quarters for the development of an indigenous South Korean nuclear weapons program.[31] These pressures were resisted by the United States. Washington feared that any such ROK capability would fatally compromise escalation control in future Northeast Asian conflicts and precipitate an arms race on the peninsula that heretofore had been fairly well tempered, if only tacitly, by the two Koreas' superpower arms patrons.

The Carter and Reagan Years: Burden Sharing vs. Realpolitik

Growing U.S. budgetary constraints, along with a conviction held by many within Congress that an acceptable military balance between North and South Korea had evolved, led to a reexamination of the U.S.–ROK alliance in early 1977. President Carter was prone to view the Korean commitment negatively because of his distaste for authoritarian tendencies in South Korean politics and his commitment to more rigid human rights standards in foreign policy. In early 1977, he announced that all remaining U.S. ground combat forces would be removed from the ROK over a four-to-five-year period. To compensate for this withdrawal, the United States pledged to deploy additional fighter aircraft in South Korea and (once again) to upgrade its military assistance to Seoul.[32] The Carter administration was signaling that its Korean deterrence commitments were of diminished importance in the context of the recent Soviet military buildup opposite NATO Europe.

This withdrawal plan was suspended in July 1979, however, when new intelligence data pointed to far greater North Korean land combat capabilities than previously estimated. Moreover, President Carter had clearly underestimated the intensity of Japan's negative response and the widespread opposition of the American Congress to the departure of U.S. troops from the ROK.

Concurrently, the Nixon Doctrine's "flexible commitment" postulates were being tested by the succeeding Democratic administration and found to be inadequate given the still high level of strategic interdependence required by U.S. global alliance systems and given the military power of the Soviet Union and its allies in Europe and Asia. By way of example, Vietnam had just humiliated China in a military showdown along the two countries' border in February without needing substantial levels of Soviet assistance to do it. Western European conventional defense modernization efforts were being circumvented by the Soviet deployment of a new generation of intermediate nuclear forces, including the SS-20 missile and Backfire bomber. It had become apparent that while U.S. air and sea power could provide a mobile, flexible response at the outset of a renewed Korean conflict, a *sustained* and ultimately successful defense of the ROK would remain dependent on the United States' ability to join in a land war with South Korean forces. The creation of a Combined Forces Command (CFC) in 1978 reflected Washington's awareness that, in forging a tacit strategic coalition with China to supplement its alliance with Japan and South Korea, the U.S. was strategically committed to the security of the Asian landmass to an extent that a solely offshore U.S. military presence would be inadequate for achieving success.[33]

The Reagan administration reversed the Asia-Pacific retrenchment trend by restoring the traditional postwar American strategic emphasis on Japan's security and by gradually downgrading China's *strategic* (as opposed to political) significance in the theater. Once more, the Korean peninsula was viewed primarily in terms of denial—precluding a hostile power from using it as a staging area from which to threaten the Japanese mainland. The Reagan administration's preoccupation with the growth of Soviet nuclear capabilities and conventional force projection capabilities in Asia drove it to strengthen American offshore power in the region as a part of its comprehensive effort to restore the United States' global strategic supremacy over the Soviet Union. Geostrategic asymmetries working in the United States' favor—the regional naval balance and the techno-economic superiority of Washington's Asia-Pacific allies—were to be reinforced as a "competitive strategy," exploiting American and allied force strengths against the Soviet Union's and its allies' military weaknesses. In the case of South Korea, the "extended reach" of American naval power and the ROK's widening economic advantages over the DPRK would work to create what the Reagan administration viewed as favorable long-term prospects for security on the peninsula and for Japan as well.[34]

During President Reagan's last years in office, the costs of the U.S. military buildup in the early 1980s and Mikhail Gorbachev's overtures to replace super-power bipolar strategic competition with a new strategic posture of "reasonable sufficiency" while concentrating on domestic reform, combined to again change American strategic perceptions and postures in the Asian-Pacific. In December 1988, the Soviet leader announced plans to reduce the USSR's land forces by half a million troops, including 200,000 personnel from areas east of the Ural mountains. Soviet Pacific Fleet deployments and maneuvers also appeared to be on the decline, although qualitative improvements took place in the Soviet submarine fleet and in the USSR's tactical air capabilities attached to its Pacific theater of operations.

Soviet force cutbacks, however, failed to translate into total restraint by Moscow in arming its North Korean ally during Gorbachev's early years in power. The Soviets continued to supply Pyongyang with state-of-the-art offensive air power by initially transferring Mig-23 jet aircraft in 1985 and, in 1988 and early 1989, shipping more advanced Mig-29s and SU-25s to Pyongyang. The latter two aircraft were deemed by military analysts to be a match for the F-16C/Ds shipped by the United States to the South Korean air force during the same period. As late as January 1991, Soviet deputy premier Maslyukov acknowledged that the Soviet Union was still supplying the North Koreans with very limited supplies of "defensive" weapons systems.[35] Following the USSR's ultimate dissolution later that year, Russian analysts noted that such assistance was based on the USSR's determination—even at this late juncture in superpower relations—to conduct Soviet–North Korean relations on the basis of "class principles."[36] As will be noted below, however, little other incentive for military assistance remained since North Korea could offer no foreign exchange in return for its importing of Soviet weapons.

Soviet policy motives concerning Northeast Asia during the last years of Mikhail Gorbachev's regime are best understood as reflecting a desperate effort by the USSR to establish itself as an indispensable player in any security and arms control arrangements to be implemented on the peninsula and throughout the region. This strategy was reflected in Gorbachev's proposal advanced during his April 1991 visit to Seoul to discuss a five-power collective security system in Northeast Asia including the United States, the Soviet Union, Japan, China, and India. None of the other proposed guarantors responded positively to his suggestion as they waited to see what fate lay in store for the Soviet leader's own country. Even Soviet commentators were skeptical of the plan, noting that Moscow's credentials for providing security guarantees to others at such a critical time in the USSR's own history at best appeared questionable.[37]

In fact, it was obvious to all that South Korean capital and investment held the greatest allure for the struggling Soviet economy, and this reality led the Soviet Union to normalize diplomatic relations with the ROK in September 1990. By then the USSR had increased its trade volume with the South Koreans to a very substantial $U.S. 900 million and had lured sizable investment funding from South Korean banks ($U.S. 3 billion for 1991–93 alone). Some reports even claimed the Soviets offered to supply South Korea with "defensive" weapons systems as a means of obtaining desperately needed hard currency (although no evidence exists that Seoul ever seriously considered such an offer).[38] In short, the unraveling of the USSR's domestic economy and that country's entry into a highly uncertain era of domestic political reform necessitated a wholesale reevaluation by the Gorbachev regime of North Korea's politics of confrontation. Soviet (now Russian) policy planners have concluded that Kim Il-song's formidable military capabilities purchased at the expense of his country's continued economic deterioration can only intensify North Korea's status as an international pariah state and decrease any value it might originally have had as a regional ally. They would have preferred to see North Korea pursue a similar path to that adopted by the USSR during its own transition to democracy—to integrate North Korea's economy and society into the processes of dynamic change taking place in today's Asia-Pacific.[39]

In partial response to the warming of Soviet-American ties and to the gradual disintegration of the Soviet–North Korean military alliance, U.S. strategic planners have begun to forge a new approach to Northeast Asian security. The updated U.S. posture has become known as the "balancing wheel" strategy. It was initially outlined by the commander in chief of the U.S. Forces, Pacific (CINCPAC), and commander of U.S. Forces, Korea, in April 1989. Access to forward basing locations in the Pacific theater of operations would be maintained to protect critical sea lanes of communication. In accordance with a decline in the superpowers' global rivalry, Washington would work closely with South Korea and other regional allies to strengthen these allies' indigenous forces and to maintain a regional power balance in line with both U.S. and allied interests. In specific reference to the Korean peninsula, American extended deterrence strategy applied against the prospect of North Korean aggression would remain intact with sufficient force capabilities deployed to ensure that any inter-Korean conflict would terminate on grounds favorable to the United States and ROK.[40]

Military planning and policies, however, could not be put into effect independent of South Korea's own maturity as an economic and political force in Northeast Asia. Throughout 1988–89, significant shifts were taking place in Washington's diplomatic outlook toward ongoing events in the Koreas. For much of the 1980s, U.S.–ROK relations had grown more strained over trade issues and as a result of intensified nationalism in South Korea. These strains led to legislation in the U.S. Congress calling for greater ROK defense burden sharing. They also led to South Korean pressures for restructuring the Combined Forces Command under a Korean general, for moving the headquarters of the United States Forces, Korea (USFK) out of Seoul, and for redefining the Mutual Defense Treaty's Status of Forces Agreement (SOFA) in areas of criminal jurisdiction, for greater rights for South Korean employees attached to U.S. basing operations in the ROK, and for base jurisdiction.[41]

While not intending to link increased alliance tensions with South Korea to such initiatives, the United States nevertheless began to establish limited contacts with Kim Il-song's regime. In late 1988, the Reagan administration announced three changes in long-standing U.S. policy toward the DPRK: (1) permitting "humanitarian trade" on a case-by-case basis; (2) initiating limited contacts between American and North Korean diplomats; and (3) liberalizing visa policies for American and North Korean citizens desiring to visit each other's countries.[42]

The Bush Years: From Global to Regional Threat Assessment

Faced with rapidly accelerating shifts in the global power balance from the bipolarity of the Cold War to a more complex multipolar framework, the United States was confronted with the need to formulate a new national defense strategy that reflected a focus on countering regional threats. Throughout 1990, President George Bush and his policy representatives delivered a series of public statements confirming that the future size and composition of American forces would be shaped by U.S. projections of what would be needed for responding effectively to future regional crises and retaining a force infrastructure to rebuild strategic capabilities quickly should the planned 25 percent reduction of U.S.

military power slated to occur by the mid-1990s prove to be premature.[43]

In April 1990, Washington introduced a specific timetable for reducing its combat forces from South Korea and from other points in the Pacific theater with the aforementioned EASI. The plan called for "measured reductions" in U.S. land and air power in the ROK as South Korean military capabilities are projected to improve between the years 1990 and 2000. It envisioned a "transition [of] U.S. forces on the Peninsula from a leading to supporting role" by streamlining those forces in three phases over a ten-year period in accordance with then-existing strategic circumstances. More specifically, it tied proposed levels of U.S. force reductions to South Korea's Force Improvement Program III, which should yield "steady improvements in ROK defense capabilities." The North Korean threat and the Korean peninsula's overall military balance would be assessed periodically to gauge further U.S. force reductions.[44] The EASI was, at least in part, the Bush administration's effort to neutralize growing congressional demands for greater South Korean defense cost sharing. It was a direct response to the Nunn–Warner Amendment, passed in July 1989, which called for a comprehensive review of U.S. military commitments throughout the Asia–Pacific region.

South Korea had already been targeted by American legislators concerned about future U.S. ability to maintain current force levels in allied countries. Senate Bill 1264 introduced in June 1989, for example, called for the immediate reduction of 10,000 U.S. Army personnel stationed in South Korea. Its premise was that a continued extensive American presence in the ROK was "an irritant" to South Korean democratic forces attempting to establish a national consensus on security questions, an unnecessary drain on U.S. financial resources given South Korea's increased national prosperity, and an impediment to ongoing North–South Korean unification talks.[45] Such arguments were usually linked to what appeared to be a decreased Soviet motivation to project military power in the region and to more general questions about the continued rationales for U.S. alliance commitments in Asia with the diminution of tangible regional threats.[46]

The South Koreans have recently proved willing to underwrite more of the costs of alliance operations with the Americans, with their cost sharing increasing from $U.S. 70 million in 1990 to $U.S. 150 million in 1991.[47] In return, however, Seoul demanded greater acknowledgment by Washington that the ROK had achieved "equal status" in U.S.–South Korean security relations. In November 1990, a new Wartime Host Nation Support Agreement (WHNS) was signed at the annual U.S.–ROK Security Council Meeting. The revised Wartime Host Nation Support Agreement committed the United States to reinforce the peninsula by swiftly deploying combat units while the ROK pledged to supply such reinforcements with necessary munitions and logistical support. From South Korea's vantage point, this revised demarcation of responsibility symbolized the ROK's willingness to meet U.S. defense burden-sharing concerns by footing a larger share of total alliance operating expenses in return for Washington's acceptance that "the ROK will no longer be a passive nation that merely responds to the U.S. demand for sharing the defense cost but will conceptually become a nation that actively supports the U.S. as host nation."[48]

To a greater extent than any of his predecessors, President Bush has been forced to confront the issue of arms control as it pertains to Korea. This is necessary because Russia and China have tempered their security relations and commitments to the DPRK and because of Kim Il-song's efforts to compensate for this development by moving toward an indigenous North Korean nuclear weapons capability. Estimates vary as to how close North Korea is to becoming a nuclear power: in early 1992, the director of the U.S. Central Intelligence Agency predicted such a capability could be achieved "within a few months," while U.S. State Department sources countered that initial operating capability for a North Korean nuclear force was still several years away.[49] More certain was that any North Korean merging of nuclear warheads with an already formidable medium-range ballistic missile capability would intensify both South Korea's and Japan's threat environment at the very time that the winding down of Cold War competition offers hope for a peaceful resolution to the Korean dispute. Pyongyang's 1993 withdrawal from the IAEA was a disturbing portent.

Korean Negotiations

A third round of North–South contacts designed to facilitate reunification began in September 1990 with a meeting between the prime ministers of the ROK and the DPRK. While the first two rounds (conducted in 1971 and 1984, respectively) were unsuccessful, hopes for greater progress during the latest set of negotiations were strengthened by preliminary indications that both sides were prepared to modify their past differences. North Korea was economically decimated by the loss of its traditional Soviet support base while the ROK had adopted a more careful approach to the reunification question after observing the socio-economic traumas experienced by a newly reunified Germany. The Bush administration facilitated the spirit of accommodation when, as noted above, it announced in September 1991 that it would remove all land-based theater nuclear weapons deployed on foreign soil, thereby unilaterally removing its land-based nuclear forces from South Korea without ever officially admitting to their presence. In December 1991, a breakthrough in negotiations was achieved with the two Koreas signing a nonaggression pact, complete with provisions for the strengthening of cooperation in the areas of commerce and transport. The agreement also called for the replacement of the armistice that ended the Korean War with a formal peace treaty, but provided no specific guidelines as to how this would be effected.

The warming trend in intra-Korean ties continued immediately following the signing of the accord. South Korea announced that it would cancel the annual *Team Spirit* joint military exercises with the United States on a one-year trial basis. The DPRK reciprocated by declaring it would ratify and comply with International Atomic Energy Agency (IAEA) safeguards built into the Nuclear Non-Proliferation Treaty (NPT) that permit on-site IAEA inspections—a condition of the treaty that the DPRK had been resisting since it signed the NPT in 1985.[50]

North Korea's accommodation in these negotiations was a direct result of its increased sense of isolation and vulnerability. The DPRK's economy was coming under severe strain, leading Kim Il-song to reconsider seriously the short-term advantages of cultivating at least limited Western—and, by extension, South Korean—investment in North Korean enterprises. In addition, Kim was unable to engage in his classical tactic of playing off Moscow against Beijing. The demise of the USSR in late 1991 led to a severe cutback of the DPRK's energy supplies (the Soviet Union had been the chief source of North Korean petroleum at heavily subsidized and therefore much reduced levels from world market prices). China's surprising acquiescence to joint Korean membership in the United Nations in 1991 was a quid pro quo for South Korea's willingness to develop a lucrative trade relationship with the PRC.

Pyongyang's overtures toward establishing a more normal relationship with the United States have already been noted, but formal diplomatic relations between the United States and DPRK have remained elusive. The North Koreans delayed ratification of their adherence to IAEA inspection formulas until mid-April 1992. A separate bilateral treaty signed by North and South Korea the previous month established a Joint Nuclear Control Commission to be staffed by military experts from both sides. It called for the development of a specific timetable for each country to inspect the other's possible sites for nuclear weapons production and deployment.[51] North Korea failed to specify a precise timetable for enacting either the IAEA inspections or those stipulated by the bilateral accord, prompting continued American and South Korean suspicions that Pyongyang was adopting delaying tactics until such time that it could produce and deploy its own nuclear weapons. These suspicions endure despite subsequent reports that both Kim and U.S. officials were seeking ways to upgrade their diplomatic contacts.[52] In early May 1992, for example, North Korea submitted a report to the IAEA that seemed to confirm the presence of a reprocessing center capable of producing large volumes of weapons-grade plutonium.[53] In the meantime, North Korea's domestic affairs remain under the control of an uncompromising authoritarian government, with Kim determined to transfer power to his son, Kim Jong-il, and to resist the type of internal political reform that has recently swept away other communist regimes.

Implications of Regional Change

Given the recent shifts in the United States' security posture, the dissolution of the Soviet Union, and visible progress in inter-Korean negotiations, what does the future hold for military developments on the peninsula and throughout Northeast Asia? At first glance, the growing preoccupation by the key players in the Korean conflict with domestic politics and economic issues would appear to reduce prospects for future warfare on the peninsula. Several important considerations, however, temper such optimism.

Countering North Korean Brinkmanship

Reduced tensions in Northeast Asia will still largely depend on further North Korean politico-strategic moderation. Despite numerous pledges from North Korean leaders that they will allow nuclear inspections and fully disclose any nuclear weapons-related production capabilities, fears remain strong in Washington and Seoul that North Korea will drag out the process of establishing inspection procedures until such time as it can build and deploy an indigenous nuclear force.[54] A North Korean leadership that feels more isolated ideologically and cut off from its traditional sources of external economic and military support could still opt for higher levels of confrontation, perceiving that the DPRK's survival and legitimacy can be salvaged only through developing more self-reliant and lethal military capabilities.[55] While the December 1991 reconciliation agreement requires the North Korean government to institute social and economic liberalization, all political and military factions currently in line to support or challenge Kim Jong-il's authority after the elder Kim departs from the scene would be far better off with the preservation of a separate North Korean state.

It should be noted in this context that Kim Il-song's greatest concern is that the politics of Korean unification could emulate the experience of East Germany, which was politically assimilated by its far more powerful and wealthy West German neighbor. The DPRK's reluctant decision to apply for UN membership in the aftermath of all but certain Soviet and Chinese support for South Korea's entry into that body by mid-1991 was predicated on Kim Il-song's determination to maintain North Korea's separate existence.

South Korean defense officials argue that a military imbalance favoring North Korea remains the predominant threat to peace and stability on the peninsula. In terms of numerical comparisons, such arguments appear valid. ROK intelligence estimates have concluded that South Korea remains "the underdog in terms of regular active forces readily available for the initial phase of war."[56] Modern warfare is characterized by rapid mobility and intense firepower applied before an enemy can mobilize all its war reserves. During the late 1980s, various ROK defense officials estimated that the joint military forces of South Korea and the United States could achieve a defensive military capability of only 70 percent effectiveness against North Korean military power by 1991 and a "deterrent capability of 80 percent" by 1996.[57] Western estimates attribute to North Korea over a million active duty personnel compared to South Korea's 650,000. The North also enjoys a 2.5:1 advantage in armor and a 2.6:1 advantage in artillery over ROK combat power. North Korea's navy features submarines, fast-attack patrol boats, and other vessels that are fully capable of conducting extensive amphibious operations in support of future North Korean land offensives; the ROK has no equivalent surface ship or submarine capability. As late as mid-1990, U.S. defense officials confirmed that warning time for U.S. troops based in South Korea was still in the process of being reduced following increased deployments of North Korean troops, artillery, and rocket launchers along the demilitarized zone (DMZ) separating the two Koreas. The commander in chief of U.S. Forces, Pacific (CINCPAC), noted in April 1991 that North Korean forces were still clearly superior in quantitative military strength to their South Korean counterparts. Most Western strategic analysts maintain that the combined military strength of South Korean and American armed forces deployed in the ROK is only marginally sufficient to deter and/or defend successfully against the North Korean military threat.[58]

The most worrisome aspect of DPRK force capabilities is its potential to strike South Korean and Japanese targets with nuclear or chemical warheads from missile launching sites deployed near the DMZ. From such sites, recently deployed advanced versions of the Scud-B missile—designated the *Rodong No. 1*—could reportedly be launched against virtually all of South Korea's urban areas and could reach the Japanese cities of Osaka, Kyoto, Hiroshima, Fukuoka, and Kagoshima.[59] The possibility that such deployments could accelerate is an obvious source of deep concern for South Korean, Japanese, and American military planners.

Nevertheless, the U.S. performance in the Persian Gulf conflict demonstrated the ability of modern command-and-control systems and advanced weapons systems to overwhelm marginal strategic warfighting capabilities and outdated blitzkrieg tactics, which typify the military infrastructures of most Third World powers. Even the South Korean Defense Ministry has acknowledged the widening economic gap between the Koreas in the ROK's favor and a growing South Korean advantage in force "sustainability" (its forces' ability to fight over a period of time). Accordingly, some recent Western accounts have indicated that North Korea is looking for "new options" to break out of its regional diplomatic and economic isolation and is determined to avoid provoking the Americans and South Koreans into conflict for the time being.[60]

With prospects for further U.S. force reductions on the peninsula, and in the interest of avoiding unnecessary military expenditures to keep pace with the DPRK's bloated defense spending (even Pyongyang reportedly reduced its 1992 defense expenditures to their lowest level in twenty-seven years, at about 11.6 percent of the total national budget), South Korean analysts are examining various alternatives to the postwar U.S.–ROK deterrence trip wire as potentially cost-effective means to defray future North Korean attacks. One concept under discussion is the replacement of the trip wire's "line defense"—configured to seal off invading North Korean forces with the application of American and

South Korean firepower—with a "strongpoint defense" featuring mobile defensive units applying maximum firepower at points where the invader is anticipated to penetrate during the initial hours and days of a blitzkrieg. Advocates of this approach contend that an indigenous South Korean Army of roughly half its current size could implement this posture effectively.[61] Other South Korean defense observers argue that the ROK has no choice but to adhere to an "offensive-defensive" strategy based on its use of high-technology weapons systems against DPRK forces, and incorporating elements of the U.S. "Airland Battle Doctrine" to destroy the enemy's command-and-control and reinforcement capability well to its rear. Mobility is incorporated here as well, but a linear defense supported by massive firepower is still needed to prevent opposing forces from breaking through one's own front lines and conducting enveloping or flanking attacks.[62] In both these cases, however, it is conceded that U.S. offshore force capabilities may well remain the decisive component of battle.

Over the near term, therefore, it appears that conventional deterrence strategy and capabilities employed by ROK and remaining U.S. firepower deployed on the peninsula will be the most likely means for preventing North Korean aggression. At issue is the extent to which the United States will need to remain involved as a contributor to that strategy. This question will intensify as American global military resources are pared by scheduled military budget reductions throughout the 1990s, stretching remaining U.S. force assets to the limit to meet security interests and commitments in other regions. The progress of unification talks and the South Korean economy's continued rate of growth, affecting its capacity to support a more self-reliant defense posture, also loom as key factors in the DPRK's future propensity to confront or to negotiate with the ROK. Yet another important question will be how well South Korea can adjust to a short-term North Korean military—even nuclear—threat while waiting for the passing of Kim Il-song's regime and, hopefully, the DPRK's eventual political liberalization.[63]

The Japan Factor

One of the most critical ramifications of continued U.S. force reductions in the Asia-Pacific theater is Japan's policy response. An increased Japanese security role in the region, independent of the American strategic umbrella, would not be a welcome development in Seoul or other Asian capitals, where memories of Japanese wartime behavior are still strong. South Koreans characterize their ties with the United States as an "alliance" and those with Japan as "friendly and cooperative." With unusual candor, one South Korean analyst recently explained the basis behind the differentiation:

> The fact that the [South Korean] government sets its relations with Japan one step lower than those with the United States intensely reflects its concern that Japan will become a major military power. This is the standpoint of a country that suffered from Japanese aggression.

... As for the Japanese moves to send Self Defense forces to the Persian gulf, the [South Korean] government made clear its position that the ROK is concerned about Japan becoming a major military power and hopes that it will send economic assistance instead. However, the fact that the government decided to set its relations with Japan at the level between those with the United States and those with China and the Soviet Union reveals its desire to maintain close relations with Japan. These relations are more than mere economic cooperation, such as winning Japan's support for ROK foreign policy.[64]

Throughout much of the postwar timeframe, South Koreans have justifiably believed that the United States was committed to ROK security largely as an adjunct of Washington's more intense concern for denying Japanese territory and economic assets to any other would-be regional hegemonist.[65] With the prospect of an American strategic retrenchment from Northeast Asia now imminent, Japan is viewed in Seoul and elsewhere throughout the area as the most likely candidate to be that hegemonist. In late 1991, South Korea's Defense Ministry released a White Paper which explicitly warned that any Japanese military buildup taking place in the aftermath of increased U.S. force withdrawals would destabilize regional security.[66]

Recent Japanese governments have adopted what thus far must be viewed as a sensitive posture concerning the issue of Japan's rearmament. Far from intending to reemerge as an independent military power, Japan seems most comfortable adhering to its postwar security relationship with Washington, arguing that a regional power vacuum that still underlines the need for the U.S.–Japan Mutual Security Treaty could develop in Northeast Asia in the post–Cold War era. Japanese policy leaders remain visibly reluctant to institute systematic defense planning arrangements with the ROK, despite intermittent episodes of Japanese service chiefs suggesting that such cooperation should be established on a limited and low-key basis.[67] An objective assessment of Japan's present military power yields the conclusion that regional fears about Japanese remilitarization are clearly premature. As John Endicott has recently reminded us, "by selective standards, Japanese defense spending may be ranked third highest in the world, but that in no way makes Japan the third ranking military power. One should remember that the two Koreas have more powerful armies, by several times, than their neighbor to the East. Spending alone . . . does not make a military power."[68]

A more likely development is that a new division of labor between American, Japanese, and South Korea forces will evolve in accordance with revised threat perceptions and with the need to underwrite any subregional confidence-building measures. More specifically, the Japanese and South Koreans, under American supervision, could begin to collaborate in intelligence sharing on military traffic patterns in critical sea lanes of communication and air corridors overlapping the approaches to the Korea Strait and the Sea of Japan. They could also jointly monitor military capabilities of Russia, China, and North Korea, not so much with the intent of containing them, but to better supplement whatever levels of sea-lane surveillance and control the United States deems necessary in Northeast Asia in the revised post–Cold War context of the region's security. At least one respected American expert on Northeast Asian security affairs has recently suggested that South Korea could more effectively "localize" its national defense posture by developing greater offshore military capabilities of its own. In doing so, it is asserted, the ROK would be drawn into "a strategic framework shared by Japan" but still controlled by Washington.

Japan and South Korea could both move, over time, to coordinate more effectively a Northeast Asian component of what the United States has labeled as appropriate "out-of-area" contributions to the Western defense alliance in other regions such as the Persian Gulf. Both Japan and Korea, for example, could move toward upgrading host nation force agreements similar to those now existing between the United States and its NATO partners, providing for their assumption of broader defense missions in Northeast Asia if U.S. forces stationed in either or both countries were needed to quell future Third World crises. Such arrangements could materialize, of course, only after Japan has reconciled its own extra-national and extra-regional defense role with its self-imposed constitutional limitations, and after ROK leaders have reconciled the need for such burden-sharing efforts with their still overwhelming preoccupation with the North Korean threat.[69]

Regional Confidence-and-Security Building: Tempering Military Confrontation on the Peninsula?

The level to which future allied security cooperation and coordination occurs in Northeast Asia hinges upon Washington's ability to make the case that traditional threats underlying the bilateral defense treaties between the United States and its traditional Northeast Asian allies have still not been reduced to a degree that makes those arrangements strategically irrelevant. Recent trends point to an ambiguous situation in this regard.

The Soviet Union has been transformed—at least temporarily—from an imperialist global power with a self-appointed mission to underwrite the forces of international communism into an economically crippled, if still militarily powerful, decentralized commonwealth of independent states. Russian leaders have demonstrated an interest in tapping into the Asia-Pacific network of trade and investment which, barring the future spread of unmanageable domestic political chaos, should drive them toward adopting increasingly capitalist-oriented marketing and development strategies. The military alliance forged between the USSR and DPRK in July 1961 is, for all intents and purposes, extinct. The new Russia perceives no real leverage to be extracted from continuing its observance now that the United States and Japan are moving on their own to establish qualified diplomatic relations with the North Koreans, and it has no spare resources to underwrite continued military support for Kim Il-song. According to recent South Korean reports, Moscow stopped shipping offensive weapons systems to the DPRK in late 1989 and no Soviet military exercises with DPRK forces have been carried out since September of that year.[70]

China also remains preoccupied with its own political and economic reforms. In October 1991, Kim Il-song visited the PRC to solicit economic and military assistance and, reportedly, to urge the conservative Chinese leadership to regenerate and lead a Marxist security coalition of the PRC, the DPRK, Vietnam, and Cuba. He returned to Pyongyang almost empty-handed. While China reportedly upgraded its military assistance program to North Korea from $U.S. 300 million to $500 million and agreed to train several thousand North Korean troops annually, Kim's requests for economic assistance were rejected as was his proposal to forge an international alliance of remaining communist states. In fact, Deng Xiaoping and other Chinese leaders reportedly instructed Kim to study China's own experience of opening more extensive economic relations with the West.[71] Clearly, as one analyst of Chinese foreign policy has recently noted, "China sees its regional strategic interests as best served by encouraging reform in North Korea, helping North Korea relax its hostility to the outside world, and discussing tension reduction measures for the Korean peninsula with the U.S., the USSR [now Russia] and North and South Korea."[72] Indeed, following his discussions with IAEA officials in Vienna, which took place just prior to Kim's visit to China, Chinese foreign minister Qian Qichen publicly declared that the PRC wanted neither North nor South Korea to possess nuclear weapons (a point reportedly reiterated to Kim in Beijing a few days later), while Jiang Zimen, general secretary of the Chinese Communist Party, intimated to Japanese journalists that Chinese–North Korean fraternal ties could no longer be translated into a formal defense alliance—an apparent refutation of the 1961 Sino–North Korean defense accord.[73]

Until its demise, the USSR was highly active in promoting confidence-and-security-building measures (CSBMs) for Northeast Asia and, more specifically, for the Korean peninsula. Prior to 1991, much of this could be attributed to the USSR's continued alarm about a Northeast Asian military balance unfavorable to itself, especially regarding maritime power. In his landmark address on Asian security delivered at Vladivostok in July 1986, Mikhail Gorbachev proposed that CSBMs recently adopted to defuse military competition in Europe could serve as a useful precedent for easing tensions in the Asia-Pacific region as well. Regarding Korea, Gorbachev advocated the establishment of a nuclear-free zone, called for a reduction of U.S. antisubmarine warfare (ASW) capabilities in the Pacific, and supported the DPRK's long-standing proposals for dialogue and confederation as steps to guarantee conflict avoidance on the peninsula and throughout the region.[74] By mid-1991, however, the Soviets had accepted the notion that U.S. forces in Korea had actually played a stabilizing role on the peninsula.

Washington has rejected North Korean proposals to remove all U.S. forces from the ROK on the grounds that the United States is responsible as a guarantor to the United Nations Armistice Agreement ending the Korean War, and on the basis that such forces continue to be needed in fulfilling the terms of the U.S.–ROK Mutual Defense Treaty. Drastic reductions in force levels are also viewed skeptically without a commensurate set of verification procedures being defined that are acceptable to both sides. Just after President Bush announced his administration's plans to remove both its ground- and sea-based tactical nuclear weapons from South Korea and other overseas locations, American defense officials announced that the United States would reduce the level of its ground forces on the peninsula by 6,000 troops in compliance with the scheduled Phase II of EASI, leaving just over 30,000 ground forces in South Korea by the mid-1990s. Continued fears of North Korean nuclear weapons development, however, led U.S. secretary of defense Dick Cheney to announce a postponement of this troop strength reduction when he attended the annual U.S.–ROK Security Consultative Meeting in Seoul during late November 1991. Cheney and his South Korean hosts argued that conventional deterrence strategy needed to remain credible and effective until such time as the North Korean nuclear program was more thoroughly addressed in the context of its long-term implications for regional security.[75]

The key question about CSBM implementation on the Korean peninsula, as Thomas Wilborn has cogently argued, is to what extent CSBMs would add any real strategic reassurance to their adherents, who are usually adversaries, in lieu of the state of deterrence that is already operative between such adversaries.[76] Kim Il-song and his South Korean counterparts have been precluded from renewing their conflict either because their opponents' military capabilities or those of their allies have been viewed as sufficiently formidable to make the costs and risks of a conflict clearly outweigh its strategic benefits. Can a specific combination of CSBMs be derived to provide the same incentive for conflict avoidance in a more positive context than the element of fear underscoring the effectiveness of deterrence postures on the peninsula?

If the momentum of Korean nationalism continues to intensify among South Korea's electorate the answer may well have to be a qualified "yes." Clearly, the American extended deterrent has become regarded in a growing number of South Korean circles as an uncomfortable reminder of Seoul's postwar strategic dependency on an outside power. The dilemma facing ROK leaders is how to appear responsive to unification aspirations without falling into the trap of prematurely assimilating the DPRK into its own politico-economic infrastructure. Such premature assimilation could have the same ramifications for instability that are now facing a single Germany mired in industrial disputes, confronting painful social readjustments, and challenged by the possible rise of national extremist groups.

The process of confidence-and-security building on the peninsula has, to some extent, already commenced in the form of those intra-Korean accords negotiated during 1991 and early 1992 and as a result of independent political trends. The level and intensity of military exercises on the peninsula have decreased. The elimination of land-based U.S. nuclear-capable delivery systems deployed on South Korean soil has reportedly been completed and North Korea has committed itself to IAEA supervised inspections of its nuclear facilities. If a de facto nuclear-free zone is truly to be established on the peninsula, however, the United States, Russia, and China will need to agree to a formal arms transfer control agreement by which none of them would transfer state-of-the-art aircraft or other weapons systems to either Korea.

Eventually, both Koreas and the four major outside powers concerned with the peninsula's security could replicate the "Two-Plus-Four" agreement reached with Germany in 1990 that facilitated an overall culmination of Cold War politics in that region. Such an arrangement has already been proposed by the United States and could become more possible when Japan normalizes relations with North Korea as China did in 1992 with the ROK.[77] Over time, this type of diplomacy could provide for the phased withdrawals envisioned by EASI, with commensurate phaseout of DPRK and ROK military units, and become a basis for the peninsula's eventual unification.

Conclusion

Upon reflection, the conditions underlying Northeast Asia's geopolitical environment in the early 1990s are remarkably similar to those found in the late 1940s when NSC 48/1 mandated the United States' first postwar withdrawal from the Korean peninsula. Russia's current leadership crisis promises to complicate its contemporary political and economic transformation just as Stalin's last years in power foreordained far-reaching changes in the USSR by his successors. In the late 1940s, China and Japan were approaching historic crossroads, with the former opting to embrace Marxist central planning and the latter beginning to rebuild its wartorn industries and regional markets ultimately to new heights. Almost a half-century later, China is attempting to reconcile central authoritarianism with Western national development strategies, and Japan is still resisting direct military involvement in international security ventures while its neighbors continue to fear its remilitarization. Then, as now, American strategic planning was preoccupied with other theaters of operation (then Europe; at present the Persian Gulf). Japan was—and still is—regarded as the linchpin for American strategy in the Asia-Pacific region, an outlook that was resented by Washington's Korean allies. Both communist and noncommunist political factions were active in promoting their own versions of Korean unification; little has changed since.

It may be that as the United States' resource base declines proportionately to that of other powers in the contemporary international framework, it will be destined to accelerate the very painful process of selecting priorities among a number of important strategic commitments, as originally anticipated by the

Nixon Doctrine. Traditional and highly valued allies such as South Korea could be asked to assume ever more substantial responsibilities for meeting what are still formidable regional security challenges. Yet, indulging in premature judgments that U.S. force levels will no longer be necessary or affordable to sustain a minimum credibility of deterrence commitment to Seoul could be tragically counterproductive if such perceptions are based solely on the need for responding to short-term American domestic political pressures. The EASI correctly states that the scale of such commitments must be determined on the basis of threat assessment. It is, however, too optimistic in its assumptions that South Korean economic advantages over the North will automatically translate into ROK defense capabilities to deter those that can be fielded by the DPRK. Little analysis is offered as to how deterrence on the peninsula would be affected by the potential North Korean deployment of indigenous nuclear weapons or as to what future configuration of U.S. forces remaining in the ROK can best guarantee future North Korean restraint. A more comprehensive and systematic discussion in this regard by Washington's highest officials is needed.

The success of future CSBM initiatives directed toward the peninsula will ultimately depend on the continued success of the United States and South Korea to balance incentives with firmness against the Kims' continued intransigence and efforts to resist political change. In this sense, the problem of Korean conflict avoidance remains more than a local security question; the stakes are immense for regional and global security as well. Pyongyang has demonstrated just a trace of political moderation by its willingness to talk directly with South Korean negotiators when forced into a corner by Seoul's tactics of *Nordpolitik* and by its overwhelming need for access to the West's hard currency. Its political ethos nevertheless remains tainted by a rigid ideology, unquestionably hostile to the idea of North Korea's becoming transformed to a more orthodox, less bellicose, participant in the community of nations.

Only more consistent collaboration by the United States, Russia, China, and Japan in their relations with the DPRK will be effective in permanently neutralizing tensions on the peninsula. Such great power collaboration may be hard to achieve, however, in the aftermath of China's crackdown on its own political reformers, Boris Yeltsin's tenuous position relative to his own country's reactionary forces, Japan's inability to erase the animosity of either North or South Korea toward the Japanese, and Washington's apparent ambitions to play the role of a unilateral enforcer of a new world order. The recent "Defense Planning Guidance," authored by U.S. Defense Department analysts, envisions the United States maintaining a regional balance of power in Northeast Asia and is illustrative in regard to the last point. This document speculates that "enhanced [security] roles" on the part of Japan or Korea could lead to greater destabilization of the region unless Washington is able to maintain a defense alliance with a unified Korea.[78] Such reasoning appears to undercut the Bush administration's initiatives during 1991, more readily than before the Soviet Union's demise, to explore and facilitate regional confidence-and-security-building initiatives.

The time to take advantage of the winds of democratic change in Northeast Asia may be rapidly ending. This is especially the case if Russia is destined either to disintegrate economically and politically or to retrogress strategically into a reactionary state of global confrontation. On the other hand, if Northeast Asia's four major powers were now to undertake a special joint effort to add a permanent settlement of the Korean problem to the superpower legacy of creating a post–Cold War Europe, there are prospects for a more enduring regional security order in the Asia-Pacific.

Notes

1. For a report on the recently declassified Chinese cables to Stalin, see Seth Faison, "In Secret Cable, Mao Noted Risk of Invading Korea to Foil U.S. Power," *International Herald Tribune,* February 27, 1992, p. 5. Bruce Cumings's landmark study on the Korean War concludes that Chinese involvement in the war intensified only as American involvement in the defense of South Korea deepened during the fall of 1950. See his *Origins of the Korean War,* volume 2, *The Roaring of the Cataract 1947–1950* [hereafter cited as *The Origins of the Korean War,* vol. 2] (Princeton, NJ: Princeton University Press, 1990), especially pp. 652–655. Excellent assessments of the comparative Soviet and Chinese positions are also provided by Hao Yufan and Zhai Zhihai, "China's Decision to Enter the Korean War: History Revisited," *The China Quarterly* no. 121 (March 1990), pp. 94–115.

2. U.S. Department of Defense, *A Strategic Framework for the Asian Pacific Rim: Looking Toward the 21st Century* (Washington, D.C.: USDOD, April 1990); and President George Bush, "Initiative on Nuclear Arms: Changing the Nuclear Posture," *Vital Speeches of the Day* 58, no. 2 (November 1, 1991), pp. 34–36, reprint of an address to the nation, Washington, D.C., September 27, 1991.

3. In addition to Cumings' previously cited volume, see his earlier work, *The Origins of the Korean War: Liberation and the Emergence of Separate Regimes* [hereafter cited as *The Origins of the Korean War,* vol. 1] (Princeton, NJ: Princeton University Press, 1981), pp. 214–264. Also see Chae-Jin Lee, ed., *The Korean War: 40 Year Perspectives* (Claremont, CA: The Keck Center for International Studies, 1991); Rosemary Foot, *The Wrong War: Dimensions of American Policy and the Korean Conflict, 1950–1953* (Ithaca and London: Cornell University Press, 1983); John Lewis Gaddis, *Strategies of Containment* (Oxford: Oxford University Press, 1982); and Robert Jervis, "The Impact of the Korean War on the Cold War," *Journal of Conflict Resolution* 24, no. 3 (December 1980), pp. 563–592.

4. Bruce Cumings, *The Origins of the Korean War,* vol. 1, pp. 113–114; and related memoranda under the title "Interest of the United States in the Future Status of Korea and the Question of Recognition of a Provisional Korean Government," (Washington, D.C., April 1943); reprinted in *Foreign Relations of the United States (FRUS),* vol. 3, *The British Commonwealth, Eastern Europe, The Far East* (Washington, D.C.: USGPO, 1963), pp. 1090–1096.

5. Soon Sung Cho, "American Policy toward Korean Unification, 1945–1980," in Tae-Hwan Kwak, John Chay, Sopon Sung Cho, and Shannon McCune, eds., *U.S.-Korean Relations 1882–1982* (Seoul: Kyungnam University Press, 1982), p. 66.

6. The most complete account of this process is by Bruce Cumings, *The Origins of the Korean War,* vol. 2, especially pp. 35–78.

7. Michael C. Sandusky, *America's Parallel* (Alexandria, VA: Old Dominion Press, 1983), p. 238.

8. After a briefing from General Douglas MacArthur in Tokyo, Representative Robert F.L. Sikes reported that "Russia is maintaining about five times the number of occupation troops [in the Far East], mostly in Korea. . . ." See "Soviet Aims Alarm U.S. Group in Japan," *New York Times,* September 1, 1946, p. 4.

9. Cumings, *The Origins of the Korean War,* vol. 2, pp. 37, 59–61; and Ralph N. Clough, *Embattled Korea: The Rivalry for International Support* (Boulder and London: Westview Press, 1987), p. 17.

10. James F. Schnabel and Robert J. Watson, *The History of the Joint Chiefs of Staff,* vol. 3 in *The Korean War,* Part 1 (Wilmington, DE: Michael Glazier, 1979), p. 12.

11. The 60,000 KPA force strength figure is advanced by Robert Scalapino and Chong-Sik Lee, *Communism in Korea* (Berkeley: University of California Press, 1972), p. 928.

12. "Memorandum to General J. Lawton Collins, Chief of Staff, U.S. Army by Sihn Sung Mo, Minister of Defense, Republic of Korea, October 20, 1949 [Top Secret]," *Declassified Documents System* (1978), 52-A.

13. Schnabel and Watson, *The History of the Joint Chiefs of Staff,* pp. 26–27.

14. Thomas H. Etzold and John Lewis Gaddis, eds., *Containment: Documents on American Policy and Strategy, 1945–1950* (New York: Columbia University Press, 1962), pp. 255, 263–264.

15. Cumings, *The Origins of the Korean War,* vol. 2, pp. 178–179. Also see Samuel F. Wells, "Sounding the Tocsin: NSC and the Soviet Threat," *International Security* 4, no. 2 (Fall 1979), pp. 116–158.

16. Gaddis, *Strategies of Containment,* pp. 114–115; and William E. Berry, Jr., "Alliance Commitments and Strategies in Asia," in Schuler Foerster and Edward N. Wright, *American Defense Policy,* 6th ed. (Baltimore and London: The Johns Hopkins University Press, 1990), p. 222.

17. Cumings, *The Origins of the Korean War,* vol. 2, p. 409. Also see Alexander George and Richard Smoke, *Deterrence in American Foreign Policy: Theory and Practice* (New York: Columbia University Press, 1974), pp. 146–149.

18. McGeorge Bundy, *Danger and Survival* (New York: Random House, 1988), pp. 240–241; and Roger Dingman, "Atomic Diplomacy during the Korean War," *International Security* 13, no. 3 (Winter 1988–89), pp. 86–87.

19. For a comprehensive account of events leading to the withdrawal of all but two divisions of U.S. ground forces from Korea to Japan, Hawaii, and the continental U.S. by December 1954, see Robert J. Watson, *History of the Joint Chiefs of Staff,* vol. 5, *The Joint Chiefs of Staff and National Security Policy 1953–1954* (Washington, D.C.: JCS Historical Division, 1986), pp. 229–233. Also see Lee Suk Bok, *The Impact of U.S. Forces on Korea* (Washington, D.C.: National Defense University Press, 1987), p. 59.

20. Clough, *Embattled Korea,* pp. 100–101; and Gregory F.T. Winn, "National Security," in *North Korea: A Country Study* (Washington, D.C.: American University, 1981), p. 221.

21. Clough, *Embattled Korea,* pp. 24, 40. By mid-1953, Rhee's aggressive posture may have been prompted as much by his desire to push the U.S. as far as he could to win more military and economic assistance from the Americans as by any real intent to perpetuate the war.

22. Marc Trachtenberg, "A 'Wasting Asset': American Strategy and the Shifting Nuclear Balance, 1949–1954," *International Security* 13, no. 3 (Winter 1988/89), pp. 46–47.

23. " 'Atomic Target' Possible in Korea, Taylor States," *New York Times,* April 24, 1954, p. 3.

24. "Radford to See Rhee," *New York Times,* August 3, 1956, p. 2.

25. Joo-Hong Nam, *America's Commitment to South Korea* (Cambridge: Cambridge University Press, 1986), pp. 87–88.

26. Princeton N. Lyman, "Korea's Involvement in Vietnam," *Orbis* 16, no. 2 (Summer 1968), pp. 565–566; Seunggi Paik, "United States–South Korean National Security Relationship: 1945–1972," Ph.D. Dissertation, Southern Illinois University, Department of Government, August 1973, pp. 54–55; and Se Jin Kim, "South Korea's Involvement in Vietnam and Its Economic and Political Impact," *Asian Survey* 10, no. 6 (June 1970), p. 524.

27. Lyman, "Korea's Involvement," pp. 566–567.

28. Joo-Hong Nam, *America's Commitment to South Korea*, pp. 98, 100.

29. Research Institute for Peace and Security, *Asia Security 1980* (Tokyo: RIPS, 1980), p. 137; and Robert Scalapino, "The Development of Security Ties," in Academy of Korean Studies and The Wilson Center, *Reflections on a Century of United States–Korean Relations* (Lanham, MD: University Press of America, 1982), p. 282.

30. Gregory Henderson, "Korea: Militarist or Unification Policies?" in *Reflections on a Century of United States–Korean Relations*, pp. 146–147.

31. Following a trip by Kim Il-song to China in April 1975, and the discovery of extensive North Korean tunnel systems under the DMZ, South Korean leaders put the United States on notice that they were prepared to develop indigenous nuclear weapons if Washington failed to reaffirm existing extended deterrence commitments to Seoul. Indeed, it was revealed in early June that France was prepared to sell nuclear bomb production components to the ROK. President Ford and Secretary of Defense Schlesinger responded that the United States was fully prepared to use nuclear weapons in South Korea's defense. Meanwhile, U.S. officials worked behind the scenes to discourage any propensity by South Korea to develop its own nuclear force. See Spencer Rich, "Paris Giving Atomic Plants to 4 Nations," *Washington Post,* June 4, 1975, pp. A-1, A-7; Rowland Evans and Richard Novak, "Korea: Park's Inflexibility," in ibid., June 12, 1975, p. A-19; and *Keesing's Archives,* June 1975, p. 27273.

32. For background, see A Report to the Committee on Foreign Relations, United States Senate, *U.S. Troop Withdrawal from the Republic of Korea,* 95th Cong., 2nd Sess., January 9, 1978, p. 21.

33. Scalapino, "The Development of Security Ties," pp. 278–282.

34. Caspar W. Weinberger, Secretary of Defense, *Annual Report to Congress, Fiscal Year 1988* (Washington, D.C.: USGPO, January 12, 1987), pp. 32, 35; and Report of the Commission on Integrated Long-Term Strategy, *Discriminate Deterrence* (Washington, D.C.: USGPO, January 1988), pp. 30–31.

35. Stephen Blank, "Soviet Perspectives on Arms Control in the Korean Peninsula," *The Korean Journal of Defense Analysis* 3, no. 1 (Summer 1991), p. 127.

36. Vasily V. Mikheev, "New Soviet Approaches to North Korea," *Korea and World Affairs* 15, no. 3 (Fall 1991), p. 448.

37. See, for example, V. Golobnin, "Will They Help Our Pacific Policy?" *Izvestiya,* June 20, 1991, p. 5, as translated and reprinted in *Current Digest of the Soviet Press* 43, no. 25 (1991), pp. 19–20.

38. "Moscow Makes Known Its Readiness to Supply Arms to South Korea," *International Herald Tribune,* January 23, 1991, p. 2.

39. See, for example, Mikhail Titarenko, "The Situation in the APR [Asia-Pacific Region] and Soviet–South Korean Relations," *Far Eastern Affairs* no. 5 (1990), pp. 7–8.

40. Testimony of Admiral Huntington Hardisty, U.S. Navy, Commander-in-Chief, U.S. Pacific Command, and General Louis Menetrey, U.S. Army Commander, U.S. Forces, Korea, in Hearings before the Committee on Armed Services, United States Senate, *International Security Environment (Strategy)* 100th Cong., 1st Sess., April 19, 1989, especially pp. 612–613, 624.

41. Research Institute for Peace and Security, Tokyo, *Asian Security 1989–1990* (London: Brassey's, 1989), pp. 18–19.

42. Don Oberdorfer, "In Bow to Seoul, U.S. Eases Some Restrictions on North Korea," *Washington Post,* November 1, 1988, p. A-28.

43. The critical policy statement setting the context for U.S. force reduction policies and revised force doctrine is "President George Bush's Speech to the Aspen Institute Symposium," August 2, 1990, reprinted as Appendix E in *Report of the Secretary of Defense to the President and the Congress* (Washington, D.C.: USGPO, January 1991), pp. 131–134. Also see General Colin S. Powell, Chairman of the U.S. Joint Chiefs of Staff, "The Eisenhower Centenary Lecture: Military Realities and Future Security Prospects," *RUSI* 136, no. 1 (Spring 1991), pp. 17–21.

44. *A Strategic Framework for the Asian Pacific Rim,* pp. 15–17. Also see Denis Warner, "Phased Reduction in Asia," *Asia-Pacific Defence Reporter* 17, no. 2 (August 1990), p. 14.

45. See, for example, testimony of Senator Dale Bumpers reprinted in *Congressional Record (Senate),* September 26, 1989, S-11850/S-11853.

46. Susumu Awanohara, "Friends and Enemies," *Far Eastern Economic Review* 150, no. 50 (December 13, 1990), p. 26.

47. Statement of Admiral Charles Larson, Commander-in-Chief, United States Pacific Command, before the Subcommittee on Defense, Committee on Appropriations, U.S. House of Representatives, *Department of Defense Appropriations for 1992* , 102nd Cong., 1st Sess., April 9, 1991, p. 76.

48. Yi Kye-song, "Pact Shows Equal Partnership," *Hangyore Sinmun,* December 30, 1990, p. 3; translated and reprinted by Foreign Broadcast Information Service—*East Asia* (hereafter cited as *FBIS-EAS*), January 15, 1991, p. 35.

49. Elaine Sciolino, "State Dept. Disputes CIA's Korea Stance," *International Herald Tribune,* March 11, 1992, p. 5.

50. Leslie Helm, "2 Koreas Sign Agreement on Reconciliation," *Los Angeles Times,* December 13, 1991, pp. 1, 16; and David Sanger, "38 Years Later, Korean War to End," *International Herald Tribune,* December 13, 1991, pp. 1, 4; and Shim Jae Hoon, "Early Signs," *Far Eastern Economic Review* 154, no. 45 (November 7, 1991), which assesses Pyongyang's economic motivations for agreeing to negotiate the accord.

51. "North Korea Signs Atom Pact," *International Herald Tribune,* April 10, 1992, p. 4; and "New Nuclear Pact by 2 Koreas Stirs More Suspicion of North," in ibid., March 6, 1992, p. 4.

52. On April 18, 1992, U.S. assistant secretary of state for East Asian and Pacific Affairs Richard Solomon reportedly told Japanese reporters that if the North Koreans submitted to inspections under two arrangements—the IAEA and bilateral understandings negotiated between North and South Korea in December 1990—the U.S. would raise the level of political dialogue with the North. At the same time, Kim Il-song was reported to have welcomed the eventual diplomatic normalization of U.S.–DPRK relations. Consult "U.S. Sees Progress on Ties with North Korea," *International Herald Tribune,* April 18–19, 1992, p. 3.

53. Tai Ming Cheung, "Checking for Bombs," *Far Eastern Economic Review* 155, no. 20 (May 21, 1992), p. 20; and David Sanger, "North Korea Unexpectedly Reveals Nuclear Details," *International Herald Tribune,* May 7, 1992, p. 4.

54. In late February 1992, a senior U.S. State Department official was quoted by the *Washington Post* as noting that the Bush administration was getting the impression that North Korea was "jerking us around." Don Oberdorfer, "North Korea Close to Bomb, U.S. Fears," *International Herald Tribune,* February 24, 1992, p. 3.

55. The linkage between heightened North Korean feelings of international isolation and prospects for greater North Korean bellicosity are ably covered by Larry A. Niksch, "Kim Il-song's Kingdom under Seige," *Asia-Pacific Defence Reporter* 18, nos. 6/7 (December 1991/January 1992), pp. 33–35.

56. The Ministry of National Defense, The Republic of Korea, *Defense White Paper 1989.* English language edition produced by Korean Institute of Defense Analysis (Seoul: MOD, 1989), p. 145.

57. Tae-Hwan Kwak, "Military Capabilities of South and North Korea: A Comparative Study," *Asian Perspective* 14, no. 1 (Spring–Summer 1990), p. 113.

58. Menetrey testimony in *International Security Environment (Strategy)*, pp. 625–627; testimony of Carl W. Ford, Jr., Principal Deputy Assistant Secretary of Defense for Asian and Pacific Affairs, in Hearing before the Subcommittee on Asian and Pacific Affairs of the Committee on Foreign Affairs, House of Representatives, *Developments in United States–Republic of Korea Relations*, 100th Cong., 1st Sess., 26 July, 1989, pp. 18–20; testimony of Spencer Richardson, Director for Korean Affairs, U.S. Department of State in a Hearing before the Subcommittee on Asian and Pacific Affairs of the Committee on Foreign Affairs, U.S. House of Representatives, *Korea: North–South Nuclear Issues*, 101st Cong., 2nd Sess. 25 July 1990, p. 34, and *Department of Defense Appropriations for 1992*, p. 70; and Tae-Hwan Kwak, "Military Capabilities," pp. 113–143.

59. "North Korea Test Fires a Long-Range Missile," *International Herald Tribune*, October 5–6, 1991, p. 4; and "Fears Grow in Japan over Missile's Reach," in ibid., March 11, 1992, p. 5.

60. Gary Klintworth, "Beleaguered, Bewildered, but Looking for New Options," *Asia-Pacific Defense Reporter* 17, no. 2 (August 1990), pp. 16–17. Klintworth was reporting on a briefing given to a delegation from The Australian National University by North Korean officials. Also see Awanohara, "Friends and Enemies," p. 26, which asserts that "there are signs that Pyongyang, under pressure from its erstwhile patrons in Moscow and Beijing, will seek to normalize its standing in the world even before its leader Kim Il-song disappears from the scene. A regional solution involving North and South Korea . . . is no longer unrealistic."

61. See Chi Man-won, "North and South Korea Can Reduce Their Armies to 300,000 Each," *Wolgan Chosun* (July 1990); as translated and reprinted in *FBIS-EAS*, July 12, 1990, pp. 25–31.

62. Chae-Ha Park, "A Grand Strategy for Korea's Defense," *The Korean Journal of Defense Analysis* 1, no. 2 (Winter 1989), especially pp. 189–192.

63. For a provocative analysis of this factor, see Andrew Mack, "Seoul Might Prefer to Live with a Pyongyang Bomb," *International Herald Tribune*, May 13, 1992, p. 6.

64. O Tae-Kyu, "Government Policy on Major Power Viewed," *Hangyore Sinmun*, December 30, 1990, p. 3, translated and reprinted in *FBIS-EAS*, January 3, 1991, p. 35.

65. Background on this point is provided by Edward Olsen, *U.S.–Japan Strategic Reciprocity: A Neo-internationalist View* (Stanford, CA: Hoover Institution Press, 1985), passim.

66. "South Korea's Fears Outlined," *Jane's Defence Weekly* 16, no. 20 (December 12, 1991), p. 937.

67. Sheldon Simon cites a *Korean Times* report noting that in March 1990 representatives of the Japanese Air Self Defense Force approached the South Korean air force to discuss personnel exchanges. Such educational interaction, however, falls far short of the levels of cooperation needed to replace the departure of American personnel from Korea and Japan who often served as intermediaries between the Japanese and South Korean militaries on such issues as controlling air space and very occasional joint naval exercises such as RIMPAC, where both Japanese and South Korean

units have participated. See Sheldon Simon, "Security and Uncertainty in the North Pacific," *Korean Journal of Defense Analysis* 2, no. 2 (Winter 1990), p. 81.

68. John Endicott, "Japanese Security Policy: Stability in an Era of Change?" *Korean Journal of Defense Analysis* 2, no. 2 (Winter 1990), p. 109.

69. Sheldon Simon again provides the most relevant analysis, noting that precedents exist which allow U.S. forces headed toward the Middle East to have access to Japanese bases and that the Nakasone government approved, in principle, U.S. Special Forces detachments stationed in Okinawa to be redeployed to Middle East crisis points. Sheldon Simon, *The Future of Asian-Pacific Security Collaboration* (Lexington, MA, and Toronto: Lexington Books, 1988), p. 144.

70. "Soviets Said Stopping Weapons Shipment to North," *Chungang Ilbo,* October 30, 1991, p. 1, translated and reprinted in *FBIS-EAS,* October 30, 1991, p. 18. The report linked the cessation of Soviet assistance to North Korea with South Korea's approval of a $U.S. 3 billion economic loan to the USSR. It is alleged that the Soviets' discontinuing such military assistance to the DPRK was a condition of approval.

71. See a *Yonhap* report broadcast on October 16, 1991 citing the Hong Kong newsmonthly *Dongxiang* and reprinted in *FBIS-EAS,* October 16, 1991, p. 31.

72. Gary Klintworth, "Arms Control and Great-Power Interests in the Korean Peninsula," *Korean Journal of Defense Analysis* 3, no. 1 (Summer 1991), p. 165.

73. On Qian Qichen's statement, see Choe Maeng-ho, "PRC Minister Cited on North Nuclear Program," *Tong-A Ilbo,* October 5, 1991, p. 5, as translated and reprinted in *FBIS-EAS,* October 8, 1991, p. 27. The general secretary's remarks on PRC–DPRK alliance relations were relayed by a Korean Broadcasting Television Network report, translated and reprinted as "PRC's Jiang Zimen Cited on Ties with North," *FBIS-EAS,* October 9, 1991, pp. 17–18. A less sanguine account of the meetings between Kim Il-song and Chinese leaders is offered by Dong-Bok Lee, "The Soviet Events and Inter-Korean Relations," *Korea and World Affairs* 15, no. 4 (Winter 1991), pp. 632–633. Lee asserts that what Kim and his hosts discussed in the context of military relations remains uncertain.

74. See *Dialogue with North Korea: Report of a Seminar on "Tension Reduction in Korea"* (Washington, D.C.: Carnegie Endowment for International Peace, 1989), pp. 47–50, for a translation of North Korea's 1987 confederation proposal and the "Communiqué of the Joint Meeting of the Central People's Committee, Standing Committee of the Supreme People's Assembly and Administration Council of the Democratic People's Republic of Korea," released in 1988 in *Dialogue with North Korea.*

75. The text of the joint U.S.–ROK communiqué released at the end of the Security Consultative Meeting is found in "Source Material," *Korea and World Affairs* 15, no. 4 (Winter 1991), pp. 780–783.

76. Thomas Wilborn, "Arms Control and ROK Relations with the DPRK," *Korean Journal of Defense Analysis* 2, no. 2 (Winter 1990), pp. 135–136..

77. See U.S. Secretary of State James Baker, "America in Asia: Emerging Architecture for the Pacific," *Foreign Affairs* 71, no. 1 ((Winter 1991/92). Author is citing from p. 9 of United States Information Agency reprint.

78. Patrick E. Tyler, "Pentagon's New World Order: U.S. to Reign Supreme," *International Herald Tribune,* March 9, 1992, pp. 1, 2.

5

The Diplomatic Dimensions of the Korean Confrontation*

Edward A. Olsen

The diplomatic and military dimensions of the Korean confrontation are a "chicken and egg" phenomenon—mutually causal. Nonetheless, they are treated discretely in this volume in order to emphasize the ways in which each theme shapes the context of the other.

The division of Korea in the immediate wake of the Second World War was a diplomatic and geopolitical decision in which Koreans had no significant voice. Liberated from the consequences of Japan's imperial struggle with the West, Korea was involuntarily thrust into a new global struggle that evolved into the Cold War. That act created the "Korean confrontation," which became a major focus of postwar Asian international relations.

Divided Korea

Though Americans frequently treat the liberation of Korea in 1945, the founding of the Republic of Korea (ROK) in 1948, and the subsequent rescue of South Korea from North Korean aggression from 1950 to 1953 as displays of selfless behavior on the part of the United States, Koreans seldom see things that way. Needless to say, North Koreans perceive virtually all those actions in a negative manner, believing themselves to have been victimized by American "imperialism." Relatively few South Koreans share those perceptions.[1] Nonetheless,

---

* The views expressed in this chapter are solely those of the author and do not represent the position of any U.S. government agency.

many—perhaps most—South Koreans *do* share with their northern brethren a sense of Korea's victimization. While many Koreans have been, until recent years, reluctant to be candid about their feelings of having been victimized for fear of alienating their American benefactors, the reexaminations of the Cold War that are flourishing in the wake of that era are permitting Koreans the candor many long supressed.[2]

Whether or not South Korea was a beneficiary or victim (along with North Korea) of U.S. and Soviet diplomatic and military actions is an important theme in the confrontation between the two Korean states. It is a theme to which we shall return in conclusion. The reason it is raised at the start of this analysis is not because of its intrinsic importance for contemporary Korea but because it is a major indicator of the key characteristic of the formative phase of modern Korean diplomacy. In short, the first couple of decades of post–World War II Korean diplomacy were profoundly beyond the control of Koreans. Though intimately involved in the consequences of the decisions made about Korean affairs, Koreans essentially were frustrated bystanders in the decision-making process.[3]

Certainly for the first decade of the Cold War (1945–55) Korea was a theater in which the superpowers overwhelmingly set the stage, wrote the script, and directed the movements of the actors. Americans, Soviets, and the Chinese communists, either visibly or in the wings, controlled virtually the entire show. Most Koreans on each side were spear carriers. A relative handful of Koreans on each side enjoyed secondary but supporting roles. None possessed the ability to determine his own fate. Their destiny again was in the hands of outsiders. The Japanese had been ousted, only to be replaced by Americans and Russians who now called the shots. During the Korean War the Chinese communists also helped shape the geopolitical environment, but in a manner constrained by Moscow's preeminence in the socialist camp. Though some Koreans tried to take matters into their own hands in the early postwar period, they ultimately failed.

The best the Koreans were able to do at that point was to fall back upon a technique some Koreans had used successfully with the Japanese; namely to make the best of a bad situation by adapting pragmatically to the circumstances. Consequently, a cadre of "leaders" emerged in the South and the North whose primary claim to power rested upon their political connections with the new *wae gook in* (overseers) stemming from their experiences as exiles during the Japanese colonial era. In the North, this meant Russian-speakers who had some affinity for Marxism-Leninism, accepted Moscow's revolutionary primacy, and often possessed military experience. In the South, this usually meant civilian English-speakers who had some knowledge of democracy and capitalism. Because many of the latter Koreans gained that background though American and other missionary-sponsored education, they also tended to be part of the Christian minority in a country that was largely Confucian and Buddhist. Thus, the two halves of Korea gravitated toward divergent foreign-oriented cultural, ideological, and/or religious influences.

These budding foreign-oriented leadership groups in the North and South of Korea generally shared with their more nationalist and xenophobic contemporaries an aversion to being subservient to outsiders. Nonetheless, they were sufficiently pragmatic to confront in an accommodating manner the reality of powerful foreign presences in their midst. Rather than let the foreign interests that Japan's defeat had imposed upon Korea totally determine their fate, these Koreans offered their services to the Americans and Russians as a way to gain some influence over the decisions Washington and Moscow might make. Many, if not all, were also motivated by personal ambitions. Incrementally this realistic approach enjoyed limited success.

The most concrete early example of this success was the creation of the rival Korean states in one divided nation. This was, however, a bitter victory at best. While the ROK and DPRK (Democratic People's Republic of Korea) became vehicles for Koreans to exert a voice in their lot and help shape superpower decisions, this was achieved through the institutionalization of a Korean confrontation about which few, if any, Koreans were enthusiastic. In short, even the process of gaining some say in their own affairs was achieved at the cost of allowing foreigners to determine the agenda of issues. Equally important, it was achieved at the cost of sacrificing most Korean autonomy. No Koreans, on either side, could persuasively claim to be masters of their own geopolitical destiny. Instead, in the diplomatic, military, and economic terms that define a state's status in world affairs, both Koreas became client states of their respective superpowers.

Internationally this yielded widespread imagery of the two Koreas as puppets of the superpowers that obediently took their cues and behaved like proper little proxies. North Korea was widely perceived as a Stalinist stooge, in orbit as a satellite of the Soviet Union. It became an abject member of the Soviet bloc, toeing the Moscow line on orders. Prior to the Korean War, South Korean leaders had displayed flashes of assertiveness, but that war served as a constraint reining in such sentiments. The ROK would have been defeated by the DPRK had the United States not rescued it. Moreover, its military, economic, and diplomatic viability as a client state protégé had to be recreated from the rubble of war. After the war, South Korea became a classic "friendly tyrant" in a growing network of docile right-wing allies of the United States within the free world camp, whose anticommunist credentials were considered more important than any supposed commitment to Western pluralistic values.

A profound consequence of these separate developments was the growth of a pariah diplomatic quality regarding each Korea. In pursuit of political influence over each's superpower backer, the two Koreas earned a reputation for being flunkies of the main Cold War antagonists. Neither was taken seriously as an independent actor in international diplomacy. Each Korean state had replaced Korean colonial subservience to Japan and its long-standing tributary subordination to China, which preceded the colonial era, with a new servility regarding the superpowers.

This status had profound domestic consequences in each Korea that reinforced the client statism of both. North Korea evolved toward a particularly rigid form of Leninism-cum-Stalinism. In time, this ideological orientation ossified in such a stolid manner that it failed to keep pace with changes elsewhere in the Marxist world. This thereby caused many of the contemporary frictions in North Korea's foreign policy which shall be addressed below; but in the late 1940s and for most of the 1950s, North Korea's international flunkyism and domestic totalitarianism were eminently compatible. Just as North Korea was a loyal client, the Kim Il-song regime demanded and enforced rigid domestic obedience.

In South Korea the situation was not as stark, but there too domestic authoritarianism grew in a geopolitical climate that placed a premium upon loyalty to anticommunism. The Syngman Rhee government fostered a centralized civilian strongman model that scarcely tolerated dissent. Compounded by the endemic factionalism of Korea's traditional Confucian polity, the notion of a loyal opposition within a pluralistic system remained weak despite American tutelage. The subsequent military-backed regimes in South Korea did little for many years to deflect the ROK from an authoritarian course. Although today there is much dividing North and South Korea politically, in their formative years they shared a pattern of flunkyism toward foreigners (*sa dae ju ui*) that enabled each country's foreign-sanctioned leaders to develop a greater voice in Korea's client state relationships. Ironically, this shared pattern earned each Korea a minimal voice in the broader diplomatic context in which the Korean confrontation was configured.

New Patterns

Those subservient Cold War patterns began to shift a bit in the 1960s as the Cold War itself evolved. The Sino-Soviet split enabled North Korea to carve out a role for Pyongyang as a fence sitter. Perceptions that Moscow and Beijing valued North Korea's allegiance and feared its ability to tilt toward one side or the other in a diplomatic game with zero-sum overtones provided the Kim regime with useful leverage. Pyongyang proved adept at using that diplomatic leverage. It significantly increased North Korea's voice in prospective Soviet and Chinese decisions pertaining to Korea and its interests. North Korea's influence was, by design, most focused on its two bickering backers. In the early stage of the Sino-Soviet split (i.e., the late 1950s and early 1960s), when Americans tended to be skeptical that the "split" was genuine, North Korean efforts to straddle the fence were largely discounted by Americans as meaningless. As the reality of the split was accepted more widely by Americans, so too was there real appreciation for the consequences of North Korean maneuvering. While North Korea possessed virtually no direct influence over U.S. policymaking during those years (other than as a perceived threat), its burgeoning role as a fence sitter did provide it with indirect influence over American thinking. The United States had to consider the impact of North Korean leverage upon the USSR and PRC that might be an inadvertant by-product of U.S. policy toward South Korea or toward the region upon which the ROK depended. This complex of relationships added a new level of constraint in U.S. actions regarding Korea.

Developments in the early 1960s suggested North Korea's diplomatic role might prove more influential than South Korea's. In contrast to North Korea's hyperstable government (albeit a ruthlessly enforced form of stability), its relatively strong economy, which had been resuscitated after the Korean War's devastation, and its ability to influence its backers, South Korea seemed to have less going for it. In 1960 and 1961 South Korea experienced the overthrow of two governments, economic stagnation, and strained relations with its only backer that further diminished its already scant leverage in Washington. The downfall of Syngman Rhee, the subsequent aborted experiment with democracy, and a military coup d'état perpetrated by the ROK Army under the guidance of Park Chung-hee and Kim Jong-pil were enervating for ROK diplomacy both with the United States and globally. South Korea's only claim to fame, so to speak, in the international arena was its credibility as an American client state. The events of 1960 and 1961 severely undermined its utility as a client and thereby weakened its credibility.

Syngman Rhee, an American protégé, was deposed in large part because he could not make clientism pay off for South Korea. Except for the enhancment of its physical security against renewed North Korean aggression, South Korea had little to show for Rhee's clientism. Its economy was in bad shape. Its democracy was a charade. Furthermore, Rhee's prickly style of clientism had long since worn thin among his American handlers. Clientism was not producing for South Korea what it was intended to achieve, namely a major Korean voice in American policy toward Korea. Almost as bad, it was producing little for Americans as well. Instead of obtaining a proxy or steadfast ally, American protection of South Korea had yielded high costs, great risks, and a sense of entanglement that in retrospect presaged what was to come in Vietnam. South Korea was far more of a liability to the United States than an asset at that point.

While U.S.–ROK relations and South Korea's standing in world affairs seemed pretty bleak then, and it was difficult to visualize how they might get worse, they did. The brief interregnum of Chang Myun was a setback both for suppressed Korean aspirations vis-à-vis democracy and for proclaimed American ideals. South Korean democratic forces had a chance simultaneously to fulfill their domestic political ambitions and create an international identity for the ROK as a client state that could shed its clientism. Both goals were bungled. Rampant factionalism undermined whatever chance existed for genuine democracy to flourish. Political infighting worsened the already bleak economic conditions inherited from the Rhee regime. Both of these trends compelled the leaders in Seoul to embrace a new form of clientism in a quest for U.S. support of its fledgling reforms. So, instead of enhancing the ROK's diplomatic status, the Chang Myun government floundered internationally as a failed client state.

Blame for these circumstances has to be shared by the United States, which missed an enormous opportunity to reify its proclaimed goals in Korea, namely to foster a stable democratic form of government with a viable socio-eonomic system that could fend for itself against the North Korean threat. American indecision focused on ambiguity about the players in Seoul politics, uncertainty about who to back and how, and a desire to provide a stable strategic cushion without becoming excessively involved. In effect, Americans seemed to be waiting for the dust to settle politically. The diplomatic consequences of this attitude proved to be significant indeed. The military sector of South Korean society took U.S. caution as a signal that the United States shared the concern of some in the military that the disorder of the Chang Myun government threatened to unleash chaos in South Korea that would prove disastrous for ROK and U.S. security interests. Partly using such perceptions as a pretext, partly from a sense of genuine concern, and partly due to political ambitions on the part of a relative handful of ROK army officers who shared a very different vision of South Korea's future, the Park Chung-hee coup was carried out in 1961.

Diplomatically, these events, and the political nuances they symbolized in U.S.–ROK relations, represented a drastic worsening of conditions. This can be seen in two respects. The more widespread view at the time, which survives largely unscathed today among critics of alleged "U.S. imperialism" in Asia, perceived the coup as a U.S.-backed or, at least, U.S.-sanctioned occurrence. It became for some analysts[4] a classic example of the United States backing a "friendly tyrant" for Cold War purposes, largely disregarding the ideals of self-determination and pluralism for which the Cold War was being waged. This is a very difficult charge to address because, over a longer period of time (i.e., the remainder of the 1960s) circumstances did lead Washington to accept the Park regime as essentially legitimate and very much a useful component of U.S. strategy in the Pacific. This was entirely in keeping with a far broader theme in U.S. policy toward Asia dating from the earliest postwar days and the start of the Cold War, which saw Americans placing a distinct priority on military factors rather than political or economic elements.

These attitudes clearly skewed American diplomacy throughout the entire region toward a military focus. In the 1940s and 1950s this tendency was so pronounced in Korea, where the U.S. military establishment dwarfed the American diplomatic presence, that most Koreans assumed the military played the dominant role in U.S. decision making. Americans within the country team and in Washington knew otherwise, and understood U.S. civil-military relationships in ways that few Koreans did. Even these Americans, however, recognized that U.S. civilian decision making regarding Korea was extraordinarily influenced by military factors, and that political and economic concerns usually took a back seat.

A much less understood perspective on the Park coup, and American reactions to it, focuses on the short-term responses. To put it mildly, American officials felt betrayed by the actions of Park, Kim, et al. There was no automatic sanctioning of the coup. In fact, the senior U.S. military and diplomatic officials on the scene in Seoul went to great lengths to rebuff the coupmakers and distance the United States from their actions. Great animosity arose between Washington and American officials in Seoul and the coupmakers. This was true of both U.S. civilian and military officials. The latter especially felt betrayed because they thought their ROK military counterparts had been absorbing what was being transmitted to them about U.S.-style civil-military relations. So, the widespread perception that Americans backed, or at least tolerated the Park coup, is grossly misleading. Actually, the eventual U.S. acceptance of the new ROK regime was grudging, not enthusiastic.

Acceptance and sanctioning did emerge on the American side, but not before a couple of years in the early 1960s when U.S.–ROK relations were severely strained. Those tensions had great diplomatic consequences for South Korea. In the short run, South Korea found itself diplomatically disadvantaged versus North Korea's relatively successful diplomacy at the time. The ROK under Park was initially a classic pariah state, not even relished by its only benefactor; this marked a low ebb for South Korea's diplomatic standing. Though the ROK clearly survived that experience and has rebounded with considerable success, that low point did leave one lasting legacy for U.S.–ROK relations. It sowed a level of distrust of Koreans among Americans that had not been there before. There had been a sense previously that Koreans might be devious, capricious, and headstrong at times—best exemplified by Syngman Rhee's antics—but virtually no Americans had reason to consider Koreans untrustworthy or unreliable. The Park coup altered that mindset, probably permanently. It introduced a level of American caution, skepticism, and second-guessing regarding Koreans that reappears periodically to this day.

In a sense, this subtle but profound change in the atmosphere of U.S.–Korean relations was positive because it served to balance a longstanding Korean tendency to harbor doubts about American reliability. Stemming from late nineteenth- and early twentieth-century U.S. diplomacy, which to Koreans treated Korea as a pawn on a large chessboard, Americans bore a reputation among Koreans that is best expressed by an old children's jump-rope chant:

> Don't be cheated by Russians,
> Don't rely on Americans,
> The Japanese are rising again,
> So, Koreans, be careful.[5]

In these terms the negative reactions by Americans to the Park coup, and subsequent rapprochement as Washington learned to accept the Park regime for what it was, signaled the real beginning of a long-term process of bilateral diplomatic maturation. The process began slowly, but over the years has gradually fostered an increasingly distinct and separate identity for South Korea in world affairs. This has had major diplomatic consequences that shall be assessed below.

For the remainder of the 1960s, however, South Korea experienced considerable growing pains. The Park coup, and the government it spawned, used a process of trial and error to put the ROK on a developmental course that proved very beneficial economically. Park and the economic technocrats he acquired to guide South Korea opted for a very different course than Syngman Rhee traversed. Instead of following the lead of the United States' brand of capitalism and the warmed-over Japanese colonial vision for southern Korean development—which was essentially agricultural—that Americans had relied upon, the Park government modified the American style of capitalism by adapting it to the export-led, highly centralized approach to development that the Meiji-era Japanese leadership had used for Japan. Park reinforced that national development approach by his push for normalized diplomatic relations with Japan, which were achieved in 1965, despite volatile opposition within Korea.

Park's diplomatic approach seemed straightforward enough. He was bent upon retaining the essential support provided by the United States. All else was a distant second, including the newly important relations with Japan. South Korea's sole meaningful support internationally was the United States. Park wanted to restore the ROK as a client state in good standing in the Cold War, which intensified in the mid to late 1960s because of the conflict in Vietnam. However, the motives behind his efforts were significantly different from those of Syngman Rhee. Park's regime envisioned achieving enough economic growth and military self-reliance that it could become a partner-client rather than a puppet-client. In short, the uncertainty attendant to U.S.–ROK relations when Park seized power made it imperative that the ROK refashion its clientism in a more sophisticated manner. The then small relationship with Japan mainly provided another (economic) outlet for enhancing South Korea's value to the security network headed by the United States.

Korean Initiatives

In the mid-1960s those relationships were very tentative. By the late 1960s and early 1970s, however, they had been transformed into a diplomatic factor not envisioned at the outset. Facilitated greatly by access to the Japanese economy and by profits spun off from the Vietnam War, the South Korean economy moved rapidly toward what many have called the "miracle on the Han." Narrowly speaking, the economic consequences of that success story are beyond the scope of this analysis, but in diplomatic terms South Korea's rapid growth from 1965 to 1975 was tremendously important. Bilaterally, the newfound economic wherewithal of South Korea enabled Seoul to make a far more persuasive case to Washington that South Korea was a potential regional partner of genuine substance, albeit more junior than Japan. This enabled Seoul to begin to break out of its "client-itis." It also enabled Seoul to make a stronger case that the ROK could actually do for itself, with declining U.S. assistance, what the South Vietnamese then were proving unable to do—cope with a regional communist adversary. In short, South Korea under Park was en route to making itself a real ally of the United States.

In broader terms, however, the ROK leadership was also engaged in policies that were at cross-purposes with the primary diplomatic goal of solidifying ROK–U.S. relations. As South Korea's economy flourished, it became an instrument for diversification of South Korean relations with many other countries. Though initially facilitated by access gained as a result of being part of the U.S.-led collective security network, once South Korea's economic diversification accelerated, it assumed a momentum of its own. That was important in several ways. It introduced a multilateral economic motive into Seoul's foreign policy calculations, which had previously been overwhelmingly dominated by security concerns and fixated on U.S.–ROK relations. Other countries, notably Japan, now loomed larger than they had to South Koreans since the ROK's founding.

These diversified relations assumed redoubled importance to Seoul in the early to mid-1970s for reasons having little to do with economics. As the United States experienced setbacks in Southeast Asia, South Korean confidence was severely shaken by U.S. failures and by domestic American reactions to those failures. The South Korean response was basically twofold. Seoul tried tentatively to hedge its bets a bit internationally by looking toward diversified economic contacts for their value as political and military assets. Though that movement established a precedent which, in retrospect, is very important for today's South Korean diplomacy, it bore little immediate fruit. So Seoul relied upon a ham-handed effort to shore up its bilateral ties with the United States. Its crude lobbying efforts eventually blew up in Seoul's face, yielding the "Korea-gate" episode.[6]

During 1965–75, when Seoul was experimenting at home and abroad economically, it experienced a new high and low in U.S.–ROK relations (as an ally in Vietnam and via its clumsy lobbying, respectively), and its status versus North Korean diplomacy generally improved. While North Korea retained the levels and style of influence it enjoyed in the early 1960s, and its ruthless image was not much worse than that of the hard-line Park regime, Pyongyang experienced severe reversals as a result of the relative economic gains made by South Korea. The DPRK was doing about as well as many Third World developing states, especially within the communist "bloc," but in comparison to South Korea's rapid gains it was slipping seriously. On balance, therefore, South Korea's circle of friends was expanding and North Korea's was relatively static. This led to a diplomatic bean-counting competition between Seoul and Pyongyang that was taken quite seriously by both sides. North Korea seemed to understand that a qualitative change was afoot in the diplomatic aspects of the confrontation between the two halves of Korea, and treated diplomacy as a deadly serious struggle with its adversary. For its part, South Korea displayed growing confidence that events might actually go its way, and redoubled its efforts.

From the mid-1970s to the mid-1980s the diplomatic confrontation between the two Koreas moved to a new plateau. It thereby reflected the ways in which each Korea was in domestic transition. North Korea posed a less dramatic example of change because it clung to a Stalinist paradigm. Pyongyang, however, introduced a new wrinkle to that approach via Kim Il-song's nepotistic innovations. In short, Kim put in motion the mechanisms that he designed to assure that Kimism would outlive Kim in a way that neither Stalinism nor Maoism long survived their namesakes. The "Great Leader" Kim Il-song installed the "Dear Leader" Kim Jong-il as his overt heir apparent, thereby creating the first communist hereditary line. The birth of the Kim Dynasty was greeted with much international skepticism, but the senior Kim has made it work so far domestically by gradually transferring power to the junior Kim.

By the mid-1980s the "Kim Dynasty" was an embarrassment to many of North Korea's friends, notably the Brezhnev regime in Moscow and its short-lived series of successors. Nonetheless, they tolerated the North Korean dynasty despite its ideological inconsistencies. More damaging for North Korea were the diplomatic repercussions stimulated by foreign ridicule of Kim's nepotism. These only compounded international dislike of North Korea's harsh totalitarianism. Still worse for Pyongyang, these adverse factors were magnified by a growing recognition that North Korea was falling further and further behind South Korea. By the mid-1980s South Korea's economic successes had earned it the right to host the Asia Games in 1986 and the Olympics in 1988. These were graphic symbols of South Korea's arrival in the world and a slap in the face for North Korea, demonstrating the way in which much of the world visualized Korea. Seoul was at the center of Korean identity internationally, not Pyongyang.

The cause of this transformation in global perceptions was a major period of flux in South Korea. From 1975 to 1985 the ROK unambiguously surpassed the DPRK as a player in international economics. The North was virtually a non-actor, while South Korea had moved from being a spear carrier, through the chorus, into and out of bit parts, and had assumed a truly major role. Over the course of these ten years the ROK economy became world-class. Equally important from a diplomatic perspective, the South Korean political, bureaucratic, and business elites who guided the ROK to its success also were widely recognized as world-class leaders. Gaining this enhanced status was not simple. Much of the world remained skeptical about South Korea's political standing. During the same decade, the South Korean polity was wracked by tensions and disruptions that repeatedly threatened to derail the economic miracle.

The final years of the Park regime were politically tumultuous, contributing to events that led to his assassination. Carter-era tensions over human rights and the "Koreagate" fiasco brought U.S.–ROK relations to a new low, exacerbated by Seoul's fears about the consequences of the post-Vietnam syndrome in the United States for Korean security. The subsequent failed effort at an openly democratic political campaign, the 1979–80 usurpation of democratic aspirations by another military takeover in 1980, and the profoundly destabilizing upheaval in Kwangju and its aftermath sent terrible signals to much of the world. So, too, did the enthusiastic acceptance of Chun Doo-hwan's regime by the Reagan administration in 1981. Despite all those traumatic political factors, South Korea nonetheless emerged by 1985 in a relatively solid position diplomatically, thanks to its economic performance.

Economic prominence was undoubtedly *the* major factor behind the ROK's enhanced international position, but other domestic factors also helped in somewhat perverse ways. The very fact that South Koreans could traverse the tumultuous times they experienced from 1975 to 1985 without devastating economic setbacks was itself a positive factor. It demonstrated an innate stability within ROK society that was appreciated by the international community and gave South Korea's trading partners new confidence that South Koreans could overcome whatever they confronted politically. Despite an assassination, a quasi-coup, much domestic political violence, and serious strains in U.S.–ROK relations, South Koreans had remained committed to economic progress and hopeful about their chances to achieve genuine political pluralism. They were coping with serious political problems and achieving great economic success simultaneously. The ability to manage this delicate juggling act earned South Korea much of its enhanced standing in world affairs as of 1985. The economy, reinforced by political resilience, may have been the means to this diplomatic end, but alone they would not likely have produced its enhanced standing.

Korean Diplomacy

Starting in the late 1970s the Park Chung-hee government made significant efforts to reorder ROK foreign policy ambitions. Partly as a consequence of new levels of nationalistic self-confidence, and partly as a result of greater U.S. latitude for its allies to take the intiative, South Korea began to envision its junior partner role becoming more meaningful and mutually beneficial. Since this fit well with the long-standing U.S. diplomatic boiler-plate about the importance of U.S.–ROK relations and "vital" American interests in Korea, Washington did nothing to disabuse such exaggerated rhetoric on Seoul's part. Seoul also pressed for greater autonomy in its foreign policy. While remaining a member of a U.S.-led coalition internationally, Seoul devised initiatives—especially regarding North Korea—that helped to set the pace. In doing so, the Park government cautiously started to break out of the client state pattern. In its foreign policy, South Korea was no longer content to be solely a reactive participant and strove to be an initiator on occasion. This was in stark contrast to its neighbor, Japan, which remained far more passive though by no means a client state. The irony here was that South Korea remained a partial client state (and its leaders wanted it this way) even as it challenged the client relationship.

The Chun government may have been a reactionary throwback in terms of political legitimacy, but in foreign policy it accelerated the fledgling steps toward a role as an international initiator begun under Park. Encouraged by the revived bilateral stability permitted by the Reagan administration's tolerance for Chun's domestic political excesses, Seoul was able to devise and implement a very flexible and innovative foreign policy. Chun and his foreign policy establishment enjoyed great success at broadening South Korea's diplomatic horizon.[7] Unlike Park, who sought diversification partially to *compensate for* his weakened ties with the United States, Chun persisted in, and then expanded, the ROK's quest for greater international economic and diplomatic diversification to *supplement* U.S.–ROK ties. This represented an important qualitative change. Thus, the Chun government intensified and changed the process of bilateral maturation that Park had inadvertently sparked through his coup. Ironically, while Chun's foreign policy was designed to supplement and reinforce ROK–U.S. relations, and was generally supported by Washington in those terms, it actually spurred the maturation process toward a divergence of paths. Despite a carefully cultivated (by Koreans *and* Americans) mythology that the United States and South Korea share many common interests, the 1980s tended to underscore the way in which the two countries' interests overlap but are not truly "common." For example, both countries share stakes in bilateral trade, defense (of the peninsula and the region), and diplomacy, but the contributions each makes are disproportionate to the benefits each receives. This, in turn, generates frustration among Americans who feel the United States has been taken advantage of, and resentment among Koreans who feel the United States picks on the ROK.[8]

From 1985 to 1992 Korea's international status has been transformed in an almost unbelievably rapid fashion by the end of the Cold War and Korean responses to that seminal event. Since Korea constituted a key theater during the formative phase of the Cold War, and was Asia's prime Cold War theater for four decades, it naturally remained an important factor in the process of Cold War termination.[9] When the Gorbachev government was established and new signals began emanating from Moscow that serious change might be imminent, neither Seoul nor Pyongyang were any more prescient than the rest of the world regarding the rapid shifts in world politics that were about to unfold. Actually, both Koreas were more cautious than most countries. North Korea seemed unable to visualize the scope of the revolutionary events that would shake the foundations of its prime backer or their consequences for international communism. South Koreans were similarly conservative in the ways that they assumed no fundamental changes in the Cold War–based global security system, of which they felt the ROK was an integral part, could possibly be on the horizon. Both Seoul and Pyongyang could not have been more wrong. The divided world to which they had grown accustomed throughout the years since the 1940s was about to dissolve.

The first hints that something profound might be in the offing were evident leading up to and during the Asia Games, and more obvious in the Seoul Olympics. In the course of those sporting events major diplomacy was conducted. ROK–PRC and ROK–USSR contacts mushroomed. While Seoul's connections with China were important, and have had major significance for South Korean–PRC economic relations and—in turn—PRC–DPRK diplomatic ties,[10] they were dwarfed by the shift in ROK–USSR relations that subsequently occurred. The first time Soviet flags flew in Seoul at Olympic sites it caused quite a stir. Memories of Soviet involvement behind the scenes in the Korean War and the Soviet attack on KAL Flight 007 in 1983 were revived. Consternation was transparent among the conservative anticommunists who were the political bedrock in Seoul. On balance, they seemed to accept the symbolic Soviet inroads into South Korea largely as an unavoidable price of hosting the Olympics. Virtually no South Koreans foresaw the possibility that ROK–USSR ties might blossom overnight, though many academics speculated about the ways that marginal improvements might occur.

The years 1988–91 were particularly formative for Korean diplomacy. Against the background of a continuation of trends from 1975 to 1985 that thrust South Korea ahead of North Korea, Seoul seized the opportunity to forge a newly innovative foreign policy. Those trends included an acceleration of South Korea's economic lead over North Korea, which put the ROK so far ahead that for all practical purposes the contest had been forfeited by Pyongyang. By mid-1992 the North Korean economy was showing signs of severe problems.[11] South Korea's lead became still more acute as the Soviet Union's enormous economic problems were abjectly exposed, compounding both the reality of North Korean economic weaknesses and the vulnerability of the Marxist model it relied upon. In economic terms South Korea emerged as one of the victors of the Cold War and North Korea as one of the losers.

Politically, too, the South loomed larger than the North. While Pyongyang stagnated, Seoul—at long last—seemed on the road to achieving genuine democratic and pluralistic reforms. After the ouster of Chun Doo-hwan in 1987 and the dramatic political refurbishing subsequently conducted by the Roh Tae-wu government, South Korean politicians finally seemed to have gotten their act together. While by no means had they created a placid state politically, and it remained during 1988–92 a dynamic polity in flux, there was a sense that the rhetoric about democracy and human rights was being realized. In conjunction with great economic advances and the Olympian spotlight on Seoul's political dynamism versus Pyongyang's political repression, South Korea very clearly surpassed North Korea as a credible state internationally. There was no more talk about South Korea being a pariah, and very little reference to it as a puppet of the United States.

An additional trend from the late 1970s and early 1980s that accelerated during 1988–92 was the maturation of U.S.–ROK relations. South Korean clientism was rapidly disappearing. In a perverse way, the April 1992 Los Angeles riots that partially targeted Korean-Americans accentuated South Korean awareness of differences with the United States. In South Korean eyes, clientism no longer exists in a credible way, though some South Koreans seem unable to shake old subservient habits. Recognition of this trend is less noticeable in American leadership circles, where the notion that South Korea is a client state that should heed American directives lingers. One can see it clearly in prevalent U.S. ideas about defense burden sharing, criticism of Korean trade practices, and ethnocentric proclamations about human rights. In the United States, too, however, it is becoming increasingly obvious that South Korea is not the kind of fawning client state it once was. If it is a "puppet," it is Pinnochio-like in that it has acquired a life of its own. If it is a "client," it is one with many other masters, which no longer obediently asks "How high?" when told to jump by Americans.

Cumulatively, these trends have enabled Seoul to design and implement a foreign policy in which the reactive factors are greatly diminished and the initiator roles are in the ascendancy. One can see this in both broad diplomacy and, importantly, in the ways in which diplomatic means are being introduced into formerly narrow security concerns. On the broad end of the spectrum, Seoul's innovations are crystal clear in the ways it has adapted speedily to changes in the former Soviet Union, Eastern Europe, and Germany. In the wake of the Olympics, Seoul seemed to sense that seizing an opportunity for improved ROK–USSR relations might lead to unpredictable benefits. In the face of greater caution in the United States and Japan, the Roh government took a calculated risk of incurring superpower instability on the Korean peninsula and heightened North Korean animosity by plunging into a concentrated effort to improve ROK–USSR ties. This clearly was an attempt to do an "end run" around North Korea. It also clearly had U.S. sanctioning. However, none of the parties—as of 1988—was so insightful as to foresee the collapse of communism and the consequent edge that development would provide to Seoul in its relations with Moscow.

As the Berlin Wall tumbled, the Warsaw Pact fell into disarray, and longstanding weaknesses in the Soviet economy exposed the deepening vulnerabilities and inadequacies of the Soviet system, it soon became evident that the ROK's preliminary diplomatic moves regarding the USSR and its then allies in Europe had positioned Seoul to take advantage of the end of the Cold War. South Korea was in the right place at the right time. The Roh government acted speedily. Seoul pressed forward diplomatically on several fronts, seeking to chip away at the diplomatic ties North Korea had so arduously achieved over many years. Despite enormous efforts by Pyongyang to shore up its network in a once rock-solid socialist bloc, one by one it failed.

The first sign of what was to come was Seoul's success at enticing Hungary into formal diplomatic relations, announced February 1, 1989.[12] Initially, Hungary seemed certain to be an exception likely to reinforce the rule of steadfast DPRK ties with the remainder of Eastern Europe. After all, Hungary—hyperconscious that it was Central not Eastern European—long had been an anomaly anyway, often in the vanguard of social and economic experimentation. Surely the others would not follow this aberrant path. Had the Soviet Union remained strong and resolute, able to stymie the collapse of its external satellites, such a prognosis might well have prevailed. The years 1989–90 fostered a different history, however, that saw state after state in the European socialist bloc experience revolutionary change. As the Communist parties were either overthrown or so discredited (as in the Soviet Union) that they were in danger of being replaced, or transformed out of existence, there was a universal turn toward the Western world.

The main focuses of those countries' attention unquestionably were the United States, Western Europe, and Japan. Led by the United States, they were the clear victors in the Cold War. Most Western attention during this period was on the impact of these shifts upon Western countries. Much self-congratulation occurred, commending Washington and various European capitals for their steadfastness throughout the long Cold War years. Japan was usually included as a virtual afterthought. This almost certainly was, and is, a major mistake. A plausible case can be made that changes in the former socialist bloc were precipitated equally by the economic challenge posed by Japan to the United States and the European Community, which served to underscore in Soviet and Eastern European minds how far behind their societies actually were. In any event, the losers in the Cold War certainly were well aware that the victors included Japan and the coterie of dragons in its neighborhood. Therefore the turn to the "West" also included a turn toward all of East Asia's advanced economies.

This shift in orientation was ideally timed for South Korea because Seoul had prepared itself to make an outreach to those states in order to undercut North Korea. As the Cold War ended, however, Seoul soon found itself with a new audience diplomatically. Instead of being the exception that proved a rule, Hungary's bold move became a precedent that all of Eastern Europe (except Albania and East Germany) quickly followed.[13] They all forsook North Korea and embraced South Korea. Albania and North Korea long were like-minded regimes, so that temporary exception was not surprising, but it fell too. This was a particularly bitter pill for Kim Il-song. East Germany, of course, was a truly special case with enormous significance for Korea, North and South. The prospect of German reunification precluded any need for the DDR to follow the example of its neighbors and embrace the ROK diplomatically and economically. Once it became part of a unified Germany it would, and of course did, become part of a state with full relations with South Korea rather than North Korea.[14]

Korea and Russia

The main formal holdout was the Soviet Union, though it, too, made moves in 1988–89 that were taken by Seoul to represent de facto diplomatic recognition.[15] During that period, however, Moscow continued to reassure Pyongyang—despite evident tensions—that the USSR would not abandon it.[16] Despite those assurances, the Soviet Union surprised much of the world by holding a summit with the ROK in September 1990. The brief summit between Roh and Gorbachev in San Francisco was short on substance, but long on symbolism. The fact that it was held at all, much less in the United States, sent an unambiguous signal that something was afoot. In its own right that meeting was as important diplomatically for the Korean Cold War (and its larger Asian context) as the first cracks in the European iron curtain.[17] It seemed only a matter of time before the promise of improved ROK–USSR relations hinted at by the summit would be realized. Most projections after the San Francisco summit suggested the next step might occur within a couple of years at the earliest. Both Seoul and Moscow went out of their way to deflate expectations. Moscow continued to reassure Pyongyang that it need not be unduly concerned. Seoul seemed equally intent upon preempting a sense of rising expectations in South Korea. The so-called spin doctors were busy indeed.[18]

Actually, the atmosphere in South Korea by that time had changed significantly. Prior to the Olympics, South Korea tended to be wary of the Soviet Union. This was partly because of the Soviet Union's past and continuing assistance to North Korea, its behavior regarding KAL 007, and the overall tenor of the Cold War. Most South Koreans may not have considered the Soviet Union an enemy bent on inflicting harm on the ROK, but they clearly treated it with the apprehension deserved by the key adversary of South Korea's main protector. Moreover, South Korea's domestic anticommunism had been so entrenched and pervasive that expression of interest in any communist state was risky for average South Koreans. The ROK was in a self-imposed vacuum regarding communism and those who espoused it. The Gorbachev era, the Olympics, and Seoul's early outreach efforts brought about major changes indeed.

In order to understand these rapid changes in atmosphere, one must recall that Korean history does not have a strongly rooted sense of anxiety about Russians. The children's chant cited above dates from early in the century and yet seems relevant to contemporary South Koreans and their recent dealings with Americans and Japanese. The notion of Russians "cheating" is real to many in the West, but is someone else's history to contemporary South Koreans who, until very recently, had virtually no experience with Russians. This is very much unlike Japan's experiences with the Soviet Union. Consequently, the Russian threat has often been seen as a distant, almost secondhand one to many South Koreans. They could grasp it intellectually as an abstraction, but—except for KAL 007—they normally had not personalized it on an emotional level.

So, when the Olympics took place, against an undercurrent of growing anti-Americanism that stemmed from bilateral economic frictions and the Reagan administration's enthusiasm for the then recently deposed Chun regime, many Koreans were well disposed to react warmly to the visiting Soviet team precisely because it was not American. This was exacerbated by visible U.S.–ROK sports frictions during the Olympics. On balance, therefore, South Koreans proved to be enthusiastic hosts for the Soviet teams and for various cultural, economic, and political hangers-on. That level of enthusiasm soon took on remarkable momentum, considering the relative vacuum that had prevailed. Olympic fever, and its accompanying goodwill toward the Soviet Union, rapidly spread and mixed with the sense of popular anticipation that was aroused by media speculation about the ways in which ROK–USSR relations might unfold.

To put it bluntly, it became "in" for South Korean policymakers and scholars to be advocates of closer ROK ties with the Soviet Union. Red carpets were rolled out for a long series of visiting Soviet emissaries. The media were filled with their comings and goings. Whereas once it was most common in the media to see reportage of miscellaneous ROK–U.S. scientific, commercial, and scholarly meetings, they were substantially replaced by their ROK–USSR equivalents. In short, a faddish atmosphere emerged in which unrealistic expectations, especially regarding prospects for trade, were so common that the ROK government felt compelled to dampen them. Nonetheless, the boom continued. The collapse of the Soviet Union did not deter Korean enthusiasts. There are few signs of this enthusiasm being seriously diminished. Even the possibility that the Gorbachev and Yeltsin reforms may give way to an authoritarian reversal did not sour the ardor of most South Korean elites. They seem as convinced that there is a "Great Russia Market" for South Koreans to exploit as Americans are fascinated by the "Great China Market" mythology.

It was in such an atmosphere that Seoul and Moscow announced formal diplomatic relations on December 30, 1990; these were subsequently transferred from the Soviet Union to the Russian Republic.[19] This heightened the fad and propelled South Korea further toward a Russia-oriented diversification of its foreign policy. Improved ROK–Russia ties had to overcome hurdles such as the Unification Church's efforts to be an intermediary[20] and recurrent questions about KAL 007.[21] On balance, these proved to be sideshows, and the leaders in Seoul and Moscow retained their emphasis on trade. This was underlined during President Roh's landmark visit to Moscow in December 1990. Burgeoning economic relations produced estimates that ROK–USSR trade would reach U.S. $10 billion annually by 1995.[22] This will be modified by the dissolution of the Soviet Union, but presumably the total estimates for South Korean trade with the now separate republics will prevail. More concretely, this emphasis yielded an agreement in January 1991 under which Seoul would provide Moscow with about U.S. $3 billion in economic assistance that the Soviet Union was to use for trade and joint ventures with South Korea.[23] That has been retained with Russia. The strength of Seoul–Moscow ties was cemented in graphic terms by the brief visit of President Gorbachev to Cheju-do in April 1991. The first visit of any Soviet head of state to anywhere in Korea, it sent an unambiguous signal to Pyongyang that Moscow–Seoul relations were solid. This was underscored by the relative failure of Gorbachev's much ballyhooed trip to Japan prior to visiting the ROK. The meetings between Gorbachev and Roh in San Francisco, Moscow, and Cheju-do mark a profound breakthrough in East Asian international relations.[24]

Those developments and the promise of continued improvements in ROK–Russia ties almost certainly has sealed North Korea's diplomatic fate. In those terms the Kim Il-song regime lost its peninsular version of the diplomatic Cold War. There was, and is, a sense in South Korea that the end of the global Cold War, and its spillover into improved ROK–Russia ties, has essentially sealed North Korea's strategic destiny too. Although there continues to be apprehension regarding North Korean armed potential—marked by fear that the Kim Il-song regime might behave irrationally if it finds itself cornered with no chance of escape or no survival as a separate entity—that concern is greatly diminished compared to a few short years ago.[25] Consequently, the second major aspect of the broad end of the diplomatic spectrum concerns changes in ROK–DPRK nuances from 1988 to 1992. Prior to these years there had been many ups and downs in North–South diplomacy, leading nowhere in terms of concrete steps toward tension reduction and the eventual reunification of Korea. A basic reason for this lack of meaningful progress was that neither Korea had much incentive to alter its behavior. During 1988–92 this changed significantly.

North Korea discovered that its world was changing. No matter how much it might criticize the former Soviet Union or various Eastern European states for succumbing to the pressures embodied by the end of the Cold War,[26] Pyongyang was unable to hold back the tide. The DPRK became increasingly out of step with a changing world. The absorption of East Germany by West Germany, on Bonn's terms, was a profound shock to the Kim regime. Coming in the wake of China's Tiananmen upheaval, Ceausescu's fall in Romania, and Gorbachev's wayward ways in Moscow, German reunification was a nightmare come true for Pyongyang. It posed a precedent that was as abhorrent to Pyongyang as it was appealing to Seoul. As the East European states, then the Soviet Union, got into line to knock at Seoul's door seeking trade, investment, and technology, Pyongyang found itself cut out of the game. It could not hope to compete. With China very reluctant to get entangled again in a Korean conflict in support of North Korea, and cozying up to the ROK in a relatively discreet but undeniable manner, Pyongyang had to face the fact that it had no foreign backer left to reinforce it militarily. The Soviet Union clearly was out of that business, and shortly thereafter it was totally "out of business," a traumatic event for North Korea. North Korean fence-sitting leverage had dissipated along with the thawing Cold War. Neither China nor Russia had genuine reason any more to be seriously concerned that Pyongyang might tilt toward either Moscow or Beijing.

To the extent it can still be called leverage, the main "leverage" Pyongyang possessed was the threat to enter a suicidal war with the South that might endanger its neighbors. That was not very usable or persuasive leverage.

North–South Overtures

South Korea's reaction to North Korea's dilemma has been remarkable. Unlike years past when one might have expected Seoul to gloat openly, rub in its victories through propaganda, and press for North Korean capitulation, Seoul has adopted a statesmanlike commitment to gradual negotiations with Pyongyang. Progress has occurred in terms of more meetings and higher-level contacts (i.e., starting with the September 1990 exchange between prime ministers).[27] Some progress has either been quirky, such as Seoul's idea for a "Unipeace City" in the DMZ,[28] or small and long overdue, such as the February 1991 agreement to form joint sports teams.[29] Most important, however, is Seoul's evident confidence that the long-term prognosis for its side is almost inevitably positive. In effect, South Korea has shifted from a bitter zero-sum diplomatic war to a far more patient and mellow diplomatic war of attrition versus North Korea. As ROK foreign minister Choi Ho-joong noted in November 1990, when he announced the planned closure by 1992 of ten window dressing–type small ROK embassies, there was no longer any need for the ROK to engage in wasteful diplomatic competition with North Korea.[30] As of this writing in spring 1992, significant progress had been made in late 1991 and early 1992 regarding a nonaggression pact and nuclear arms control.[31]

The handwriting seems to be on the wall for the Kim regime and, at a minimum, Seoul seems prepared to wait for Pyongyang to tire of the struggle. South Korean diplomacy toward North Korea has become far more upbeat and outgoing. Instead of being standoffish and hypercautious, South Korean diplomats are reaching out to North Koreans in a friendly manner. Compared to the former cold formality, political contacts on the peninsula and overseas tend to be consciously gracious. The author witnessed very friendly interaction between North and South Korean mainstream scholars at the University of Hawaii in June 1991, which was warmly applauded by the ROK's consul general (Ambassador Sohn Jang-nai), who formerly was considered a hardliner.[32] This attitude reinforced the ROK's flexible diplomatic pressures at the United Nations where Seoul developed momentum toward ROK membership in late 1990 that was completed in September 1991 when both Koreas joined the UN General Assembly.[33]

Seoul's approach is commendable and almost certainly will prevail. Pyongyang, however, is not passively accepting the changes going on around North Korea. Though it can do little about improved ROK ties with former supporters of the DPRK, Pyongyang has been fully capable of rebounding by using South Korea's innovative diplomatic techniques. This is precisely what North Korea has done vis-à-vis Japan and is attempting to do with the United States. Despite strong South Korean objections, Japan—guided by Liberal Democratic Party kingmaker Kanemaru Shin—responded to North Korean diplomatic overtures. Overcoming persistent Korea–Japan animosities that cloud DPRK–Japan relations as much as ROK–Japan relations, Tokyo and Pyongyang at long last began normalization talks on January 31, 1991.[34] These talks promise to be difficult. To buffer the impact of this major Japanese foreign policy shift, the Kaifu government behaved in a conciliatory manner toward South Korea. Prime Minister Kaifu visited Seoul in January 1991 for ROK–Japan summitry, paying his respects at a monument to anti-Japanese independence fighters, and promising to end onerous fingerprinting of Korean residents of Japan.[35] The Kaifu government played a calculating game with the Koreans. Unlike past and present U.S. administrations, various Japanese administrations have never allowed Seoul to exercise any meaningful veto over Tokyo's Korean options. Although Tokyo usually tilted toward Seoul on Korean issues, it also maintained a semblance of impartiality regarding the existence of two Koreas. This was reinforced by popular Japanese dislike of both Koreas. Tokyo has now moved its Korea policy to a higher level of evenhanded sophistication by establishing closer relations with *both* Koreas, thereby addressing Pyongyang's newfound desires for an alternative diplomatic lever and Seoul's vulnerability regarding Japan's very real power to influence Korea's fate.

Tokyo seems to be taking action in support of peace and stability on the Korean peninsula, and in that sense it deserves credit for becoming a more active player in Korean affairs despite the Japanese public's distaste for getting entangled again in its neighbor's problems. Nevertheless, there also is a feeling in Korea that Japan is once more being manipulative regarding Korea, and actually is doing all it can to perpetuate the status quo in order to minimize the prospects for Korean unification. Many Japanese have harbored doubts about the desirability of the two Koreas' becoming one, though Tokyo and most Japanese political leaders say they support that goal. This duality, and Korean suspicions about Japanese intentions, were crystallized in the fall of 1990 when a well-known author and TV personality, Tanemura Kenichi, reportedly said, "An all-out invasion of Japan by Korea is inevitable if Korea is reunified . . . therefore it is in Japan's best interest to help North Korea economically so the Korean peninsula remains divided as now."[36] This comment caused controversy in South Korea and denials by Tanemura, but it symbolized the suspicions that exist on both sides.

Despite mutual doubts, the net result of these developments is simultaneous movement by Japan toward South Korea's vaunted "cross-recognition" formula for Korean tension reduction, and by Pyongyang toward new flexibility in North Korea's foreign policy. While both Seoul and Pyongyang seemingly benefited, in the short run North Korea gained more. Seoul lost a bit of leverage when Tokyo did not ask South Korea's permission to improve Japan–DPRK relations. To the extent that played into North Korean hands, it was a net gain for

Pyongyang. As much as North Korea wanted movement in this direction, however, it also exposed the DPRK's need to seek alternatives to shore up its diplomatic and economic weaknesses. The fact that it had to turn for succor to hated Japan, which Pyongyang long has accused of sinister designs on Korea, only serves to underline the North Korean dilemma. So, even as Seoul frets about Japanese actions and their motives, there is a sense that in the long run these developments will benefit South Korea, too. This is reinforced by Japan's sensitivity to both U.S. desires that Tokyo not undermine Seoul and, more important, Tokyo's anxiety about North Korea's nuclear potential.[37] On balance, this is one more example of Seoul's more relaxed attitude regarding competition with Pyongyang.

North Korea's overtures to the United States have not met with anything like the success enjoyed with Japan. Much to Seoul's relief, Washington has not been willing to respond to North Korean initiatives.[38] Though diplomatic movement on this front may be inevitable as major power relations with both Korean states in the post–Cold War era become more balanced,[39] it is clear that Seoul is ambiguous. Although Seoul says it encourages improved U.S.–DPRK ties, it actually seems to want to delay that prospect as long as possible. Tellingly, the more Seoul's nervousness about the possibility of improved U.S.–DPRK relations becomes evident, the more Pyongyang's desire for such ties becomes obvious. There are graphic signs that North Korea wants improved relations with the United States. Pyongyang's reluctant decision on May 28, 1991, to seek admission to the United Nations in tandem with South Korea reversed a long-standing position. While it had virtually no choice, because standing idly by would have allowed South Korea to be the only Korean state able to represent Korea in the UN, Pyongyang's move still nudged it toward a more accommodating diplomatic stance likely to be appreciated by the United States.[40] Another illustrative example was provided at the Hawaii conference cited above when the head of the North Korean scholars' group emphasized twice in his paper that "the United States is the only superpower remaining in the world."[41]

Evidently, both Koreas are still thinking in a virtual zero-sum context when it comes to diplomacy with the United States. In reality, North Korean desires vis-à-vis the United States are yet another example of Pyongyang reluctantly adjusting to new circumstances not of its choosing. Seoul need not be so anxious about American reliability and Washington need not be so sensitive to South Korean paranoia. One positive demonstration of U.S. flexibility regarding representatives of the DPRK in the United States was the attendance of U.S. flag officers at a dinner for the North Korean scholars who visited Hawaii.[42] The U.S.–ROK relationship would not be jeopardized by the United States routinely responding cautiously yet positively to North Korea's dilemma. Nonetheless, as of this writing the United States and North Korea remain the odd men out in an overall climate of diplomatic normalization. This reassures Seoul and motivates Pyongyang to persist with its new found option of doing with its superpower adversary what South Korea did with the former Soviet Union. Despite the uncertainty over how these relationships will play themselves out in the very long run, for the time being Seoul remains overwhelmingly confident that the trends are positive for South Korea.

Fading Client State

The first and second facets of change in South Korea's broad diplomatic spectrum have been widely noticed and recognized as important. Far less noted have been the ways in which these events have influenced U.S.–ROK relations. On the surface the impact has been tremendously positive. American officials emphatically support South Korea's initiatives, albeit with occasional grousing that the ardor of South Koreans for things Russian may be excessive, naive, and unseemly. Less noticeable, but no less real or important, however, have been the ways in which these recent shifts have reshaped the context of U.S.–ROK relations. The new relative emphasis on Russia and a variety of other states underlines the importance of diversification for contemporary South Korea. The remnants of client statism are being shredded by Seoul's new options. The process of maturation in U.S.–ROK relations is accelerating very rapidly indeed.

South Koreans no longer think of the United States as the foundation of South Korea's international security network. Dr. Kim Chong-whi (senior Blue House aide for Foreign and National Security Affairs) in December 1990 accurately referred to the United States as the "cornerstone" of ROK foreign policy.[43] ROK officials are adamant that Seoul places the highest priority on U.S.–ROK relations. For example, Foreign Minister Lee Sang-ock noted in January 1991 that improving ties with Washington topped Seoul's diplomatic agenda for that year.[44] In keeping with that goal, Information Minister Choi Chang-yoon announced possible plans for a Korean Information Center in Washington that would help Americans to understand Korea better.[45] In a sense, the renewed level of attention Seoul is devoting to U.S. affairs is a sign that the process of maturation is accelerating so fast that South Korea needs to shore up areas of the relationship that frictions have eroded.

Though Americans have paid far more attention to a right-wing Japanese who urged his countrymen to say "no" to Americans as a sign of national assertiveness, they have scarcely noticed the upswing in nationalistic South Koreans' willingness to say "no" to the United States on trade issues in particular. South Korean behavior on GATT issues aroused considerable U.S. ire in 1990–91. American officials and businessmen were unable to hide those frictions.[46] During the Persian Gulf War, U.S. animosity toward Japan's self-centered reluctance to lay Japanese lives on the line generated less visible animosity toward the ROK's very comparable cautious attitudes. In this case, however, U.S. officials limited the damage.[47] As these and other incidents indicate, a gap is emerging in the once close U.S.–ROK relationship. Little brother has grown up and wants to be accorded greater parity and respect within a still hierarchical relationship. As important, big brother is growing frustrated and impatient with little brother's self-indulgent attitudes.

While the United States is still the "cornerstone," other countries also represent blocks in the ROK's international foundation. For example, South Korea is building upon its expanded ties with Western Europe, the Middle East, and various former socialist bloc countries by still broader overtures to Latin America and Africa. The ROK plans to become a major donor of economic aid throughout the 1990s, shoring up its own economic prosperity as other countries have by using tied aid.[48] Seoul also has launched its own version of the Peace Corps.[49] Both of these efforts will focus on Asia initially, but they are profound indicators that South Korea harbors broader ambitions diplomatically.

This combination of three broad aspects in current ROK diplomacy points to a significant change in ROK security perspectives. As I elaborated in an analysis done for the Cato Institute in 1990,[50] South Korea is changing its approach to and appreciation for security. In the not too distant past, Seoul thought exclusively in terms of large ROK ground forces and limited air forces, supported by token U.S. ground "trip wire" forces and a large American reservoir of ground, air, and maritime power, all focused on a tangible North Korean threat. To be sure, that perception persists in South Korea, but it is increasingly offset by three other views: (1) South Korea faces as much of a real threat to its economic security as it does militarily from North Korea; (2) South Korea needs to cultivate its air power and, especially, its sea power if it is to be taken seriously as both a regional power and an entity capable of sharing burdens with any ally or coalition partner;[51] and (3) South Korea requires a multifaceted perspective on security. In short, South Korea today is using broader aspects of a diversified diplomacy on its strategic front to fashion its own version of what the Japanese call "comprehensive security." This takes on added significance when juxtaposed to South Korea's growing recognition that U.S. global strategy is in the process of adapting to a post–Cold War environment that poses a sharply reduced threat to the United States.

These major shifts in South Korean foreign policy and the reactions they precipitated in North Korea define the current state of play on the diplomatic dimension of the Korean confrontation. While North Korea enjoyed a slight edge diplomatically during the late post–Korean War recovery period (i.e., from the late 1950s through the mid-1960s), its advantages have been eroding since the mid-1960s. The process of erosion was gradual for roughly two decades. As of the mid-1980s, North Korea was behind diplomatically, but its position was still tenable internationally. It had a chance of catching up to the ROK diplomatically, if not economically, by holding itself out as a legitimate alternative model of Korean development. Since 1985, however, revolutionary world trends, compounded by a very facile and innovative South Korean foreign policy, have greatly accelerated the erosion of North Korea's international position. North

Korea's diplomacy and the supporting features of its society simply are not working as well as South Korea's. The ROK is prevailing in the contest.

Prospects and Options

Although South Korea is very much in the lead diplomatically, economically, politically, *and*—especially if viewed from a "comprehensive" perspective—strategically, there remain significant uncertainties regarding the future. I shall address several long-term and broad problem areas. To begin with, however, it is worthwhile to raise one relatively narrow domestic Korean issue that has repercussions in diplomacy: both Koreas confront a leadership problem.

North Korea's succession issue has been widely discussed. The only thing certain about it is that Kim Il-song is not immortal. Sooner or later, he will die and be replaced. In terms of North Korean defense and foreign policies, this shift almost certainly will have major implications. The defense policy alternatives are routinely raised by speculators on the successor. Put succinctly, North Korea may not change, or it might: (a) become more aggressive under a leader trying to live up to Kim Il-song's standards, or (b) become more flexible and less prickly under a leader who recognizes that the game is over. Far less noticed amid all this speculation is the impact succession may have on the overall tenor of North Korean diplomacy. For all his warts, Kim Il-song is an international persona. There is a consequent aura of gravity and purpose embodied in his foreign policy. When he is gone, the chances of Pyongyang (under anyone's leadership) perpetuating that aura seem slim. In short, the next North Korean leader is unlikely to be as successful as Kim Il-song still is at papering over the abject weakness of the North Korean diplomatic position. Instead, North Korea will likely have to come to grips with the reality that it is losing the Korean version of the Cold War.

South Korea's short-term domestic political problems are not as severe as North Korea's, but they are nonetheless real. For all of its vaunted international successes, the Roh Tae-wu administration has not been able to transform those successes into domestic political capital. Roh remains a politically weak president. As long as the ROK retains the level of political pluralism it has established from 1987 to 1991, Roh and the ruling Democratic Liberal Party are not assured of maintaining control of the government. The 1990s could prove to be a dynamic period for South Korean politics, producing a successor generation of leadership whose names have been overshadowed by Roh and the "three Kims" (Kim Dae-jung, Kim Jong-pil, and Kim Young-sam).

As of this writing, Roh has two ways to alter this situation. One option seems politically untenable. He cannot afford to oversee a reverse course politically in which he would sanction greater military control, decision-making centraiism, and institutionalized authoritarianism. It could occur, of course, and some analysts detect signs of a reactionary reversal already, but a major swing in that direction would be immensely damaging to all the international gains Roh has achieved. In fact, such a shift would play directly into North Korea's hands. Roh's best hopes rest with the other option, namely convincing the South Korean electorate that his government's foreign policy leadership is so necessary that allowances should be made for the shortcomings of those domestic policies that produce very low ratings in the polls.

In short, Roh might learn from presidents Bush, Gorbachev, and Yeltsin to make a virtue of necessity. Roh candidly admitted that he (like they) is less interested in, or adept at, domestic issues when he said in 1989 that he would rather be a president in charge only of foreign affairs.[52] Instead of fumbling with this weakness, Roh may yet prevail politically by stressing his strengths and those of the ruling party. On balance, however, Roh's problems and the far more significant problem of North Korea's succession remain short-term issues. One way or another, answers to them will emerge fairly quickly. As this occurs, the two Koreas must confront several long-term major problems that shall be outlined briefly here.

The most basic problems concern the way in which the end of the global Cold War will be transferred to Korea. Resolving the division of Korea, arranging its prospective unification, disposing of two heavily armed adversaries, reintegrating two societies (and their economies, which have grown grossly disparate) into one nation again, and reestablishing one Korea in world affairs, cumulatively compose a stupendous agenda. In other words, it is one thing to rejoice that the Cold War is over and recognize that Korea is being brought into the process, it is entirely different to flesh out the details. For better or worse, the two Koreas will have to perform the bulk of this work. Eventual success seems likely, but it is not assured.

As Koreans address that set of problems, they will need to cope with the other ways in which their foreign relations may change. Perhaps most tangible to Koreans is their fear (shared by South and North) that Japan will again loom large on Korea's horizon. Both Seoul and Pyongyang frequently show their anxiety about the prospective reassertion of Japanese power in the Pacific. Tokyo's disavowals notwithstanding, there is a profound sense among Koreans that Japan is moving inexorably toward a position of regional leadership. It already dominates economically and may transform that form of power into political and military instruments. Few possibilities stir Korean emotions more. In short, Koreans—as separate states or in a unified country—had better learn to co-exist amicably with a powerful Japan.

As dramatic as this problem may seem, it points to larger shifts in western Pacific power that could have equally profound meaning for Korea. The region seems on the verge of what could be considered a return to normalcy. For much of the post–Second World War period, the United States has wielded a disproportionate level of power and influence. For years, that was warranted in light of American preeminence in the Western camp of the Cold War. Today, however, neither that preeminence nor the Cold War exist any longer. For all the display of U.S. armed power in the Persian Gulf War, this power must be measured against a new dependence on foreign funding and imported technology.

On balance, we have a relatively less powerful United States retrenching in the western Pacific as it confronts two realities: (1) its allies (and sources of funding and technology) also are competitors who pose a post–Cold War challenge to U.S. national interests, and (2) the dissolution of the ideological glue of the Cold War years raises serious questions about the rationales for collective or coalition security. In short, the American role in the Pacific is being slowly but steadily transformed.

To the extent the transformation is a predictable part of Washington's policies, it causes little apprehension in Korea (South or North) or elsewhere in Asia. There is, however, a sense that the transformation is not fully purposeful or controllable by American leaders. In other words, just as various Asian states— pointedly including South Korea, Japan, and the PRC—are moving away from reactive policies and toward initiator roles diplomatically, the United States and Russia are being compelled to adopt more reactive roles and act less regularly as initiators.

For Korea, especially South Korea, this shift in relative power and decision making raises the strong likelihood that the existing gap in U.S.–ROK relations will widen. In short, the process of bilateral maturation is likely to wipe out the remnants of client statism, clarify and emphasize the ways in which U.S. and ROK interests do not coincide, strengthen Korean xenophobic feelings of victimization, and expose more regularly the areas of friction in the countries' relationship. If this actually occurs, the next ten to fifteen years are likely to produce a reordering of defense priorities in both countries, with South Korea diversifying its sources of security beyond what is visualized here and the United States focusing largely on economic goals and downplaying sharply any military roles that hurt U.S. economic interests. This does not mean that there will be a rupture in U.S.–ROK relations, but it does mean that each side is likely to be more objective and dispassionate about the other's utility. In conclusion, this would amount to a watershed lessening of the vaunted special relationship in favor of a more normal level of international relations.

Notes

1. Nonetheless, those who do are often extremely vocal and violent, epitomized by the radical street demonstrators in the spring of 1991 who evidently detected the hand of "U.S. imperialism" behind the Roh Tae-woo government, which they were trying to oust. For coverage of those events, see the *Far Eastern Economic Review* (*FEER*), May 23, 1991, pp. 10–11.

2. For examples of Korean candor, see: Nam Joo-hong, "U.S.–ROK Security in the 1990s: A Challenging Partnership," *Journal of East Asian Affairs*, Summer/Fall 1990, pp. 243–255; and Ahn Byung-joon, "Decision-Sharing in Korea–U.S. Relations," *Korea and World Affairs*, Spring 1990, pp. 5–15.

3. For insights into the frustrations of Koreans at that time, see: Bruce Cumings, *The Origins of the Korean War* (Princeton, NJ: Princeton University Press, 1981).

4. See, for example, Bruce Cumings, *The Two Koreas,* Headline Series No. 269 (New York: Foreign Policy Association, 1984).

5. Quoted in *U.S. News & World Report,* February 27, 1989, p. 35.

6. For details on "Koreagate," see: Robert Boettcher, *Gifts of Deceit* (New York: Holt, Rinehart and Winston, 1980).

7. The author assessed that shift in its formative stage in Edward A. Olsen, "The Evolution of the ROK's Foreign Policy," *Washington Quarterly,* Winter 1983.

8. The author examined this theme in greater detail in Edward A. Olsen, "U.S.–ROK Relations: Common Issues and Uncommon Perceptions," *Korea and World Affairs,* Spring 1989.

9. The author addressed Korea's role in the termination of the Cold War in Edward A. Olsen, "Ending the Cold War in Korea," *Journal of East Asian Affairs,* Winter/Spring 1990; "Special Report—The Korean Cold War, 40 Years Later / The Post–Cold War Era: An American Perspective," *The World and I,* July 1990; and "The Impact of the End of the Cold War on Northeast Asian Security," *1990 Pacific Symposium Proceedings* (Washington, D.C.: National Defense University Press, forthcoming). For alternative perspectives see: Tim Shorrock, "How Long Yet for Korea's Cold War?" *The Nation,* January 28, 1991, pp. 82–85; and A. Plotkovskiy, "Korea: An Equation with Two Unknowns," *Komsomolskaya Pravda,* November 29, 1990, p. 3, in Foreign Broadcast Information Service: Soviet Union (hereafter *FBIS–SOV*), November 30, 1990, pp. 22–24.

10. After lengthy negotiations the ROK and PRC witnessed the opening of a South Korean trade mission office in Beijing, January 31, 1991, under the auspices of the Korean Trade Promotion Corporation (KOTRA). Although the ROK treats the office as a de facto embassy and the PRC adamantly insists it is not, there is much speculation that it is indeed a precursor to formal ROK–PRC diplomatic recognition. See the *Korea Herald,* January 31, 1991, pp. 1, 11; and February 1, 1991, p. 2.

11. For comparative data on the two economies, see the annual "South and North Korean Economies," published by the ROK National Unification Board. For a particularly devastating assessment of the weaknesses of the North Korean economy, see *FEER,* May 30, 1991, pp. 38–40. See also *FEER,* May 28, 1992, p. 30; and *Korea Herald,* May 5, 1992, p. 5; and May 10, 1992, pp. 1–5.

12. For background on Hungary's move, see: Foreign Broadcast Information Service: East Asia (hereafter *FBIS–EAS*), November 1, 1988, pp. 13–14; December 19, 1988, pp. 29–30; January 13, 1989, p. 16; January 26, 1989, pp. 27–28; February 1, 1989, pp. 26–27; and October 21, 1989, p. 35.

13. For background on these countries' moves toward diplomatic relations with South Korea, see: *FEER,* December 8, 1988, pp. 20–26 and November 9, 1989, p. 16; *Hangook Ilbo,* October 4, 1989, p. 3; *Chungang Ilbo,* January 11, 1989, p. 5; and *FBIS–EAS,* October 25, 1989, pp. 22–23; December 28, 1989, pp. 21–22; March 22, 1990, pp. 21–22; and March 30, 1990, p. 19.

14. *FBIS–EAS,* March 8, 1990, p. 31.

15. *Korea Herald,* July 13, 1990, p. 6; and July 22, 1990, p. 2.

16. *FBIS–EAS,* May 17, 1990, pp. 8–9; and July 9, 1990, p. 17.

17. For representative coverage of the San Francisco summit, see: *New York Times,* June 7, 1990, p. A3; *FBIS–EAS,* June 8, 1990, pp. 15–26; and June 13, 1990, pp. 16–20; and *FEER,* June 14, 1990, pp. 10–11. For the author's post-summit analysis, see "Kan-so samitto igo; watakushi wa ko miru," *Sankei shimbun,* June 8, 1990.

18. Examples of the "spin doctors'" craft are *New York Times,* June 6, 1990, p. A3;

and *Korea Herald*, July 28, 1990, p. 6; August 8, 1990, p. 1; August 12, 1990, p. 5; and August 15, 1990, p. 1.

19. *Korea Herald*, October 2, 1990, p. 1.

20. *New Republic*, November 19, 1990, pp. 7–10. See also, *Korea Herald*, July 28, 1990, p. 7; and *FEER*, May 17, 1990, p. 24.

21. *U.S. News & World Report*, January 14, 1991, p. 19; *FEER*, January 17, 1991, p. 12; and February 14, 1991, p. 15; and *Korea Herald*, February 5, 1991, p. 2.

22. *FEER*, September 20, 1990, p. 86; and *Korea Herald*, November 18, 1990, p. 1; December 14, 1990, p. 1; December 15, 1990, pp. 1, 9; December 16, 1990, p. 10; and December 19, 1990, p. 1.

23. *Korea Herald*, January 20, 1991, pp. 1, 5; and *FEER*, February 7, 1991, pp. 44–45.

24. For coverage of Gorbachev's Cheju-do trip, see *FEER*, May 2, 1991, pp. 11–13; and *The Roh-Gorbachev Summit on Cheju* (Seoul: Korean Overseas Information Service, Policy Series, 91–2).

25. For a thorough analysis of why Seoul perceives the North Korean threat to be receding, see *FEER*, January 3, 1991, pp. 15–19.

26. For examples of North Korean criticism of its former steadfast supporters, see: *FBIS–EAS*, September 19, 1990, pp. 14–15; November 3, 1990, pp. 6–7; and November 27, 1990, pp. 10–11; *FEER*, March 29, 1990, pp. 16–17; and *Korea Herald*, November 30, 1990, p. 1; and December 23, 1990, p. 3.

27. For coverage of the first prime ministerial meeting, see *FEER*, September 13, 1990, p. 11, and September 20, 1990, pp. 24–25.

28. *FEER*, December 20, 1990, p. 32.

29. *Korea Herald*, February 13, 1991, p. 1.

30. *Korea Herald*, November 29, 1990, p. 1.

31. *Korea Herald*, December 13, 1991, p. 1; December 14, 1991, p. 1; and February 19, 1992, p. 1.

32. University of Hawaii, Center for Korean Studies, "United States/North Korea 1st Binational Exchange Conference," June 3–6, 1991. This event also was notable for the consul general emotionally singing traditional songs with the North Korean scholars and three prominent mainstream South Korean scholars who attended as observers: Kim Dal-joong (Yonsei University), Koo Young-nok (Seoul National University), and Hong Sung-chick (Korea University).

33. *FEER*, December 6, 1990, p. 15; and *Korea Herald*, September 18, 1991, p. 1.

34. *Japan Times Weekly* (International Edition), February 11–17, 1991, p. 3; and *Korea Herald*, February 1, 1991, p. 1.

35. *FEER*, January 31, 1991, pp. 36–37.

36. Ibid., p. 39.

37. Japan's (and others') concern about North Korea's nuclear potentials are asssessed in Leonard S. Spector, "North Korea's Nascent Nuclear Threat," *Asian Wall Street Journal Weekly*, April 27, 1991, p. 12; and Andrew Mack, "North Korea and the Bomb," *Foreign Policy*, Summer 1991, pp. 87–104.

38. For coverage of North Korean outreach to the United States and American responses, see *Seoul Shinmun*, September 29, 1990, p. 1; and *FEER*, May 24, 1990, p. 1; and June 21, 1990, pp. 22–23.

39. The author addressed American interests in pursuing this option in Edward A. Olsen, "Chill between U.S. and Pyongyang Is a Mistake for Both Sides," *Asian Wall Street Journal Weekly*, November 5, 1990, opinion page.

40. For coverage of the UN decision, see *FEER*, June 6, 1991, p. 15.

41. Suk Chang-sik, "On the Role of Scholars in the Improvement of DPRK–U.S. Relations and Academic Exchange," pp. 2, 5.

42. A formal dinner hosted on June 3, 1991, by University of Hawaii president Albert Simone at his residence was attended by R. Adm. L. Vogt (USN) and M. Gen. Wm. Matz (USA) from CINCPAC staff, both of whom socialized amicably with the North Koreans.

43. From interview in *Korea Update*, February 4, 1991, ROK Embassy Information Office (Washington), p. 6.

44. *Korea Herald*, January 25, 1991, p. 1.

45. *Korea Hereald*, January 31, 1991, p. 2.

46. For coverage of U.S.–ROK frictions over GATT and related market access issues, see: *Korea Herald*, December 22, 1990, p. 2; January 10, 1991, p. 7; January 12, 1991, p. 6; January 15, 1991, p. 1; and February 2, 1991, p. 3; *FEER*, November 22, 1990, pp. 54–56; and "Pillars of Protectionism in Korea," American Chamber of Commerce in Korea, Seoul, August 1990.

47. For a sense of the controversy about ROK reluctance to play a larger role in the Gulf War, see *Korea Herald*, January 19, 1991, p. 2, and January 20, 1991, p. 2. For Ambassador Gregg's damage control, see *Korea Herald*, January 30, 1991, p. 1.

48. *FEER*, December 27, 1990, p. 30.

49. *FEER*, May 4, 1990, p. 26.

50. "Korean Security: Is Japan's 'Comprehensive Security' Model a Viable Alternative?" in Ted Galen Carpenter and Doug Bandow, eds., *The U.S.–South Korean Alliance* (New Brunswick, NJ: Transaction Publishers, 1992).

51. See also, "In Search of Enemies," *FEER*, January 3, 1991, pp. 16–19; Kim Dal-choong, ed., *Hangook gwa haeryag anbo* [Korea and maritime security] (Seoul: Yonsei University, Institute of East & West Studies, 1989); and Kim Dal-choong and Cho Doug-woon, eds. *Korean Sea Power and the Pacific Era* (Seoul: Yonsei University, Institute of East & West Studies, 1990).

52. Quoted in *FEER*, December 27, 1990, p. 6.

6

China's Asian Policy in the 1990s: Adjusting to the Post–Cold War Environment*

Paul H.B. Godwin

China and the Cold War:
Adversaries, Allies, and the Balance of Power

The emergence of the Sino-Soviet dispute in the late 1950s was a seminal development in the Cold War, for it tore apart one of the most feared alliances in the East–West global conflict. The rupture led to a pattern in Beijing's security analyses where the balance of power between the United States and the Soviet Union became the principal determinant of Chinese foreign and defense policies. Nonetheless, the Moscow–Beijing rift was not static, but constantly evolved, adding new components as the dynamics of the international system and the East–West confrontation intersected with China's internal politics and Beijing's interpretation of its security environment. It was this evolution over the duration of the Cold War that restructured the strategic balance between the United States and the Soviet Union in the early 1970s, with China playing a central role. By the mid-1980s, however, changes in the leadership of both the USSR and the United States combined with changes in China's interpretation of the global balance of power led to yet another permutation of China's basic security strategy. China moved from tilting toward the United States to a position more

---

* The views expressed in this chapter are those of the author and are not to be construed as those of the National War College, the National Defense University, or any other Agency of the United States Government.

definitely self-reliant in anticipation of an increasingly multipolar global distribution of power.[1]

By the early 1990s, however, Beijing faced a totally unanticipated set of events. Détente between the United States and the Soviet Union, the collapse of the East European communist regimes, and disintegration of the Warsaw Pact were accompanied by political and economic stresses in the USSR that ultimately led to the disintegration of the Soviet Union itself. Entering the 1990s, Chinese security analysts face a condition where the United States and its coalition of industrialized Western democracies, including Japan, are preeminent in the international system. The balance of power in the international system, Chinese strategists fear, is tending more toward unipolarity than multipolarity.

In brief, removal of the East–West dimension from both historical and incipient conflicts in the Asia Pacific Region (APR) is interpreted by Beijing as potentially creating less rather than more regional stability. In the analyses of Chinese security strategists, the absence of superpower competition permits local conflicts to arise where previously they had been suppressed by the dominant East–West pattern of conflict. To this dilemma Chinese analysts in the 1990s had to add the potential effect of a unipolar international system dominated by a United States–led coalition of Western industrialized democratic states.

The Sino-Soviet Dispute and China's National Security

The deterioration of the Sino-Soviet alliance came about over a decade and reflected a variety of disagreements between Soviet and Chinese leaders. The dispute is too complex for simple summaries, but its essence was a fundamental issue of national security. Less than one year after its founding in 1949, the People's Republic of China had become dependent on the Soviet Union for its security against the United States because of the Korean War. Nonetheless, Beijing became concerned by 1956 that Khrushchev's policies of "peaceful coexistence" with the United States could lead to a superpower condominium inimical to China's interests. Khrushchev sought Beijing's acceptance of his security policies through both persuasion and coercion. As a carrot, Khrushchev used military and economic assistance, including a cooperative nuclear weapons program. When these failed to gain China's support for his goals and policies, Khrushchev canceled the nuclear weapons program in 1959 and withdrew all military and economic assistance in the summer of 1960.

These punitive actions failed to coerce Beijing into accepting Soviet national security objectives as those of China, and the final years of the Khrushchev era saw Beijing and Moscow move even further apart. The Sino-Indian border war of 1962, the Cuban missile crisis of the same year, and the 1963 treaty banning atmospheric nuclear weapons tests all widened the Sino-Soviet rift. With Khrushchev's political demise in 1964, there was a short period when Brezhnev sought to return China to the fold. Trade between the USSR and China increased as the Soviet Union terminated its economic warfare against Beijing, and Zhou Enlai went to Moscow to initiate discussion of the issues dividing the two communist powers. The talks came to naught. Moscow and Beijing continued their separate and conflicting paths, but under Brezhnev's leadership the dispute was militarized.

Militarization of the Dispute

Soviet forces deployed in areas adjacent to China in 1964 were modest, probably not more than twelve to fifteen divisions. Although border polemics had increased in the final two years of the Khrushchev regime, they were based not on the importance of the border issues themselves but more on Beijing's intent to demonstrate that China was the aggrieved party in the dispute and to put Moscow on the defensive. The USSR was portrayed as the direct descendent of imperial Russia and tarred with the brush of colonialism and imperialism. Border talks opened in February 1964, but Chinese demands and disagreement over drawing riverine boundaries made the issues unnegotiable. In October, the month Khrushchev was removed from office, the talks were abandoned. In that same month, China detonated an atomic weapon and joined the club of nuclear powers.

Quite possibly, the sheer size of the Chinese People's Liberation Army (PLA) and the evident success in Beijing's nuclear weapons program led Moscow to reassess the USSR's military posture along its border with China and in the Mongolian People's Republic (MPR). Even so, the military buildup began modestly, with perhaps seventeen divisions deployed by 1966. This would be sufficient for more aggressive patrolling of the border, but far less than would be required for an invasion threat to China.

Perhaps more indicative of Soviet long-range intentions, however, was the twenty-year friendship treaty signed by the USSR and the MPR in January 1966. There had been no Soviet troops in Mongolia since 1957, and the new treaty stipulated that the USSR would sustain all costs of future deployments. Within a few months, Moscow had deployed two divisions and some air units in the MPR.

There was reporting of Sino-Soviet border skirmishes in 1966, and toward the end of the year the USSR deployed SS-4 and SS-5 MRBMs in the Soviet Far East. The Soviet military buildup continued over the next two years, perhaps hastened by the political instability in China that accompanied the Great Proletarian Cultural Revolution. By 1969, the USSR may have deployed some twenty-seven divisions on territory adjacent to China, and possibly two or three in the MPR. The buildup was notable for its inclusion of tank and mechanized divisions, even though the forces deployed did not contain the latest Soviet equipment. Because China's ground forces were basically straight-leg infantry units, their combat capability was significantly less than that of their Soviet counterparts.

The USSR, nonetheless, would certainly have been troubled by China's test of a hydrogen bomb in 1967 and the initial deployment of mobile MRBMs that fall. A Chinese nuclear attack on the USSR would have been an act of national suicide, but the fact that Beijing's nuclear weapons program was progressing and deployment was under way had to be considered a significant threat by Soviet military planners and a major concern for the Soviet leadership.

The March 2, 1969, Chinese ambush of a Soviet patrol on a disputed island in the Ussuri River, called Zhenbao by China and Damansky by the USSR, led ultimately to the dramatic Sino-American rapprochement of 1972. Apparently deliberately planned and not the result of an unanticipated meeting of two patrols, the USSR responded to the ambush with a major engagement on March 15 in the same location. Considerable speculation surrounds the motivation behind the Chinese action, but the consequences are clear. The Zhenbao–Damansky clashes led to a major buildup of Soviet force deployments opposite China.

At the time of the ambush, the operational forces of the People's Liberation Army (as all three branches of the Chinese armed forces are designated) had deteriorated to the point that they were little more than a lumbering obsolescent giant. The course of the Sino-Soviet dispute had led to China's isolation from its only source of advanced military technology and its primary source of economic assistance. China's own foreign policy had led to Beijing's quasi isolation from both the East and the West, while the PLA's involvement in the domestic politics of the Great Proletarian Cultural Revolution had distracted its officer corps from the armed forces' national defense mission. Thus the domestic and foreign policies of China had left its armed forces in disarray.

By the same token, the sheer size of the PLA combined with its emerging nuclear forces and a basic military doctrine of protracted "People's War" would have made a Soviet attack on China immensely costly. Thus deterrence did exist, even though it was based upon what Allen Whiting has termed a deterrent posture of "calculated irrationality."[2]

The militarization of the Sino-Soviet dispute created a military threat that neither Beijing nor Moscow could dismiss. In Europe, the USSR was separated from the NATO alliance by the East European members of the Warsaw Pact. The pact formed a *cordon sanitaire* between the Soviet Union and its enemy. In Asia, China had fought in the Korean War to keep the United States away from its border and sustain the Democratic People's Republic of Korea (DPRK) as a buffer against the Republic of Korea (ROK) and its American ally. In the Second Indochina War, Beijing assisted Hanoi for much the same reason—to keep the United States from China's southwestern border. Along their mutual border, however, China and the Soviet Union faced each other without the separation provided by buffer states.

In addition, the MPR had become a base for potential Soviet military operations into China's northern territory. Strategically, the Soviet Far East and the MPR formed a horseshoe that surrounded northeast China and exposed the critical industrial base of Manchuria to a multipronged Soviet attack. The western edge of the horseshoe, based in Mongolia, threatened the political heart of China in Beijing. The Chinese even had a model for a potential Russian military attack on China—the August 1945 Soviet onslaught into Japanese-occupied Manchuria. Named "August Storm," the campaign was a multipronged offensive that attacked Manchuria and northern China from all sides, including Mongolia. A replication of "August Storm" was the military threat China feared most.

Sino-American Rapprochement

The March 1969 military engagements between Soviet and Chinese forces triggered the process of rapprochement between China and the United States that culminated in President Nixon's dramatic visit to China in 1972. The reasons for China's acceptance of a rapprochement are complex, but in large part they relate to Beijing's concern that the USSR had become a far greater military threat to China than it had been ten years earlier. The decade since the Sino-Soviet break had left China weak and isolated. An additional factor behind China's motivation was the strategy of Soviet-American détente pursued by the Nixon administration since 1970, which raised once again the specter of a superpower condominium where China's isolation would be a principal aspect of the accommodation.[3]

Rapprochement with the United States gave China the opportunity to gain access to the financial and technological resources of the West and seek the shelter of an American security umbrella. Accommodation with the United States would end China's isolation from the international system and its status as a pariah state among the Western powers. Rapprochement would also forestall American-Soviet détente from developing into Beijing's feared anti-Chinese condominium. The so-called "Strategic Triangle" conceptualized by President Nixon and his national security adviser Henry Kissinger gave China a link to superpower strategy that carried with it the image, if not the fact, of a strategic alignment with the United States. The relationship, however, went far beyond détente; it entered the realm of *entente*.

Sino-American Entente

Perhaps fearing a potential two-front war, where the USSR would be engaged by NATO forces in the West and a Sino-American-Japanese alliance in the East, Brezhnev continued the buildup of forces along the Sino-Soviet border and in the Soviet Far East. By the mid-1970s, 25 percent of Soviet ground and air forces were deployed where they could threaten China, and by the late 1970s the Pacific Fleet became the largest of the four fleets in the Soviet navy.

In December 1978, shortly after it signed a treaty with the USSR directed against China, Vietnam invaded Cambodia. Vietnam defeated China's client, Pol Pot, and replaced his government with one obedient to Hanoi. China responded in February 1979 with a punitive and costly expedition into Vietnam. Hanoi reacted by granting the USSR access to the base facilities in Cam Ranh Bay and Danang. In December 1979, the USSR entered Afghanistan. For Beijing, this action confirmed once again the aggressive, expansionist thrust of Soviet foreign policy.

By 1980, China's entente with the United States had produced a measure of security against the possibility of a direct attack by the Soviet Union, but the USSR was becoming an even more expansive and militarized power in Asia. This factor more than any other brought closer to fruition the possibility of strategic cooperation between China and the United States. Any chance of China's feared accommodation between Moscow and Washington faded with the Soviet invasion of Afghanistan. A heightened level of tension between the United States and the USSR, on the other hand, gave China the potential for leverage with both Washington and Moscow.

When the Reagan administration came to office in January 1981, it brought with it a view of the USSR that paralleled China's. The new administration raised the level of confrontation with Moscow, intensified support for both the Afghan resistance and the insurgent forces facing the Vietnamese in Cambodia, and spawned the "Reagan Doctrine," which sought to confront the USSR wherever Moscow had gained a position in the Third World.

China gained from two principal consequences of the Reagan administration's strategy. First, the administration agreed to transfer lethal "defensive" military equipment to China on a case-by-case basis. This was an important change from the Carter administration, which had limited military transfers to "non-lethal" equipment. This policy change was politically significant in that it clearly indicated to the Soviet Union that Sino-American ties played a major role in the new administration's strategy. Second, the aggressive policies pursued by the United States, and China's emerging role in American strategy, led Brezhnev to seek an accommodation with Beijing.

The year 1981 saw several entreaties and concessions from Moscow in search of a dialogue with Beijing. Border talks were reconvened in October 1982. Although no substantive agreement was reached on the border issues, the opening to the USSR was a clear statement of China's new "independent foreign policy" announced at the Party Congress that year. Similarly, border trade on a barter basis was reopened, initially between Heilongjiang Province and the Soviet Far East.

Even though Sino-Soviet relations were warming, Brezhnev refused to yield on any of the "three obstacles" China insisted on resolving before relations between Moscow and Beijing could be "normalized." The hurdles raised by Beijing were the Soviet forces in Afghanistan, Soviet support for the Vietnamese occupation of Cambodia, and the massive Soviet military deployment along the border with China and in the MPR. While Sino-Soviet rapprochement was being stymied by Beijing's demands, Soviet nuclear capabilities threatening China were increased by the deployment in the Far East of SS-20s and the Backfire bomber in the early 1980s. Soviet defense policy was responding to the Sino-American entente with a vengeance.

Continuing Soviet military deployments and the "three obstacles" raised by China created constraints that severely limited any real progress toward a Sino-Soviet rapprochement. But, beginning in 1984, changes in the American leadership began to recast the Sino-American linkage. Secretary of State Alexander Haig resigned and was replaced by George Shultz. Haig's assistant secretary for East Asia, John Holdridge, was replaced by Paul Wolfowitz. Haig and Holdridge were known as strong advocates of the strategic value of maintaining close ties with China. Schultz and Wolfowitz were more inclined to accept China's military and economic weakness as a sign that Beijing could not play a leading role in international politics, while at the same time China's size and military potential would act as a restraint on the USSR without any required action on the part of the United States. If anything, the new foreign policy leadership in Washington believed that China was in greater need of the United States and the Western powers than they were of China.[4] This asymmetrical dependence would ensure Chinese cooperation in areas of mutual interest and concern, such as support for the resistance groups in both Afghanistan and Cambodia, without granting Beijing special status in the American strategic logic.

Sino-Soviet Rapprochement

With Gorbachev's assumption of power in March 1985, and his revision of Soviet security policy, Asia became a major focus of Moscow's global strategic reassessment. Rapprochement with China became the primary Soviet objective in Asia, and Gorbachev's July 1986 speech in Vladivostok indicated that Soviet strategy designed to encircle and threaten China with military force was coming to an end. China, while sustaining its "three obstacles" as impediments to Sino-Soviet normalization, saw this speech as the first major step in Moscow's retreat from a predatory Asian policy. Under Gorbachev's new security strategy, relations with China rapidly improved.

In October 1986, the USSR and China agreed to resume border talks. In February 1987, Qian Qichen—then China's vice minister of Foreign Affairs—visited Moscow. He declared in April that the Soviet Union was willing to discuss the "three obstacles" to the normalization of Sino-Soviet relations.[5] These initial exchanges on the major issues dividing Moscow and Beijing inaugurated an acceleration of contacts, discussions, and negotiations that led to the Beijing summit of May 1989.

Mikhail Gorbachev and Deng Xiaoping met in Beijing for the summit that produced official restoration of ties between the Soviet and Chinese Communist parties. Relations had been "normalized" on China's terms. The USSR had withdrawn its forces from Afghanistan; had begun a major draw-down of Soviet forces threatening China; and had convinced Vietnam to withdraw its forces from Cambodia and accept a political settlement to the war. Following the Beijing summit, the USSR and China expedited settlement of their border disagreements and began a systematic process of negotiations directed at mutual force reductions and the creation of confidence-building measures (CBMs) along the Sino-Soviet border and in the Mongolian People's Republic.

Chinese analysts nonetheless remained cautious in their early 1990 interpretations of the progress made in Soviet force reductions and the implementation of Gorbachev's announced shift toward a defensive military doctrine for the Soviet Union. They saw the shift to a defensive military doctrine as yet in a transitional stage, and the massive reductions in both conventional and nuclear forces announced by Gorbachev counterbalanced by the technological upgrading of Soviet weapons and equipment, including space systems. Soviet forces, in the eyes of Chinese analysts, remained powerful and offensively postured.[6]

Demilitarization of the Border

Soviet troop reductions were, however, under way, and the first stage of withdrawal from the MPR was completed in October 1989, when three ground force divisions and one air division were pulled out.[7] By January 1991, the USSR had withdrawn all combat forces from Mongolia, including air force units, leaving only logistics regiments. Most of the forces withdrawn, according to Soviet sources, were to be demobilized. The remaining logistics units were to be out of the MPR by the end of 1991.[8]

The Mongolian withdrawal was only part of the more complex process of force reductions and CBMs agreed to at the Beijing summit. In November 1989, Soviet and Chinese diplomatic and military representatives held their first discussions of mutual balanced force reductions (MBFR) and confidence-building measures. The negotiations lasted two weeks and were the first in a continuing series of meetings that were to alternate between Moscow and Beijing.[9] April 1990 saw the premier of China and the chairman of the Soviet Council of Ministers sign a formal agreement in Moscow on force reductions and confidence building along the border.[10] Significantly, given the imbalance in combat power granted Soviet forces by the superior technology of their weapon systems and platforms, the USSR agreed that Russian reductions should be greater than those of the Chinese forces.[11] Thus, the negotiations had produced a concept of "balanced" force reductions that required the USSR to concede its technological superiority through asymmetrical cutbacks.

The MBFR/CBM negotiations were accompanied by increasing contact between the two defense establishments. Liu Huaqing, vice chairman of the CCP Central Military Commission and a leading figure in China's defense modernization programs, visited Moscow in May 1990 simultaneously with the arrival of a Soviet military delegation in Beijing. This was the first formal exchange of military visits in more than thirty years.[12] Liu Huaqing's visit, according to Chinese press reports, also opened the door to Soviet military technology transfers.[13] Soviet reports said Liu Huaqing visited a Mig-29 production plant,[14] leading to considerable speculation in the Western press that China was to purchase advanced Soviet air superiority fighters and ground-attack aircraft.[15] By 1992, China was purchasing some twenty-four Sukhoi-27 air superiority combat aircraft from the Russians and negotiating the possible acquisition of modern Russian tanks, and Mig-29 and Mig-31 fighters.

In October 1990, the MBFR/CBM negotiations had reached the point where the diplomatic and military working groups were negotiating what units and military equipment should be reduced, defining the border areas where the reductions should take place and the verification procedures to be adopted.[16] Soviet reports said that Chinese delegations were already visiting troop units and military academies in the Turkmen Military Region.[17] Neither Moscow nor Beijing chose to supply any details of the force reductions outside Mongolia.

Force reduction negotiations were conducted simultaneously with border negotiations. The sixth round of border negotiations, completed in October 1990, resulted in the signing of a preliminary agreement demarking the eastern sector of the border along the Amur River. With this agreement, the joint committee on border negotiations began work on the western sector of the border.[18] In December, the USSR reported that agreement had been reached on 90 percent of the entire 4,600-mile (7,000-plus km) border.[19]

The disintegration of the USSR one year later came as a profound shock to the Chinese leadership. Whereas Sino-Soviet relations had been proceeding along a road Beijing had long sought to travel, the Chinese leadership had not anticipated a total collapse of their erstwhile principal military threat. They could not but recognize the sense of triumph in the West as the Cold War ended and the USSR crumbled. Nor could they miss the exhilaration in the United States when its multinational coalition of Arab and Western powers crushed the armed forces of Iraq in a brief and brilliant campaign that emphasized American technological and military prowess. China now faced not the classical balance-of-power paradigm it had sought to manipulate for two decades, but a new paradigm of Western preeminence with the United States as the world's sole military superpower.

China's Interpretation of Its Security Environment: Problems in the Balance of Power

With any major military threat to China essentially removed, Beijing's perceptions of the future Asian security environment focused on U.S. security policy and the emerging dynamics of intra-regional alignments. U.S. security policy in Asia is of fundamental concern to Beijing because of its links to and influence over the future role of Japan in the region, developments on the Korean peninsula, settlement of the Cambodian impasse and the future security policies of ASEAN and Indochina, and Washington's potential influence on developments in South Asia.

Chinese strategists, however, continue to pay close attention to the balance of power. Even though the USSR and the United States had been seen as declining powers since the mid-1980s, their respective military strength was perceived as a mutual restraint limiting their freedom of action. As internal conditions in the USSR deteriorated in 1991, Chinese analysts concluded that the Soviet Union was no longer capable of acting as a balance against the United States. These strategists viewed the United States as the superior global economic, political, and military power. A security environment where the United States, even as a declining power, is predominant was not predicted by Chinese analysts. What is more, the American response to the Tiananmen tragedy of 1989 led to Beijing's interpreting the "post-containment" and "new world order" declarations of the Bush administration as threatening the Chinese leadership's core values.

Beijing views a principal goal of U.S. foreign policy in the post-containment era as seeking to subvert the remaining "socialist" states of the world through a strategy of "peaceful evolution." Peaceful evolution as a strategy seeks to undermine the values of socialism through the political, economic, and cultural penetration of socialist states that accompanies Western assistance and commerce.[20] The final collapse of the USSR is viewed in Beijing as a consequence of this American-led Western strategy of peaceful evolution. The second objective of American foreign policy as seen by Beijing is the attempt to create a coalition of Western powers dominated by the United States that will control the international system.[21] Of particular concern to Chinese analysts is Japan's role in the overall American strategy for a post-containment world. In the view of some analysts, the United States is attempting to structure a tripartite coalition with Japan and Europe to create a "new world order."[22]

Other Chinese analysts point to critical weaknesses within the coalition. In particular, trade frictions and differences over the future structure of European security will limit any systematic coordination of policies for the foreseeable future. Additionally, the coming roles of Germany and Japan cannot be foreseen at this time, therefore the United States may well be forced to align with other states to constrain Germany and Japan. Furthermore, these analysts state that China and many Third World countries will oppose the dictates of the advanced industrial powers and will seek to reinforce current regional arrangements and create new ones.[23]

U.S. global security policy is therefore seen as *potentially* threatening to China's future role in Asia. The existence of a single superpower seeking an alignment with the advanced industrialized democratic states as part of a global strategy designed to replace the East–West bipolar system with an American-led unipolar structure means that the international system is no longer balanced. One of the strongest statements of Beijing's anxiety is to be found in a front-page *Renmin Ribao* (People's Daily) editorial on September 26, 1990, a time when stresses within the USSR had clearly removed the Soviet Union from any capability or desire to actively contest the United States. The commentary said, "when the world pattern is undergoing the transition from the old to the new, new forms of hegemonism and power politics are also emerging, and are threatening world peace and security."[24] While such harsh statements are extremely rare, they do reflect a pattern of analysis found in Chinese journals focused on security issues where the collapse of the USSR and the disintegration of East European Marxist-Leninist states and the Warsaw Pact has left the United States and Western industrialized democracies dominant in the international system.

The Soviet-American balance had been at the heart of the calculations that formed the primary influence on China's foreign and defense policies in Asia. With that balance now removed, China faces a dilemma it has not confronted in twenty years.

China and Asia in the 1990s: The Question of Power

China enters the final decade of the twentieth century with a distinct sense of uncertainty. While there is no major imminent military threat to China's security, there is a high level of anxiety expressed whenever Chinese officials reflect on the remaining years of the decade. This apprehension, as Chinese officials have stated for the past several years, is based on their conviction that if China is unable to achieve its domestic modernization goals, and its economy and scientific and technological base remain weak, then Beijing faces the distinct possibility that China will enter the twenty-first century with its international influence significantly reduced.

Chinese analyses stress that the "nature" of power in the international system is changing from military to "aggregate" or "comprehensive" national power. Although military power remains important, economic strength and the scientific and technological underpinnings of an economy are becoming increasingly important. In December 1988, the Chinese foreign minister stated that China had to develop a "sense of urgency" if it was to overcome the burden of its weak economy and poor "cultural" base. China, Qian Qichen said, faced a long and difficult road if it was to catch up with the developed world.[25] Military power was not unimportant, however, for the economic, scientific, and technological strength of a country was also reflected in its military power—an interpretation considerably reinforced by the technological prowess of American arms and equipment in Desert Storm and the allied coalition's swift destruction of Iraq's defenses.

The collapse of East European Marxist-Leninist regimes, the reunification of Germany, the internal weaknesses of the Soviet Union, and the disintegration of the Warsaw Pact, led Foreign Minister Qian Qichen to observe in January 1991 that the world was in a transitional stage between the old order and the new. He was troubled that old conflicts intermingled with new ones as the international system went through a process of realignment: "In this transitional period, the international system is volatile and the world does not enjoy peace."[26] An essay in *Liberation Army Daily*, the official organ of the Chinese armed forces, made an equally concerned analysis of the future focused on the increased probability of regional conflicts and local wars.[27]

Thus Chinese analyses and interpretive statements by leading Chinese officials demonstrate that Beijing is deeply disturbed by an international environment where the potential for regional and local conflict could seriously undermine China's preeminent security goal of economic, scientific, and technological development. Beijing constantly asserts that China needs a stable international environment in which it can expand its commerce and maintain access to the technological and financial resources of the industrialized powers and international financial institutions. Major disturbances of the international system may seriously undermine the long-term development objectives upon which China's future role in global and regional politics depends.

This interpretation of the dilemmas faced by the PRC has led Chinese officials to state that their foreign policy is oriented primarily toward the resolution of conflicts globally and on China's periphery. In large measure, that orientation is reflected in actual Chinese behavior in the international system. But in some cases Chinese foreign policy demonstrates another facet of Beijing's concern: that the collapse of the USSR and the rise of U.S. influence has significantly reduced China's leverage among the great powers. At the extreme, Chinese strategists may believe that China could become marginalized by the emergence of Europe and Japan as new global power centers. Thus China has sought to resolve conflicts in which it is a participant while simultaneously asserting its status as a major regional power.

China and Asia in the 1990s:
Conflict Resolution and Great Power Status

The April 1990 publication of the U.S. Defense Department's strategic framework for a long-term draw-down of U.S. forces in Asia [28] received considerable attention from Chinese analysts. These analysts viewed U.S. military forces in the Asia-Pacific Region as primarily designed to balance and constrain the USSR. But within a broader strategic appraisal, the East–West conflict and the Soviet-American confrontation had suppressed regional conflicts and tended to restrain regional powers seeking to expand their influence, particularly Japan. Thus the end of the Soviet-American confrontation and the draw-down of forces now being undertaken by Washington creates for these analysts the danger of a regional power vacuum.[29]

The Problem of Japan

While China is confident that its northern borders will be secure and that Russia will not present a viable military threat for at least a decade, Japan's future role in Asia is of special concern. Chinese fears of Japan have been evident for many years, but with the United States committed to force reductions in the region, the potential for Japan to become a major military and political power in Asia is receiving even more attention from Chinese analysts. The United States' linkage to Japan is seen as especially important in restraining what Chinese analysts see as a "natural" evolution of Japan into a military power.

There does seem to be a consensus among Chinese analysts, not necessarily supported by those who focus specifically on military security issues,[30] that the security treaty between Japan and the United States will remain in force for at least the next decade and will continue to restrain any rapid expansion of Japanese military strength. Even without a Soviet military threat, Chinese analysts believe Japan needs the security treaty and U.S. forces to provide the confidence to develop its ties with Russia.

The security treaty also helps dispel regional apprehension about the potential expansion of Japanese military power, thereby assisting Japan in its economic and political objectives in the region. For the United States, the security treaty is seen as providing a way of constraining Japan and of retaining a military presence in the region that preserves American standing as a major military and political power.[31]

Nonetheless, and in spite of these constraints, Chinese analysts remain wary of Japan's future role in Asia. Japan's potential to become a military superpower is too great to be overlooked, especially given its history of militarism and aggression in Asia since the late nineteenth century.[32] China was undoubtedly very pleased with Secretary of Defense Richard Cheney's observation at the Japanese National Press Club in February 1990 that Japan's current military capability was now sufficient and that he saw no need for any further growth. Indeed, a major Japanese military buildup would be potentially destabilizing in the region.[33] For China's analysts, the security link between the United States and Japan is the most important factor restraining potential Japanese militarism and expansionism. Thus an American military presence based in Japan will be seen as a stabilizing factor for Asia as a whole.

Nonetheless, China remains concerned that Japan intends to increase its "political power" while remaining under the protection of the security treaty with the United States.[34] Prime Minister Kaifu's tour through Asia in May 1990, when he visited India, Bangladesh, Pakistan, Sri Lanka, Thailand, and Indonesia, received very critical commentary from Chinese analysts. The visits were characterized by one analyst as "showing Japan's intention to march into all of Asia and the world."[35] Japan's leverage is its financial assistance, which Chinese analysts say Tokyo now plans to increase and use as an instrument to gain political influence.

Kaifu's efforts to mediate in such conflicts as Afghanistan and Cambodia were viewed as a "profound change" whereby Japan's economic diplomacy was to be transformed into political power.[36]

The strategy implied by Chinese analysts was that Japan was attempting to fill the "power vacuum" created in Asia by the rapprochement in Soviet-American ties, the normalization of Sino-Soviet relations, and the changes in Eastern Europe that "rivet the gaze of all countries on Europe."[37] This power vacuum is seen as even more powerful since the collapse of the USSR. Japan's objective in offering substantial economic assistance and trade is to gain a position as "spokesman for Asia" in GATT meetings and with the seven leading Western industrialized powers. In this objective, an analyst noted, Japan will have very little success, since its position as the world's wealthiest country does not permit Tokyo to speak for the globe's poorest.[38]

Clearly, China fears that even a Japan constrained in its development of military power by the security treaty with the United States and by Tokyo's recognition of Asia's apprehension about Japanese militarism will seek to turn its economic might into a powerful source of political influence. This is precisely the kind of power China does not have and recognizes is of growing importance in international politics. What Beijing also notes is that with world attention focused on Europe, Japan could well use its economic and financial strengths to gain a very strong position in Asia. Since China stands to gain from Tokyo's economic largesse, and as long as Japan's military strength does not increase, China's criticism of Japan's efforts to transform economic power to political power will remain muted. Nonetheless, China's deep fear of an Asia dominated by Japan will persist, and U.S.'s security ties with Tokyo are viewed as critical in restraining the growth of Japan's military power. Beijing's criticism of the recent bill passed by the Diet permitting extremely constrained Japanese participation in United Nations peace-keeping operations is indicative of this primordial fear.[39]

There is, however, a logical discontinuity between Chinese analysts' apprehension about a unipolar system dominated by the United States and its coalition of Western industrialized states and their belief that America plays a crucial role in restraining Japan's nationalism and militarism. It is a dilemma that China cannot resolve to its own satisfaction.

The Korean Peninsula

The future of the Korean peninsula is crucial to China's ability to sustain a tranquil security environment in Asia. The interests of China, Japan, Russia, and the United States are all at stake in avoiding war on the peninsula and, perhaps more importantly, in ending the tension and mutual suspicion that have left the peninsula one of the most highly armed regions in the world. Changes in superpower relations since the mid-1980s reduced the probability of war to a minimum and increased the chance of a long-term settlement between North and South Korea. In addition, Sino-Soviet rapprochement, followed by the disintegration of the USSR, has eliminated Kim Il-song's capability to manipulate tension between Moscow and Beijing.

China has played an active role in bringing Pyongyang and Seoul together and in providing its good offices to encourage meetings between North Korean and U.S. officials, and between Japanese and North Korean officials.[40] China's own position on the peninsula was most clearly stated by the expansion of its trade and commercial relationship with the ROK, and the 1992 establishment of full diplomatic relations between Beijing and Seoul. The ROK's contribution to China's economic development goals is seen as far more important than the ideological ties binding Pyongyang and Beijing, even at a time when the Chinese leadership sees all socialist states as under siege from the corrosive Western strategy of "peaceful evolution."

North Korea's acceptance of dual entrance into the United Nations following Premier Li Peng's visit to Pyongyang and Gorbachev's Cheju Island summit with Roh Tae-wu was clear recognition by Pyongyang that its relations with both China and the USSR were endangered by its refusal to recognize the legitimacy of the Seoul government in the South. Similarly, North Korea's agreement to accept International Atomic Energy Agency (IAEA) inspection of its nuclear facilities came on the heels of the May 1991 Moscow summit, where Jiang Zemin and Gorbachev discussed Pyongyang's nuclear program.[41] There was clear Soviet pressure on North Korea either to fulfill its commitment to the Non-proliferation Treaty signed in 1985 or face the withdrawal of Soviet assistance for its civil nuclear programs.[42] In a Seoul interview on November 14, 1991, Chinese foreign minister Qian Qichen, who had attended the Asia-Pacific Economic Cooperation Conference hosted by South Korea, was quite specific in his statement that "there should be no nuclear weapons on the Korean peninsula."[43] While Qian Qichen also insisted that "international pressure [on North Korea] was undesirable," he was reflecting the opinion that open international pressure would delay rather than hasten Pyongyang's acceptance of inspection.

Inspection by a full-scale IAEA team in late May 1992, while not eliminating suspicion that Pyongyang has a nuclear weapons program, was the first step in removing one of the principal stumbling blocks to confidence building on the peninsula, and confidence is essential for the lengthy process of reunification to proceed. It was also a step toward Japanese diplomatic recognition of North Korea, for Tokyo has insisted that without assurance that Pyongyang does not have a nuclear weapons program, neither recognition nor large-scale trade and economic assistance can occur.

For Beijing, the critical objective is to avoid contributing to a situation on the peninsula where chaos could lead to war. Whereas a divided peninsula during the Cold War was in gridlock and armed conflict was unlikely, the absence of the restraints of the Cold War combined with a difficult political transition in North Korea creates the potential for turmoil. Beijing appears to prefer that the Koreans resolve the process of reunification themselves, while direct outside pressures are kept to a minimum. Under these conditions, China will continue to provide its good offices for continued contact among North Korea, the United States, and Japan, while seeking to limit direct public pressure on Pyongyang. With Beijing playing such a role, both sides of the DMZ may well see China as a peacemaker. The eventual reunification of the peninsula will place Beijing in appropriate position to face the new Korea. China's diplomatic recognition of South Korea in August 1992 essentially sealed China's commitment to a peacefully unified Korea, while simultaneously removing the last of Taiwan's diplomatic ties to any Asian state. As part of the normalization agreement, Seoul agreed to the recognition of only one China, and that Taiwan is part of China.[44]

Southeast Asia

In Southeast Asia, China seeks more complex goals requiring more complicated strategy. While China does seek to forge close working relationships with the six states that form ASEAN (Thailand, Malaysia, Singapore, Indonesia, the Philippines, and Brunei), Beijing also seeks to establish itself as the preeminent power in the region. The means China is using are the Cambodian impasse and territorial disputes in the South China Sea. In both cases, China is balancing its public image of pursuing a central policy of conflict resolution with insistence that its preferred solutions to both conflicts are unalterable.

Premier Li Peng visited Indonesia, Thailand, and Singapore in August 1990, centering his discussions on Cambodia. The trip was crowned by the reestablishment of diplomatic relations with Indonesia in August after a twenty-three-year suspension, and with Singapore in October.

The following December, Li Peng made yet another diplomatic foray into the region, visiting Malaysia, the Philippines, Laos, and Sri Lanka. While in Manila, Li Peng attempted to respond to the deeply felt regional apprehensions about China's future security policies when he stated that China "will not pose any threat to any country in this region in the remaining years of this century nor will it be a threat to any country in this region in the next century."[45]

These words, although important at a symbolic level, and reflecting Beijing's establishment of full diplomatic ties with all of ASEAN and the normalization of ties with Vietnam, are less consequential than China's role in the two most destabilizing conflicts in Southeast Asia. Beijing's part in finding a solution to the Cambodian dilemma and in resolving the territorial and sea boundary disputes over the Paracel and Spratly island groups is viewed as a greater measure of China's intentions. The ASEAN states see resolution of both conflicts as critical in forming the future security environment of the region.

Cambodia

Rapprochement between Moscow and Beijing released the Cambodian tragedy from its ten-year entrapment in the Sino-Soviet dispute. This release did not, however, lead to a resolution to the vicious internecine warfare that plagues this unfortunate country. Soviet inducements led to the withdrawal of Vietnamese forces from Cambodia in September 1989,[46] thereby allowing a peace process to begin. The crux of the problem remains the abiding enmity among the four factions seeking to rule Cambodia: the Phnom Penh government—initially supported by the Soviet Union and Vietnam; the Khmer Rouge—militarily the most powerful of the opposition forces, supported by China since 1975; and the two factions led by Prince Sihanouk and Son Sann, supported by the ASEAN states and the United States.

The peace plan brokered by the five permanent members of the UN Security Council at the Paris accord of October 23, 1991, shows no sign of resolving the conflict. The Khmer Rouge has thus far refused to permit its forces to enter UNTAC (United Nations Transitional Authority in Cambodia) supervised cantonments where they would be demobilized and disarmed. The other three factions have agreed to begin this process, where 70 percent of each of the forces would be disarmed and demobilized, while the other 30 percent would remain in the cantonments under UNTAC peace-keeping forces' supervision. The Khmer Rouge insists that Vietnamese forces remain in Cambodia, but will not join joint UNTAC-led teams to verify the withdrawal. Vietnam states that all its forces were withdrawn by the end of September 1989. The result is a bloody impasse. The civil war continues and Cambodia remains a killing field.[47]

While Beijing and Hanoi are now on speaking terms, China's goal of eliminating Vietnam as a contender for influence in Southeast Asia has succeeded. Vietnam was essentially coerced into working with China as a result of the Sino-Soviet rapprochement, the collapse of Marxist-Leninist regimes in Eastern Europe, and Gorbachev's retreat from entangling and expensive commitments to the Third World, including communist Third World states.

Curtailment of Soviet aid to Vietnam came at a time when Vietnam's economy was shattered and its Communist party divided. The extent of Hanoi's reliance on Soviet assistance was revealed by Vietnamese officials in December 1990 when they said that 90 percent of Vietnam's fuel, 90 percent of its steel, and 80 percent of its cotton and fertilizer came from the USSR. When agreements were signed in January 1991, credit was cut sharply and future trade was to be based on international market prices and paid for in convertible currencies.[48]

For Vietnam, the only viable solution to domestic problems is association with the West and ASEAN. It is in no condition to challenge China, and Hanoi's armed forces cannot be sustained without external assistance. For China, including the Khmer Rouge in the political settlement achieved the goal it sought in that process. Thus Beijing gains little by continuing to supply the Khmer Rouge with arms. The arms they supplied through Thailand for the past decade and more are no doubt cached and capable of sustaining Khmer Rouge forces for some time in limited guerrilla operations. For the moment, the Khmer Rouge's refusal to honor its commitments to the UN treaty process seems based more on its perception that the process is biased against its future political role in Cambodia than any support it is receiving from China.[49] Indeed, continued Chinese support for the Khmer Rouge would undermine China's delicate relations with ASEAN.

The South China Sea

Competing territorial claims in the South China Sea link Vietnam and other Southeast Asian states in a common dispute with China.[50] In the summer of 1990, however, Beijing tentatively presented a potential solution to the economic issues involved in the dispute. While visiting Singapore, Premier Li Peng proposed joint development of the economic resources under the South China Sea and a temporary shelving of sovereignty claims. There was also a suggestion that all claimants should remove their military forces.[51]

The crux of the problem is not so much competing territorial and sea boundary claims and the economic resources they cover, but growing Chinese military capability. These capabilities are now regularly demonstrated by Chinese naval exercises and the development of a Marine Brigade deployed with the South Sea Fleet of the Chinese navy.[52] These demonstrations of naval power, however, are perhaps better viewed as a form of coercive diplomacy than a display of actual naval capabilities.

The Chinese navy lacks the level of force projection capability required to conduct a full-scale naval conflict in the Spratlys, which are 600 miles south of Hainan Island. There may be a dozen older frigates assigned to the South Sea Fleet, but at that range they would have to operate without air cover. The 6,000-man Marine Brigade attached to the South Sea Fleet, although trained in amphibious warfare, could not conduct a successful campaign if faced with significant air power. Even the H-6 bomber (Tu-16 derived) would be operating at the outer edge of its combat range if launched from Hainan, and China is not known to have an in-air refueling capability. The reported development of a base in the Paracels would assist in providing air cover, but would shorten the flying distance by only about 100 miles.[53]

The acquisition of Su-27 fighters from the Soviet Union would grant Beijing the capability to conduct air operations over the Spratlys, as would an in-air refueling capability. Both of these developments were rumored for a year or more prior to their confirmation in the later summer of 1992.[54] Nonetheless, it would be perhaps ten years before either the Su-27 or in-air refueling capabilities became operational for the Chinese air forces. Similarly, the rumors of Chinese interest in the 67,000-ton aircraft carrier *Varyag* being built for the former Soviet Union in Ukraine, but now uncompleted because of a lack of funds, also heightened Southeast Asia's apprehension of an imminent Chinese increase in naval power. Purchase of this vessel has been denied by both China and the Ukraine,[55] but the fear of enhanced Chinese force projection capability remains.

With the ASEAN states engaged in the acquisition of high-technology advanced weapon systems and equipment for some years[56] and conducting more joint and combined military exercises, China's proposal of joint development of the economic resources in the South China Sea could reflect sound military judgment in addition to fitting with its preferred foreign policy objectives. ASEAN military programs were in part stimulated by the belief that the United States will soon withdraw major components of its forces from the region. The current Department of Defense plan for a long-term force reduction strategy, combined with the departure of all U.S. forces from bases in the Philippines, will reinforce that belief. ASEAN states granted American forces limited access to their military facilities in an attempt to ensure continued U.S. military presence in the region as U.S. departure from the Philippines became imminent.

Indonesia has taken the initiative in establishing a pattern of conflict resolution for the South China Sea territorial disputes. In doing so, Jakarta is consciously building on its reputation as a mediator for the region that it developed in its negotiations with Hanoi over Cambodia. Indonesia sees the South China Sea as a potential flash point, and wants to bring China, Vietnam, and the six ASEAN states into a discussion of the problem. The Indonesian Foreign Ministry hosted an annual series of informal ASEAN seminars beginning in January 1990 to discuss the South China Sea disputes.

China nonetheless remains adamant in its claim to sovereignty over the entire Paracel and Spratly island groups, as does Vietnam. Competing claims by Malaysia and the Philippines cannot be resolved as long as China and Vietnam are willing to use force. Li Peng's tentative observation in Singapore was undermined in April 1992 when China promulgated its "Law on Territorial Waters," which reasserted its claims to the disputed island groups in the South China Sea and the Diaoyutai (Senkaku) Islands claimed by Japan. Similarly, Beijing's signing of an oil exploration agreement with an American company in an area claimed by Vietnam drew a diplomatic protest from Hanoi.[57] A representative of the company stated to the *New York Times* that the company knew the leased area was in contested waters, but that he had been "assured by top Chinese officials that they will protect me with their full naval might."[58] Beijing's current attitude, therefore, is far from conciliatory and appears to be a blatant reassertion of Chinese nationalism.

The Indonesian initiative continues, however, and could be the beginning of a resolution to the economic issues involved in the South China Sea confrontation. Shelving the question of sovereignty would be a major step forward in the process of conflict avoidance, and China attended the third informal meeting sponsored by Indonesia in Yogyakarta in the summer of 1992. So long as China both maintains that the issue of sovereignty cannot be raised and continues to improve its military capabilities in the region, however, the South China Sea will remain a flashpoint.

Regional conflict resolution, however, remains a goal of ASEAN, and the invitation offered China and the USSR to join the post-ministerial conference held after the ASEAN foreign ministers' Kuala Lumpur meeting in July 1991 demonstrated this intent. China, but evidently not Russia, has been invited to send observers to the ASEAN foreign ministers' meeting again this July.[59] Currently, five non-ASEAN member nations sit at the post-ministerial meetings: the United States, Japan, Canada, Australia, New Zealand, and the European Community. South Korea has joined these six as a full-dialogue member. Thus, China's adamant insistence on its sovereignty may well have paid off in ASEAN's response, which recognizes China's central importance to the region.

South Asia

South Asia became deeply immersed in the triangular dynamics that emerged with the Sino-Soviet dispute. India developed close ties with the USSR following the Sino-Indian border war of 1962, and Moscow became the principal supplier in the construction of India's modern defense industrial complex. China, on the other hand, became Pakistan's strategic partner and principal weapons supplier after the Indo-Pakistan war of 1965. In 1971, U.S. opposition to India's role in Pakistan's civil war and its invasion of East Pakistan, followed by the Sino-American rapprochement of 1972, led Delhi to view Washington as aligned with Beijing and Islamabad. A deadly nuclear component was added when, in response to India's 1974 detonation of a nuclear device, Pakistan began its own nuclear weapons program with alleged Chinese assistance. South Asia entered a muted nuclear arms race.[60] Matters were made worse from India's point of view when in 1981 the United States began to supply high-technology weaponry to Pakistan in response to the Soviet invasion of Afghanistan—weaponry that China could not provide.

Soviet alignment with India was seen by Beijing as part of a Russian strategy to encircle China. As the alignment matured, India's potential nuclear capability and ballistic missile program, combined with its large and relatively modern conventional air, ground, and naval forces, were seen to counterbalance China's own capabilities. Conversely, Pakistan and the United States were viewed by Delhi as an alliance against India. This strategic paradigm began to unravel with the onset of Sino-Soviet rapprochement and superpower détente.

Gorbachev traveled to India in 1986 to assure Prime Minister Rajiv Gandhi that the gestures toward China expressed in his July speech in Vladivostok did not mean that the USSR's relationship with India was being sacrificed on the altar of Sino-Soviet rapprochement. In the spring of 1987, a tense situation along the Sino-Indian border alerted both Delhi and Beijing once again to the dangers involved in their mutual confrontation. China claims that after the Sino-Indian border war of 1962, India's forces gradually occupied 90,000 square kilometers (34,749 square miles) south of the McMahon Line from which the Chinese had voluntarily withdrawn in November 1962.[61] The 1987 riots in Lhasa no doubt heightened China's sensitivity to its border with India. Beijing and Delhi agreed that a border settlement was the key to normalizing their ties, and boundary negotiations begun in 1981 were reopened. This was the beginning of a process of Sino-Indian détente that appears to have kept pace with the growing warmth in Sino-Soviet ties.

Gorbachev visited India once again in November 1988, and in December Rajiv Gandhi flew to China for the first visit of an Indian prime minister in thirty-four years. His confidence in opening top-level negotiations was no doubt bolstered by his earlier meeting with Gorbachev. Although eight rounds of border talks had been held since the early 1980s, Gandhi and Deng Xiaoping admitted that no substantive progress had been made. An agreement was reached that joint working groups at the deputy foreign minister level would be established. Their task was to make proposals on how to resolve the border question.[62] It was reported that the joint working groups would bring together high military officers and land surveyors[63] in a manner similar to the working groups later adopted by the Soviet Union and China. Meetings were to alternate between Beijing and Delhi. At the second meeting, held in Delhi in July 1990, it was agreed that senior military officers from China and India would meet at the border or the "actual control line" to ensure that any infractions did not lead to an exchange of fire.[64]

Warming Sino-Indian ties were accompanied by a slow but definite rapprochement between Washington and Delhi. As early as 1981, the Reagan administration had sought to improve American ties with India when it invited Prime Minister Indira Gandhi to Washington to meet with the president. Improvement in relations was not rapid, but in 1985 the United States agreed to permit the sale of dual-use technology to India. The United States, however, was still concerned that close ties between Moscow and Delhi would result in American technology falling into Russian hands. By 1990, however, with dramatically improved Soviet-American relations, the United States agreed to clear both the General Electric 404 jet engine and fly-by-wire technology for use in India's high-technology Light Combat Aircraft (LCA) project.[65]

The United States, China, and the USSR were seeking to balance their relations with South Asia, and in the 1990 Kashmir crisis, the United States and the USSR worked together to help India and Pakistan avoid war.[66] In February, the Indian foreign minister traveled to China where he was warmly received by Li Peng. China was consistent throughout the crisis, stating that the Kashmir question was "a problem left over from history," urging both sides to solve the crisis peacefully.[67] Neither Pakistan nor India could have misunderstood the use of that particular phrase. China intended to distance itself from the dispute, and neither Pakistan nor India should assume that past ties required Chinese intervention.

Symbolic of the new and warmer relationship was the visit of a delegation from the Indian National Defense College to China in June 1990. It was the first such visit since the Sino-Indian border war, and was welcomed by General Xu Xin, the most senior of the four deputy chiefs of the Chinese People's Liberation Army General Staff Department.[68] Receiving such a delegation in the midst of the Kashmir crisis was another sign of China's warming relationship with India and provided yet another signal to Pakistan that Islamabad could not have mistaken.

Pakistan is the odd man out in the restructuring of the South Asian strategic landscape. In the fall of 1990, President Bush was unable to certify to Congress that Pakistan did not posses nuclear weapons, which resulted in suspension of Islamabad's aid package. With the USSR out of Afghanistan, U.S. strategic interest in Pakistan is significantly diminished. The overthrow of Benazir Bhutto with what may have been military collusion raised concerns in the United States that Pakistan's experiment in democracy was at an end, yet another blow to any future high levels of economic or military assistance.

With China now more eager to improve its ties with India, and the United States no longer a reliable source of military and economic assistance, Pakistan may well feel adrift. But its ratification of a treaty with India in which Islamabad and Delhi pledge not to attack each others' nuclear facilities will not ease American concerns over Pakistan's nuclear weapons program.[69] India receives no military or economic assistance from the United States, therefore it is not subject to congressional legislation that mandates the termination of assistance to any non-nuclear state receiving American aid. Pakistan's decision to ratify the treaty will serve only to further aggravate the United States at a time when Islamabad's future is none too promising. In addition, the decision will not ease China's concerns over the development of the Indian nuclear weapons program.

Improving relations with India fits China's goal of improved relations around its borders but does not relieve Beijing's apprehension over Delhi's increasing military capabilities and its use of military power to act as South Asia's hegemon. Currently, Chinese analysts applaud the efforts made by Delhi for better relations with Sri Lanka, Nepal, Pakistan, and Bangladesh, while at the same time indicating some reservations that India will be successful in its new conciliatory policies toward the region.[70]

Sino-Indian relations are now at their most congenial in over thirty years. Much of the cordiality can initially be attributed to the improved Sino-Soviet relationship and the possibility that with its northern border secure, China may feel more confident in its military position facing India. A more confident defense posture will have influenced Beijing to become more accommodating toward its powerful neighbor to the south. Such confidence is reinforced by the collapse of the Soviet Union. Nonetheless, it is clear that Russia as the successor to the Soviet Union wants to reestablish its former status as a principal supplier of arms to India.[71] Moscow has also agreed to assist Delhi in further development of rocket boosters for its space program. This at a time when India has recently successfully tested the *Prithvi* mobile surface-to-surface missile (SSM) with a range of 250 kilometers and a 250-kilogram warhead. India now plans to proceed with a test of its intermediate-range ballistic missile (IRBM), *Agni*, which has an estimated range of 1,500 km and was first successfully launched in 1989. These developments, when combined with India's recognized nuclear weapons program, suggest that while relations between India and China continue to warm, the long-term future may not be so cordial. For the moment, while China, Russia, Pakistan, and the United States have agreed to discuss a South Asia nuclear-free zone, India has rejected the proposal. Thus while relations are now more cordial than they have been in thirty years, Beijing and Delhi still face an uncertain future.

The Problem of Taiwan

The end of the Cold War and the collapse of the USSR have created a new dilemma for Beijing's aspiration to reunify China. The dissolution of all European Marxist-Leninist regimes came at a time when Taiwan was moving away from its Kuomintang (Nationalist) dominated authoritarian political system and edging toward democracy. Taiwan's move toward democracy stands in sharp contrast to Beijing's communism, and the current international environment may grant Taipei greater freedom of action than it has had since 1979. What is more, Taiwan has developed a strategy of extensive contact with the mainland that provides China both technology and financial resources that are a major contributor to the remarkable economic expansion of south China.

Beijing has paid close attention to the continually increasing trade and investment flowing from Taiwan and the general relaxation of the Taipei government toward ties with the mainland. The policies pursued by Li Teng-hui, chairman of the Kuomintang (KMT) and head of the government since Chiang Ching-kuo's death in 1988, have encouraged greater contact, trade, and commerce between the island and the mainland—a policy initiated by Chiang Ching-kuo in 1986.[72] The investment and business talent flowing into China from Taiwan have already made a major contribution to Beijing's economic development goals.

On the other hand, the extensive progress in MBFR and CBM negotiations between Beijing and Moscow must be seen as a mixed benefit by Taiwan. Free from a major military threat to its northern border, China can afford to place more and better equipped forces opposite Taiwan. In fact, Taiwan claims that just this has occurred.[73] Taipei will also feel more confident that the United States can be more supportive of Taiwan now that the post–Cold War world no longer requires Washington to be strategically tied to Beijing. President Bush's agreement to sell 150 F-16s to Taiwan has bolstered this confidence, especially when the American reaction to the Tiananmen tragedy continues in U.S. policy's emphasis on human rights abuses in China.

As China and Taiwan enter the 1990s, there is a distinct sense of frustration emerging from Beijing that could well reflect its appreciation of the mood of confidence that permeates Taipei. The "flexible diplomacy" initiated by Li Teng-hui in 1988 provides Taiwan with the de facto independence Taipei says it is not seeking. Applauded in the West for its progress toward democracy, Taiwan stands in distinct contrast to the neo-Stalinism emanating from Beijing. Indeed, Taiwan's economic accomplishments have led to expanding diplomatic ties and the upgrading of commercial relations with both the industrialized and develop-ing world.[74] Direct trade links are also being established with Russia, Vietnam, and Albania.[75]

Seen in this context, Yang Shangkun's interview with the editor of the Taipei-based newspaper *Chung Kuo Shih Bao* during the September 1990 Asian Games in Beijing is of great interest.[76] As a confidant of Deng Xiaoping and president of China, Yang's words carry great weight. An interview at this level conducted in the Great Hall of the People was designed to have policy implications. Yang said that reunification of Taiwan with the mainland should occur quickly. He noted that Taipei has taken a number of actions that contribute to eventual reunification, including its position that "fighting communism, launching a coun-terattack on the mainland, or invading the mainland" is no longer a component of Taipei's policy toward the People's Republic.[77]

While Yang viewed Taipei's policy change as a definite contribution to reuni-fication, he also noted that the older generation of both the KMT and the Chinese Communist Party (CCP) are dying, and the younger members do not fully under-stand the historical issues between the two parties. Yang made the point that it has been forty years since China was divided, and Taiwan's position has not yet been "consolidated," and there is now the danger that "foreign countries" may take Taiwan. This danger required China to maintain the right to use force. Yang stated that although military force would be used to prevent Taiwan's "separa-tion" by a foreign country, it "is absolutely not directed against our countrymen in Taiwan," for this would be fratricide.[78]

Yang Shangkun insisted that the correct approach to reunification required rep-resentatives of the KMT and the CCP to meet as equals and without precondi-tions. This approach stressing party-to-party negotiations directly counters Taipei's position that the two *governments* should follow the model that led to Ger-man reunification by recognizing each other and then negotiating reunification.[79]

This statement of Chinese policy is subject to considerable speculative inter-pretation. First, stressing the need to realize reunification quickly and linking it to the use of force to prevent "foreign countries" from permanently dividing China and Taiwan can be seen as coercive diplomacy. China may be warning Taiwan that time is running out and that it should not rely upon an American security umbrella to preserve it against the legitimate claims of Beijing. It is even possible that Beijing, observing Gorbachev's difficulties in controlling centrifugal forces within the Soviet Union in 1990, may have felt that it was necessary to underline its willingness to use military power to preserve the unity of China. Finally, by appealing to past KMT–CCP cooperation, China was presenting a more forthcoming position than it has in the past. But Beijing was also warning the KMT leadership that the democratic procedures it has legitimized could result in the loss of KMT control. The principal opposition to the KMT, the Democratic Progressive Party (DPP), is currently too fractured to be an effective opposition, but this could change. The DPP's central message is that Taiwan should be an independent state. If the DPP should gain power in the future, the consequence for Taiwan could be disastrous, for a declaration of independence would trigger a military response from the mainland.[80]

Perhaps in reaction to this coercive diplomacy, Taipei established the Foundation for Exchanges Across the Taiwan Strait (FEATS) in late 1990. Although a private, nonpolitical organization, FEATS is viewed by the government as a bridge linking Taiwan and the mainland and is supervised by a newly established set of official structures headed by the National Unification Committee chaired by President Li Teng-hui.[81] Beijing responded favorably to FEATS, seeing it as a method of upgrading contacts between Taiwan and the mainland.[82] Taiwan, however, may well view the new structure primarily as a way of coordinating business and other contacts with China while holding steadfast to its political position.

There seems to be no doubt that Yang Shangkun's interview expressed Beijing's frustration at the lack of progress toward reunification as the old generation of leaders on Taiwan and the mainland pass from the scene. The new security environment in Asia, in which the United States is both free from a strategy of containing the USSR and at the same time emerging as the globe's preeminent military and political power, does not in the short term bode well for Beijing's goal of reunifying China. Neither Beijing nor Washington are faced with a major Soviet military threat. But for Beijing, as Yang's reference to unnamed "foreign countries" suggests, this implies that the strategic logic that brought China and the United States together in the 1970s had completely faded by the 1990s. This new global strategic pattern may, in Beijing's view, free the United States from serious consideration of China's response to a closer relationship with Taipei—as the F-16 sale may well confirm in the leadership compound of Zhongnanhai.

Retrospect and Prospect

A northern border secure from any major military threat has long been a primary security objective of Beijing. This goal was achieved, however, within a rapidly changing and unanticipated global security environment. Whereas Chinese analysts in the 1980s envisioned a security environment composed of a multipolar balance in which China would have greater influence and could free itself from dependence on either of the superpowers, what emerged even before the disintegration of the USSR was a unipolar system with no balance. China is clearly apprehensive about a Western strategy of "peaceful evolution" and concerned about an American-led coalition of Western industrialized states unfettered by a counterweight. Not the least of China's concerns is the leverage it has lost as a consequence of Soviet and now Russo-American rapprochement.

Cast adrift by improved relations between Moscow and Washington and the Western response to Tiananmen Square, China has sought to reestablish itself as a major player in the international system. Beijing has sought to take advantage of conflicts once entangled in the strategic alignments spawned by East–West rivalry by pursuing policies that are a mix of conflict resolution and great-power diplomacy. Put simply, Beijing wants conflicts resolved, but on its own terms. In the same manner that China was successful in placing "obstacles" the Soviet Union had to remove before Moscow could "normalize" its relations with Beijing, so China is making its demands clear in each case.

Only with Japan and Taiwan does China face serious dilemmas. Beijing believes that restraining Japan's potential military power requires Tokyo's continuing confidence in its security ties with Washington. Similarly, Taiwan remains the single remaining "obstacle" between the United States and China. Dissipation of the East–West conflict may, in Chinese eyes, permit the United States to become more protective of Taiwan now that the need for a strategic link with Beijing has evaporated.

Stability in Asia, especially in constraining what China sees as the dangerous potential for unrestrained growth in Japanese military power, requires a continued American military presence, including a security treaty with Japan. Similarly, American cooperation is essential for a peaceful reunification of Korea, which China has to support not only to sustain stability in Northeast Asia but also to demonstrate its intentions toward reunification with Taiwan.

China and the United States are inextricably linked by Beijing's quest for the stable and peaceful international environment required to achieve its domestic economic development goals. This must be frustrating for those in Beijing who genuinely fear the strategy of "peaceful evolution" Washington is charged with pursuing.

Notes

1. Xing Shugang, Lin Yunhua, and Liu Yingna, "Soviet-American Balance of Power and Its Impact on the World Situation in the 1980s," *Guoji Wenti Yanjiu*, no. 1 (January 1983), in Foreign Broadcast Information Service, Daily Report: China (henceforth *FBIS-CHI*), no. 028 (21 July 1983), pp. A1, 12.

2. Allen S. Whiting, *The Chinese Calculus of Deterrence* (Ann Arbor: University of Michigan Press, 1975), pp. 204–208.

3. See John W. Garver's intriguing analysis in *China's Decision for Rapprochement with the United States* (Boulder, CO: Westview Press, 1982), especially pp. 153–154.

4. Robert G. Sutter, "Realities of International Power and China's 'Independence' in Foreign Affairs," *Journal of Northeast Asian Studies*, vol. 3, no. 4 (Winter 1984), pp. 14–19.

5. Beijing, Xinhua, 3 April 1987, in *FBIS-CHI*, no. 064 (26 April 1987), p. K5.

6. Wang Haiyun and Zhou Yi, "New Trends in the Soviet Army's Theoretical Study of Combat," *Jiefangjun Bao* (Liberation Army Daily), 23 March 1990, in *FBIS-CHI*, no. 075 (18 April 1990), p. 9; and Zhou Aiqun, "The Soviet Union Adjusts Its Military Strategy," *Shijie Zhishi*, no. 2 (16 January 1990), in Foreign Broadcast Information Service, JPRS Report: China (henceforth *JPRS-CAR*), no. 037 (14 May 1990), p. 12.

7. Ulanbaatar International Service, 6 October 1989; in Foreign Broadcast Information Service, Daily Report: East Asia (henceforth *FBIS-EAS*), no. 194 (10 October 1989), p. 12.

8. Moscow International Service (in Mandarin), 2 January 1991, in Foreign Broadcast Information Service, Daily Report: Soviet Union (hereafter *FBIS-SOV*), no. 015 (23 January 1991), p. 6.

9. Beijing, Xinhua, 27 November 1989, in *FBIS-CHI*, no. 227 (28 November 1989), p. 7.

10. Beijing, Xinhua, 24 April 1990, in *FBIS-CHI*, no. 080 (25 April 1990), p. 14.

11. Beijing, Xinhua, 25 June 1990, reporting Foreign Minister Qian Qichen's report to the National People's Congress on Premier Li Peng's April visit to Moscow, in *FBIS-CHI*, no. 124 (27 June 1990), p. 4.

12. Beijing, Xinhua, 1 June 1990, and Beijing, Zhongguo Xinwen She, 1 June 1990, in *FBIS-CHI*, no. 107 (4 June 1990), p. 9.

13. *Renmin Ribao*, 7 June 1990, in *FBIS-CHI*, no. 111 (8 June 1990), p. 3.

14. Moscow International Service, 9 June 1990; in *FBIS-CHI*, no. 114 (13 June 1990), p. 5.

15. See, for example, Tai Ming Cheung, "China Poised to Buy Soviet Fighters," *Far Eastern Economic Review*, vol. 149, no. 36 (6 September 1990), pp. 20–21; and Daniel Southerland, "China Seeks Technology from Soviet Military," *Washington Post*, 17 July 1990, p. 12.

16. "Current Events and Commentaries" program, Moscow (in Mandarin), 3 October 1990, in *FBIS-SOV*, no. 194 (5 October 1990), p. 14.

17. Ibid.

18. Moscow International Service (in Mandarin), 4 November 1990, in *FBIS-SOV*, no. 214 (5 November 1990), p. 11.

19. Moscow International Service (in Mandarin), 9 December 1990, in *FBIS-SOV*, no. 239 (12 December 1990), p. 61.

20. Chai Chengwen, "The Disintegration of the Soviet Union and Its Implications," *International Strategic Studies* (Beijing), March 1992, pp. 6–7.

21. Sa Benwang, "U.S. Global Strategy and Its Impact on the Global Pattern," *Shijie Zhishi*, no. 2 (14 January 1991), in *FBIS-CHI*, no. 015 (23 January 1991), p. 12.

22. Lin Huisheng, "New Trends of U.S.-Japanese-European Tripartite Coordination," *Shijie Zhishi*, no. 14 (16 July 1990), in *FBIS-CHI*, no. 155 (10 August 1990), p. 2.

23. Wan Guang, "What 'New World Order' Does the West Want to Establish?" *Liaowang Overseas* (Hong Kong), no. 37 (10 September 1990), in *FBIS-CHI*, no. 188 (27 September 1990), pp. 9–11.

24. Editorial, *Renmin Ribao Overseas Edition*, 26 September 1990; in *FBIS-CHI*, no. 187 (26 September 1990), p. 1.

25. N.A., "An Interview with Qian Qichen on New Changes in the International Situation," *Shijie Zhishi*, no. 2 (16 January 1989), *FBIS-CHI*, no. 020 (1 February 1989), p. 2.

26. Foreign Minister Qian Qichen in an interview with an unidentified reporter, *Beijing Review*, no. 1 (7–13 January 1991), p. 9.

27. Li Qinggong, "Several Characteristics of War Formation's Evolution—Development Trends of World Military Situation," (Part Three), *Jiefangjun Bao*, 29 May 1992, in *FBIS-CHI*, no. 118 (18 June 1992), p. 26.

28. *A Strategic Framework for the Pacific Rim: Looking toward the 21st Century*, April 1990, Office of the Assistant Secretary of Defense for International Security Affairs (East Asia and Pacific Region).

29. See, for example, Xia Liping, "A Preliminary Analysis of the U.S. East Asia Strategy Initiative," *Guozhi Zhanwang*, no. 8 (23 April 1990), in *JPRS-CAR*, no. 056 (27 July 1990), p. 33

30. Chen Jiehua, "Japanese Defense Perspective," *Guoji Zhanwang*, no. 2 (23 January 1990), presents an analysis that is typical of the more moderate, but yet extremely cautious, Chinese interpretations of Japanese military power and growing technologically advanced defense industrial base, in *JPRS-CAR*, no. 037 (14 May 1990), pp. 11–14.

31. Feng Zhaokui, "Where Is the U.S.-Japanese Security Treaty Going?" *Shijie Zhishi*, no. 20 (16 October 1990), in *JPRS-CAR*, no. 089 (30 November 1990), pp. 1–2; and Guo Xiangang, "Long Contemplated Readjustment—U.S. Posture in Asia-Pacific Region," *Shijie Zhishi*, no. 4 (16 February 1992), in *FBIS-CHI*, no. 057 (24 March 1992), pp. 3–5.

32. Huang Suan, "U.S.-Japanese Contention for Economic Power," *Guoji Wenti Yanjiu*, no. 3 (July 1990), in *JPRS-CAR*, no. 084 (15 November 1990), pp. 4–6.

33. Beijing, Xinhua, 24 February 1990, in *FBIS-CHI*, no. 039 (27 February 1990), p. 3.

34. Zhu Ronggen, "Japan's New Intention in Pursuing 'Big Power Diplomacy,' " *Liaowang Overseas*, no. 21 (21 May 1990), in *FBIS-CHI*, no. 101 (24 May 1990), pp. 7–8.

35. Ibid., p. 7.

36. Ibid., p. 8.

37. Ibid., p. 7.

38. Ibid., p. 10.

39. Zhang Dalin, "Japan's Bill on Cooperation in UN Peacekeeping Operations," *Guoji Wenti Yanjiu*, 13 April 1992, in *FBIS-CHI*, no. 100 (22 May 1992), pp. 4–10.

40. Zhou Bizhong, "A New Starting Point of Good Neighborliness and Friendship between Korea and Japan," *Renmin Ribao*, 2 February 1991, in *FBIS-CHI*, no. 024 (5 February 1991), pp. 9–10.

41. *Chosen Ilbo* (Seoul), 19 May 1991, reports the deputy director of the Far East Institute of the Soviet Academy of Sciences stating that inspection of Pyongyang's nuclear facilities was discussed at the summit, in *FBIS-EAS*, no. 098 (21 May 1991), p. 28.

42. See, for example, Soviet Foreign Ministry spokesman Yuriy Gremitskikh in Tass (Moscow), 18 April 1991, in *FBIS-SOV*, no. 085 (2 May 1991), p. 6.

43. Interview with Foreign Minister Qian Qichen on Seoul KBS-1 Television Network, reported in *FBIS-EAS*, no. 220 (14 November 1991), p. 7.

44. Yi Tong-min, "Seoul-Beijing Ties to Change Order in Northeast Asia," *Yonhap* (Seoul), August 24, 1992, in *FBIS-EAS*, no. 164 (August 24, 1992), p. 24.

45. Tokyo, Kyodo, 15 December 1990, in *FBIS-CHI*, no. 242 (17 December 1990), p. 11.

46. For a succinct summary of Soviet pressures and inducements on Hanoi to remove its forces from Cambodia, see Carolyn McGiffert Ekedahl and Melvin A. Goodman, "Gorbachev's 'New Directions' in Asia," *Journal of Northeast Asian Studies*, vol. 8, no. 3 (Fall 1989), pp. 15–16.

47. Murray Hiebert, "Draining the Swamp—Peace Process Grinds Slowly Forward," *Far Eastern Economic Review*, vol. 155, no. 23 (11 June 1992), p. 24.

48. Murray Hiebert, "Hard Times," *Far Eastern Economic Review*, vol. 150, no. 50 (13 December 1990), pp. 61–62; and Murray Hiebert, "Deeper in the Red," *Far Eastern Economic Review*, vol. 151, no. 8 (21 February 1991), p. 46.

49. This interpretation stems from my reading of the Khmer Rouge statement on the current impasse made in its radio broadcast on 4 June 1992: "You Can Judge Who Respects the Paris Accord and Who Does Not," *Voice of the Great Union Front of Cambodia*, in *FBIS-EAS*, no. 109 (5 June 1992), pp. 22–23.

50. For a useful overview of the issues involved, see Marko Milivojevic, "The Spratly and Paracel Islands Conflict," *Survival*, January–February 1989, pp. 70–77.

51. Michael Vatikiotis and Tai Ming Cheung, "Maritime Hegemony," *Far Eastern Economic Review*, vol. 151, no. 2 (10 January 1991), p. 11.

52. See, for example, the David Chen article in *South China Morning Post* (Hong Kong), 5 October 1989, in *FBIS-CHI*, no. 192 (5 October 1989), pp. 13–14.

53. Tai Ming Cheung, "The Growth of Chinese Naval Power," an unpublished manuscript prepared for the Major Powers in Asia Project of the Institute of Southeast Asian Studies, Singapore, September 1990.

54. See Sophie Quinn-Judge and Tai Ming Cheung, "Market Forces," *Far Eastern Economic Review*, vol. 151, no. 22 (30 May 1991), pp. 18–19.

55. Beijing, Xinhua, 11 August 1992, in *FBIS-CHI*, no. 155 (11 August 1992), p. 4.

56. Michael Vatikiotis, "Measure for Measure," *Far Eastern Economic Review*, vol. 155, no. 17 (30 April 1992), p. 18; and P. Lewis Young, "Southeast Asia: New Crossroads of World Trade," *Armed Forces Journal International*, February 1990, pp. 56–69, for a survey of ASEAN weapons acquisitions programs.

57. Voice of Vietnam Network, 17 May 1992, reported in *FBIS-EAS*, no. 096 (18 May 1992), p. 57.

58. Nicholas D. Kristoff, "China Signs U.S. Oil Deal for Disputed Waters," *New York Times*, 18 June 1992, p. A8.

59. Kyodo (Tokyo), 29 May 1992, in *FBIS-EAS*, no. 111 (9 June 1992), p. 1

60. David Albright and Tom Zamora, "India, Pakistan's Nuclear Weapons: All the Pieces in Place," *Bulletin of the Atomic Scientists*, June 1989, pp. 20–26.

61. Hu Xiaoen and Peng Zhonghuai, " 'Strengthening Border Buildup' Should Be an Important Content of Military Strategy," *Jiefangjun Bao*, 22 January 1988, in *FBIS-CHI*, no. 023 (4 February 1988), p. 10.

62. Chai Shikuan, "The Second Handshake—On Indian Prime Minister Rajiv Gandhi's Visit to China," *Liaowang Overseas*, no. 1 (2 January 1989), in *FBIS-CHI*, no. 10 (17 January 1989), pp. 12–13.

63. Robert Delfts and Rita Manchester, "Return to Realism," *Far Eastern Economic Review*, vol. 143, no. 1 (5 January 1989), pp. 10–11.

64. Beijing, Xinhua, 31 August 1990, in *FBIS-CHI*, no. 172 (5 September 1990), p. 16.

65. Hamish McDonald, "Technically Friends," *Far Eastern Economic Review*, vol. 151, no. 5 (31 January 1991), pp. 13–14.

66. "India and the Soviet Union: Fraying Knot," *The Economist*, 28 July 1990, pp. 27–28.

67. "China Hopes Kashmir Situation Calms Down," Beijing, Xinhua (in English), 8 February 1990, in *FBIS-CHI*, no. 027 (8 February 1990), p. 3.

68. Delhi General Overseas Service, 30 June 1990, in *FBIS-CHI*, no. 131 (9 July 1990), p. 11.

69. "India, Pakistan Nuclear Treaty Ratified," *Far Eastern Economic Review*, vol. 151, no. 6 (7 February 1991), p. 14.

70. For a detailed expression this view, see Zheng Ruiyang, "A Few Problems in India's Relations with Its Neighboring States," *Guoji Wenti Yanjiu*, no. 2 (13 April 1990), in *JPRS-CAR*, no. 060 (6 August 1990), pp. 12–18.

71. "Russia Offers India Joint Arms Factories," *Washington Times*, 17 June 1992, p. 2.

72. Lucian W. Pye, "Taiwan's Development and Its Implications for Beijing and Washington," *Asian Survey*, vol. 26, no. 6 (June 1986), pp. 611–629.

73. Willie Wo-lop Lam reported from Taipei that senior officials had informed him of increased troop deployments in Fujian Province opposite Taiwan and that China had reestablished the Fuzhou Military Region in order to threaten the island. *South China Morning Post*, 13 October 1990, in *FBIS-CHI*, no. 201 (17 October 1990), pp. 22–23.

74. Julian Baum, "A Trend to Friends," *Far Eastern Economic Review*, vol. 150, no. 48 (29 November 1990), pp. 12–13.

75. Commentary, "Taipei Inches toward Economic Relations with Moscow, Hanoi," Taipei International Service, 18 January 1990, in *FBIS-CHI*, no. 013 (19 January 1990), p. 52; and Taipei, CNA, 28 January 1991, in *FBIS-CHI*, no. 019 (29 January 1991), p. 61.

76. Yang Shangkun's interview was reported in *Chung Kuo Shih Bao*, 25 September 1990, in *FBIS-CHI*, no. 191 (2 October 1990), pp. 20–24.

77. Ibid., p. 20.

78. Ibid., p. 22.

79. Taipei, *Chung Yang Jih Bao*, 27 September 1990, in *FBIS-CHI*, no. 199 (15 October 1990), p. 57.

80. Li Jiaquan, "Independent Taiwan—A Road Leading to Disaster," *Liaowang*, no. 12 (19 March 1990), in *FBIS-CHI*, no. 074 (17 April 1990), pp. 51–54. Although referring specifically to a KMT-led independence movement, the message applies equally to any separatist movement.

81. Taipei, CNA, 22 November 1990, in *FBIS-CHI*, no. 227 (26 November 1990), p. 79; and Julian Baum, "Hands Across the Sea," *Far Eastern Economic Review*, vol. 150, no. 49, 6 December 1990, pp. 16–17.

82. Lian Jintian, "Taiwan's 'Three No's Policy' Unprecedented Questions," *Renmin Ribao*, 1 December 1990; in *FBIS-CHI*, no. 233 (4 December 1990), pp. 58–59.

7

The China Policy of Russia and Asian Security in the 1990s

Robert A. Scalapino

Three basic principles currently govern the foreign policies of most states, and have direct applicability to those of Russia as that nation is being newly formed at the close of the twentieth century.

First, an intimate relationship exists between domestic and foreign policies, a relationship that is at once interactive and subject to varying degrees of intensity, depending upon circumstances. To take the most obvious example, the outcome of the abortive August 1991 coup in Moscow is of great consequence to current Russian foreign policies.

Second, perceived national interests are the dominant factor in both the making of foreign policy decisions and their execution. In the perception of national interests, moreover, political elites now place very high priority on economic considerations. Security remains a vital concern, but in relative terms, economic factors—themselves a powerful element in any calculation of security today—have risen to a commanding position in most instances.

Third, despite the primacy of national interests, real or perceived, in the determination of foreign policies, there are other elements that cannot be ignored. Ideology, while declining as a critical factor, notably in the cases of Russia and China, should not be dismissed, especially as it pertains to the rhetoric surrounding foreign policy explanations and the efforts to legitimize those policies to the citizenry. Equally important, factors of tradition or history, culture, and even ethnicity play significant roles, both at elite and mass levels. Patterns of thought, historical memories, and the biases derived from these should be given far more weight than social scientists are prone to do. Geopolitical factors are also of great importance in influencing perceptions of national interest as well as in shaping national culture.

It is from this perspective that current Russian policies toward China should be viewed. Moreover, these policies cannot be viewed in isolation, separated from Russian policies toward the Pacific-Asian region as a whole or on the global level.

A brief background on the course of Sino-Soviet relations since World War II is necessary to provide the context for recent developments.[1] Rather than recount well-known events chronologically, I prefer to deal with the past analytically, noting the central elements in the relationship at key stages, and the direction as well as the nature of changes.

The foundation of the Sino-Soviet alliance that was consummated in 1949–50 rested upon the perception of a common enemy: the United States. Precisely when that perception was firmly implanted in the minds of the Chinese Communist leaders is a matter of debate. Some American observers argue that flexibility existed in Yan'an in the war years, and possibly even later. They assert that had U.S. policies been different, the nationalism implicit in Chinese communism from its beginnings would have manifested itself in a more independent stance after Communist assumption of power.[2]

The evidence currently available mostly runs against that thesis. It is true that the "indigenous" CCP leaders and those with the strong imprint of Moscow clashed and vied for power. Moreover, Mao and others on occasion thought that Moscow knew little about China and gave the wrong advice. In addition, the quality of Chinese assuredness—that sense of cultural superiority and national pride that has been the hallmark of *all* Chinese political elements—was certainly not absent in the psychological makeup of the Chinese Communists.

However, those Chinese Communists who felt most strongly about Stalinist domination had left the movement at earlier points. Throughout the Sino-Japanese war, the official CCP organs stoutly defended all Soviet actions and policies, and periodically criticized Western policies regarded as insufficiently supportive of Moscow. The evidence is strong that the Chinese Communist leaders considered themselves good Marxist-Leninists, and proud members of an international community of comrades led by "the Great Soviet Union."[3]

Moreover, most leaders, including Mao, realized that Soviet support, both economically and militarily, would be crucial in the long run, given China's geographical and ideological position. To be sure, concern about Soviet influence created doubt or ambivalence on occasion, and there were those in the Communist ranks who regarded the West as a more likely source of scientific-technological modernization for China than the USSR. But few if any Chinese Communists of this era believed that the United States would abandon Chiang Kai-shek and the Nationalist government. After all, the Pacific war between the United States and Japan had erupted essentially over the issue of Chinese sovereignty. Following the failure of the Marshall Mission and with the military defeat of the Nationalists looming near, the Truman administration sent a variety of signals to the Communists, but they were not reciprocated.[4]

If "socialism *with Chinese characteristics*" always lay deeply embedded in the Chinese Communist movement, it remained strictly subordinated to socialist "internationalism" in a period when the Communists' perception of their interests increasingly dictated affiliation with the USSR. Only after power had been attained, and extensive experience with the Russians had taken place, did the always present nationalist instincts of the CCP leaders come to the fore.

From a Soviet perspective, the picture was exceedingly complex. Stalin and his associates initially assumed that their principal relationship would be with Nationalist China in the post-1945 years. In a very real sense, they pursued a "two Chinas" policy in the early period after the war, being careful to keep official relations with the Nationalist government correct, but at the same time, providing sanctuary and assistance to the Communists in Manchuria, which they briefly occupied. Even after significant Communist military victories, Stalin assumed (and perhaps wanted) a China that would be divided roughly at the Yangtze River, with the Communists to the north, the Nationalists to the south.

It is also true that Mao Zedong was not Stalin's favorite Communist. Stalin regarded Mao with suspicion, both with respect to his understanding of Marxism, and more importantly, with respect to his attitude toward the Soviet Union. But the Russians realized that after the early 1940s at least, there were no viable alternatives within the movement. To Stalin, it was vitally important to ensure that the Soviet Union would never again be threatened with a two-front war. Thus, as a buffer-state system was being constructed to the West, it was essential to see Japan eliminated as a future menace, Korea—or at least a portion—absorbed ideologically, and China (or several Chinas) cultivated by whatever means necessary. With the onset of the Cold War, moreover, these objectives became even more important. American power—and its forward posture—had to be countered in Asia as in Europe. Thanks to the Communist victory, China became a crucial element in Soviet Asian strategy.[5]

In this period, it should be emphasized, a combination of security and political considerations took precedence over economic issues in the formulation of foreign policy, both in the USSR and in the policies of the Chinese Communists. For the Russians, the memories of a devastating war were naturally vivid, and the prospects of an anticommunist global alliance threatening. For the Chinese Communists, the principal task was to defeat the Nationalists militarily and commence the building of a new nation, preferably with minimal external threats. In this setting, ideology provided a bond, a common language, so to speak, and equally important, the Soviet Leninist state provided a model.

At the same time, the Chinese Communists were able to balance nationalism and internationalism adroitly. On the one hand, they identified themselves as a part of the global proletarian brotherhood dedicated to the unfolding socialist revolution. On the other hand, they displayed nationalist banners, proclaiming

China liberated from imperialist control and independent at last. And even with the Russians, they bargained with some toughness. A vision of the Chinese national interest, with whatever the ideological cloth draped over it, was never out of sight.

As is well known, the Sino-Soviet alliance lasted for less than a decade and ended in great mutual bitterness. The step-by-step details of its dissolution need not detain us here.[6] The fundamental causes, however, must be understood. At root, the alliance collapsed because the Soviet Union lost its credibility as an ally willing to take risks with the United States on behalf of China. Khrushchev, like another Russian leader three decades later, wanted to reduce the costs and hazards of Soviet foreign policy. He was especially anxious to seek some reduction of tension with the United States in order to give higher priority to tackling the urgent economic problems within the USSR. Thus, when the second Taiwan Straits crisis loomed in 1958, the Soviet Union refused to guarantee support for the Chinese policy of "liberating" the offshore islands. Chinese leaders regarded Soviet actions as a betrayal in much the same manner as North Korean leaders viewed Moscow's diplomatic recognition of the Republic of Korea more than three decades later.

There were other issues, to be sure. To handle the old Stalinists, Khrushchev had opened up an assault on Russia's long-time dictator, both at home and within the international communist movement. The domestic struggle took priority over all else. Without consulting foreign comrades, Khrushchev launched his famous attack on Stalin at the CPSU Party Conference of 1956. Many communist leaders—Mao prominent among them—were embarrassed, having praised Stalin lavishly before their own people. In other respects also, Soviet leaders were accused of being insensitive to the rights of other parties. Khrushchev came to be regarded as mercurial, veering from "adventurism" to "capitulation" on the international stage, and undermining Stalinism at home. Suddenly, defenses of the sovereignty and independence of every communist party began to emanate from Beijing, and a coalition of anti-Khrushchev Asian communist parties was formed, with the Chinese at its head. Nationalism interwoven with Mao Thought now emerged in Beijing in full bloom.

The rift was further abetted by the move of China away from the Soviet developmental model in certain key respects—the adoption of the commune system being one example. Toward this experiment and others like the Great Leap Forward, Russian leaders were contemptuous, insisting (correctly) that such policies would end in failure. Moreover, they deeply resented what they saw as the waste of the very large Soviet resources (material and human) that had been advanced at great sacrifice on behalf of China's modernization.

As the split widened, the Khrushchev government took the unprecedented step of halting all aid, including that going to unfinished projects, and backing away from an earlier pledge to assist the PRC in its nuclear program. Moreover, with China taking the lead, the cleavage took on a highly personal and ideological turn. Soon, in the competition for support both with their respective publics and within the socialist world, each was accusing the other of being revisionist and deserting socialism.

At a later point, some of Khrushchev's domestic opponents were to charge him with unnecessary crudeness and preemptive behavior in dealing with China and other socialist states. Unquestionably, these years regenerated deeply implanted emotional biases on both sides. Russians saw the Chinese as ungrateful, self-centered, and with a high quotient of xenophobic nationalism. Talk of "the yellow peril" was once again heard, and many unfavorable jokes about the Chinese circulated. The Chinese answered in kind. They accused the Russians of "big power chauvinism," and claimed to see a continuity with czarist imperialism: the white men again sought global dominance, with communist labels only a veneer. Thus, a great many issues supposedly buried reemerged. As one example, the proported seizure of vast tracts of land in the past, land now denominated Siberia, but "legitimately Chinese," was denounced in Beijing. The emotions on both sides reached a climax at the end of the 1960s, but they were still very strong in the 1970s—and to some degree they persist to the present.

Consequently, the decade of the 1960s saw a steadily mounting crisis in Soviet-Chinese relations, climaxed by the Ussuri River clashes at the end of the decade, and what many people on both sides believed to be the likelihood of war.[7] The USSR steadily built up its military defenses in the Far East and encircled China by strengthening its ties with North Korea, Vietnam, and India as well as Mongolia. Mao and his coterie, meanwhile, were busily alienating old foreign friends and tearing China apart in the course of the Cultural Revolution. In a state of extreme weakness and vulnerability, the PRC finally cast aside ideological reservations to accept rapprochement with the United States. Never had the primacy of national interest been so graphically demonstrated.

As is well known, the American-Chinese relationship ripened quickly into one containing not only cultural and economic components, but a low-level strategic element as well. And at the time of U.S.–PRC diplomatic recognition at the outset of 1979, Deng Xiaoping, now China's leader, was openly calling for a global alliance led by the United States to ward off "Soviet hegemonism."[8]

It is scarcely an exaggeration to assert that by the beginning of the 1980s, Soviet foreign policy in the Pacific-Asian region was a disaster. Not only were Soviet-Chinese relations still extremely hostile, relations with Japan remained as frozen as they had been since World War II. Contacts with the five nations comprising ASEAN were minimal and less than friendly. The Soviet invasion of Afghanistan had deeply antagonized much of the world, including three front-line states, Pakistan, Iran, and China—all nations of supreme importance to the USSR, and especially to its Central Asian Republics. Moscow's only allies—Mongolia, North Korea, and Vietnam—constituted a steady financial drain, and the latter two at least were privately regarded as undependable, neither behaving as good clients nor capable of being partners. India remained the sole nation of significance upon whose alignment the Soviet Union counted, but with the Indian economy undergoing changes, and its advanced sectors seeking ever higher technology, would the Soviet connection remain strong?

The rethinking of its China policy got under way in Moscow in this context, with its first manifestations in the final period of the Brezhnev era. In a speech delivered at Tashkent in March 1982, only a few months before his death, Brezhnev held out an olive branch, speaking of China in conciliatory language and offering to negotiate the border dispute. Beijing leaders were initially suspicious, regarding the Soviet efforts as insincere attempts to interfere with Chinese-American rapprochement. Signals of Russian flexibility continued to be sent out in the short-lived Andropov administration, and the Chinese made cautious responses.

At this point, the interplay of triangular relations between the USSR, the United States, and China was becoming ever more important to the policies of each of the three nations. Within the Carter administration, two broad positions could be discerned: that epitomized by Secretary Cyrus Vance, who essentially argued for an "evenhanded policy" of advancing relations with Russia and China more or less at the same pace, and that epitomized by National Security Council (NSC) head Zbigniew Brzezinski, who favored movement toward a de facto alliance with China against Russia. Naturally, Moscow was alert to and concerned about trends in the latter direction. Such trends accelerated in the aftermath of the Soviet invasion of Afghanistan, an action that undermined the Vance position. Thus, Russian leaders continued to probe means of improving relations with China, albeit with limited success. Afghanistan and Indochina proved to be major obstacles. The Chinese leaders continued to tilt toward the United States, with closer strategic ties being forged.

At the opening of the Reagan administration, however, slippage occurred. Chinese leaders were very concerned that the new conservative U.S. government would move to improve relations with Taiwan, campaign promises to that effect having been made. Deng and others had always been deeply unhappy over the Taiwan Relations Act and Washington's de facto two-Chinas policy. Now it appeared that more sophisticated arms would be sold to Taiwan. Not until they extracted from the United States the joint communiqué of August 1982 limiting arms sales to Taiwan, and by implication, promising their eventual end, was Beijing in some measure mollified.

No fundamental change in relations among the USSR, the United States, and China took place until after Mikhail Gorbachev assumed the general secretary's position in March 1985. From that time, however, a new Pacific-Asian policy for the USSR evolved with Soviet domestic priorities serving as the driving force. For Gorbachev and his associates, the task was to reduce tensions globally so as to bring down the massive Soviet military expenditures, and at the same time, to seek entry into the international marketplace and investment network so as to provide opportunities for economic revitalization. Given these imperatives, the top foreign policy priorities were obvious: first, to seek détente with the United States, with an initial emphasis upon arms reductions and various confidence-building measures pertaining primarily to West Europe; second, to reach an accommodation with China as the first step in totally revamping the Soviet Union's Asian policies.

It cannot be doubted that in the years following the advent of Gorbachev to power, significant progress in achieving these two objectives was made. It is also true to state that in the Pacific-Asian region, Russia has become a peripheral player due to domestic problems, whether the measurement be economic, political, or strategic. Indeed, the demise of the old Soviet Union and the uncertain nature of a new federation of republics suggests that for the foreseeable future, Russia will be a secondary force in the Pacific-Asian area, with its weakness rather than its strength a matter of concern.

As is well known, Soviet-American relations steadily improved after 1985 due to various developments: progress on arms limitation, notably the INF Treaty; Soviet abandonment of the so-called Brezhnev Doctrine (that no nation was free to leave socialism) and the march of East Europe toward political pluralism and a mixed economy; the advance of *glasnost* within the Soviet Union itself; unilateral Russian military cutbacks, and the decision to withdraw Soviet troops from Afghanistan; and advances in Soviet-American political and cultural relations. These developments served to create a new atmosphere in the relations between the two great military powers. One important by-product was cooperation on regional crises, from Cambodia to the Middle East.

As the decade of the 1990s opened, the prospects seemed good for a new world order in which the major states—above all, the United States and the USSR—could set aside past rivalries and build or strengthen international institutions both for peace-keeping and for economic development. Yet events in Lithuania soon provided graphic illustration of the fact that Soviet-American détente was hostage to basic economic and political developments within the Soviet Union. Was the tougher stance against the independence movement in the Baltics and the apparent rise of conservative-military elements within Soviet politics the signal that *glasnost* was being throttled, or was it merely a temporary shift in the tortuous path that the new Russian revolution had to travel? The dramatic events of 1991, including acceptance by Moscow of the independence of the Baltic states in the aftermath of the failed August coup, point to the latter thesis, at least for the present.

Nevertheless, a lineal political progression in the old Leninist states, or for that matter, in other states as well, is unlikely. The sweeping assault on the old order will bring its own excesses, and as these mount, a coalition comprising both elites and citizenry will demand responses. The call for law and order, an attack on crime, a response to corruption as well as a resentment of the inequities and uncertainties of livelihood under the new order accumulate. Authoritarian stability has been exchanged for instability, an unsettling process especially when deep ethnic, religious, or regional animosities are released. Under such circumstances, some reversal of political course generally occurs. But the new direction in turn meets resistance, and displays its own deficiencies and excesses, thus creating the basis for a reverse swing of the pendulum. The intricate pattern of political change characterizing both the constituent units of the old Soviet Union and China at present is a factor that must affect their mutual relationship, and even more certainly, the relation of each to the United States.[9]

Gorbachev's July 1986 Vladivostok speech was the first major effort to spell out to the world a new Soviet policy for Asia. In his remarks, the Soviet leader made it clear that improvement of relations with China was his highest priority. To that end, concessions with respect to key issues were signaled: troop withdrawal from Afghanistan and reductions in Mongolia; border adjustments favorable to China in the Amur River region; stepped-up economic relations including joint projects; and efforts to achieve an agreement on regional security. The Vladivostok address was not devoid of political gimmickry, but in its broad outline, it spelled out the "new thinking" that now knit Soviet domestic and foreign policy together. Economics was to be placed in command. Security doctrine was to be based on the concept of "reasonable" or "defensive" sufficiency, with unilateral force reductions undertaken. Ideological considerations were to play no role in Soviet international relations. Such were the new elements in the leadership's definition of the Soviet Union's national interests.[10]

From this base, Soviet relations with China quickly improved. There were obstacles. Deng Xiaoping, who belonged to that generation of Chinese leaders that had participated actively in the most acrimonious period of Sino-Soviet relations, continued to be suspicious. So did other Chinese. Beijing's official position remained that of asserting that the key to improvement lay in resolving "the three obstacles": Soviet military withdrawal from Afghanistan; reduction of Soviet border forces, including those in Mongolia; and resolution of the Cambodian issue.

Substantial advances with respect to each of these "obstacles" came in 1988. In April, an agreement was signed in Geneva providing for the withdrawal of Soviet troops in Afghanistan, to be completed by early 1989. At the end of the year, the Russians announced that most Soviet forces would be withdrawn from Mongolia within two years; and in the course of the year, the Russians gave evidence of good faith in urging a withdrawal of Vietnamese forces from Cambodia. Meanwhile, cultural and economic relations were growing modestly. Students, scholars, and cultural representatives were being exchanged in small numbers. Trade, much of it border trade, was rising. A few joint ventures were undertaken, and some 13,000 Chinese were working in Siberia by the end of 1990.[11]

In September 1988, Gorbachev made a second major address pertaining to Asia in Krasnoyarsk. In his remarks, he indicated again his desire for a meeting with Chinese leaders, and also outlined a detailed seven-point proposal for advancing security in the Pacific-Asian region. In January 1989, Foreign Minister Eduard Shevardnadze went to Beijing to make the final preparations for Gorbachev's visit. The path had been prepared for the summit meeting of May 15–18, 1989.

Neither the Soviets nor the Chinese could have anticipated that the continuing student occupation of Tiananmen Square, and the awkward situation thereby created, would end in disaster. Embarrassed by the fact that the Russians—and the world—were close-up spectators to Chinese disorder, a majority of PRC leaders led by Deng resolved to take a hard line on the dissenters, with a predictable chain of events following. Gorbachev, incidentally, was forced to find a position on the student protesters that would not alienate the Chinese leadership on the one hand, and not violate the principle of *glasnost* on the other hand. On this matter, he tiptoed very gently, talking to the leaders about his problems with unruly or impetuous dissenters, but not condemning the students directly.

The 1989 summit ploughed no new ground despite various agreements. Fundamentally, it served to have the highest leaders of both countries bless the new era. Now, more than three years later, it is appropriate to draw up a balance sheet on Soviet-Chinese relations and Soviet policies in the region, not merely relating to the current situation, but also with respect to the longer-term prospects.

Economic intercourse between Russia and China has grown slowly, with two-way trade reported to have been $3.4 billion in 1989, estimated to have reached $3.7 billion in 1990, and some $5 billion in 1991.[12] According to Chinese sources, local and border trade had reached an additional $700 million in 1989. The decision of the USSR to put the bulk of its trade on a hard currency basis as of January 1, 1991, has created some short-term difficulties, but over time, it may prove beneficial.

By the end of 1989, contracts covering 95 projects and labor services, and 14 additional joint ventures amounting to U.S. $240 million had been agreed upon by Soviet and Chinese negotiators.[13] Many of the projects appear to be Soviet commitments to assist in the modernization of certain plants established by them in the 1950s, and a number have subsequently been affected by the economic crisis in Russia. Some infrastructural improvements between the two nations have also taken place, notably the building of a rail link between Kazakhstan and Xinjiang, and the opening of an air route from Shenyang to Irkutsk.

On occasion, Gorbachev and other Russian leaders talked expansively about wedding Soviet resources, Japanese capital, and Chinese manpower in the development of a great Northeast Asian economic complex. In point of fact, however, Russia and China have, and will continue to have, a limited base for economic interaction. On the surface, the complementarity of the two economies seems very promising: Russian raw materials and machinery for Chinese textiles, food, and consumer goods. However, neither side has the capital nor, in most cases, the desired technology to assist the other. Soviet trade with Asia has recently constituted less than 9 percent of its total trade, that with the Asian communist states only 5 percent, and that with China between 2 and 3 percent.[14] Cross-national investment was negligible even before the worsening Russian economic crisis, despite a few well-publicized cases. In the course of Premier Li Peng's visit to Moscow of April 23–26, 1990, a "Long-Term Program for Economic, Scientific, and Technological Cooperation" between the two nations was signed, to remain in effect until December 31, 2000.[15] The agreement provides for a wide range of cooperative ventures, but sets forth no details as to funds, priorities, or timing. Naturally, domestic developments in Russia in 1991–92 created new obstacles.

There is virtually no possibility that Russia and China can be major trading or investment partners in the foreseeable future. Trade will no doubt increase if Russia and the other republics can get their own economic houses in order, and more particularly, if the Russian Republic, now given much greater autonomy, can develop its own effective economic program. Fundamentally, however, Russia must look West for its economic salvation; China must look East. The near-term future of these two societies, both of which are seeking to enter the international economic arena, hinges upon their being able to interact more effectively with the advanced market economies, thereby acquiring capital and technology as well as goods. West Europe and, secondarily, the United States, are of crucial importance to Russia. In Asia, both states will compete in some measure in seeking to attract the resources of Japan, South Korea, and Taiwan, and they will also be competing with the other developing societies of the region.

In the political realm, the situation is both complex and intriguing. In the May 1989 joint communiqué, the pledge was to develop friendship and good neighborliness on the basis of the five principles of peaceful coexistence, and settle all outstanding problems through negotiations. It was further agreed that each country was implementing reform "in a socialist way" based on its own specific conditions.[16] At the very time these lines were being written, however, the two nations were actually in the process of moving further apart politically. A growing number of Chinese leaders, and most especially the conservatives, viewed Gorbachev and his policies as providing a negative lesson. In their view, *glasnost* had been carried much too far, and *perestroika* had not gone far enough. They did not want Soviet political trends to contaminate China.

Political conservatism has dominated China's political leadership since the Tiananmen killings and the ouster of Zhao Ziyang and his supporters. China and two other Asian Leninist states, North Korea and Vietnam, have insisted upon upholding the dictatorship of the Communist party and the other "cardinal principles" of Marxism-Leninism.[17] In 1990, private memoranda were distributed to key party personnel in China excoriating Gorbachev, and pointing out the fact that had the PRC leaders acted likewise at the time of the student protests, chaos would have resulted in China as was happening in the USSR. More recent events have confirmed that opinion among the remaining Asian Leninists, including those Chinese at the top. And inner party documents make it clear that hard-line Chinese officials were disappointed that the Moscow 1991 coup failed. Both sides, however, remain determined not to allow ideological differences to become a matter of public debate. The acrimonious polemics of the 1960s have not been forgotten by either side.

To what extent will political trends in these two societies advance or retard bilateral relations? Should it be assumed, for example, that if Russia and China were to come closer together in ideological-political terms it would bring the two nations (or more accurately, the two leaderships) closer together? The evidence of the recent past scarcely supports such a thesis. The most bitter period of Sino-Soviet relations came when both states were pursuing relatively similar hard-line Leninist policies. Moreover, China's brief war with Vietnam was not a product of ideological division. On the contrary, those two societies were roughly on the same ideological wavelength at the time. Current improvements in Sino-Vietnamese relations are based partly on ideological or political considerations, but primarily they reflect a perception of national interests, especially on the part of Vietnam.

Although it appears highly unlikely at present, the reemergence to Russian political supremacy of a strongly conservative faction, especially one studded with military personalities, might actually be inimical to better Russian-Chinese relations, raising again the specter of a militarily oriented Russia determined to assert its "rights" in Asia and tough on boundary issues and similar matters.

However, if one assumes that out of the present political conflict, a "centrist" or liberal faction continues to hold power in Russia, the political status quo—namely, a setting aside of ideological differences—might be maintained. Victory for the Russian democrats, if supported with concrete economic advances, may in the medium to long term abet a similar course in China, but that is by no means certain.[18] To date, the principal sources of influence upon Chinese "progressives" have not come in the first instance from Russia, or even from East Europe, although events there have had some impact. They have come most extensively from the prosperous market economies where greater political openness also exists: South Korea, Japan, Taiwan, and even the ASEAN members, as well as the West.

Similarly, if the domestic political scene were to change in China, it is not clear that it would have a decisive influence on relations with Russia. The current leadership tilts toward conservatism politically, but it is both weak and divided. Change is likely in the not-too-distant future. If the move is further in the direction of hard-line positions, China's economic opening-up is almost certain to be complicated.[19] An open economy cannot long exist with a closed polity. That is why, sooner or later, the PRC is likely to return to the broad policies of the early and mid-1980s, and pursue a course I have labeled authoritarian-pluralist: politics constrained but not Stalinist; social institutions involving education, religion, and the family operating with varying degrees of autonomy; and the economy mixed, with the market playing a significant role.[20] Only such a system can permit growing involvement with the market economies. Moreover, this trend would not inhibit, and might assist in expanding relations with Russia.

In sum, serious ideological-political divisions might make Russian-Chinese communications more difficult and could conceivably encourage "pro-Chinese" or "pro-Russian" factions in the opposite state, factions opposing trends in their own country. In particular, the rise of a strong xenophobic nationalism could rekindle old emotions on either or both sides. It seems more likely, however, that perceived national interests will override political similarities or differences, as has generally been the case in the past.

Russian-Chinese security relations naturally take their current ambience from the other components of the relationship, and also from broader regional and global trends with respect to major state relations. Here, geopolitical considerations are vital. Officials have asserted that with respect to the 7,000-kilometer border, "90 percent of the boundary issues have been resolved." But they have added that difficult problems lie ahead in connection with the remaining controversies.[21]

The problem is made more complex because many of the remaining issues require Chinese negotiations with several of the newly formed Central Asian Republics. Meanwhile, as is well known, the Russians have been making major cuts in the ground forces stationed east of the Urals. Earlier, a reduction of 200,000 (out of some 580,000) was pledged by the end of 1991, of which 120,000 are from Far East forces.[22] During his visit to Beijing, Gorbachev announced that twelve divisions in the Far East would be disbanded or converted into defensive machine-gun divisions.[23] All Russian troops are supposed to have been removed from Mongolia by the end of 1991. Russian sources have also indicated that their Pacific Fleet had been reduced by fifty-seven naval vessels by the beginning of 1990, and that operations at sea had been significantly reduced and were being conducted only in coastal waters. In the near future, the Pacific Fleet is reportedly to be reduced by almost one-third.[24] These actions, it is asserted, have been taken under the new operative doctrine of reasonable or defensive sufficiency. The sweeping proposals regarding nuclear weapons made by President Bush in September 1991 are inducing further reductions. An agreement with Japan on the Northern Territories issue would provide major impetus for further reductions, if it could be consumated.

To be sure, qualitative improvements in the Russian military have continued as older ground equipment, ships, and aircraft are decommissioned. Nevertheless, the evidence points ever more strongly to the essentially defensive orientation of Russian military planning. Chinese military as well as civilian leaders have naturally noted that in addition to drawing down border forces, the Russian withdrawal from Afghanistan and departure from Cam Ranh Bay, accompanied by drastic cuts in economic assistance to such allies as North Korea and Vietnam, have ended the threat of encirclement. Indeed, Moscow's small Asian allies are inwardly furious over the new Soviet policies. As an ally, Russian's credibility has never been lower. The reasons, however, are well known to all. With military and related expenditures possibly taking as much as 25 to 30 percent of

GNP and the economy dreadfully ill, Russian leaders have had little choice if they wanted to pursue reform and renovation.[25]

The transformation in the security factor is the most significant change that has taken place in Russian-Chinese relations. It has affected attitudes as well as policies between the two nations. The perception of a Russian threat among Chinese leaders is not only significantly reduced but takes a different form. What if nationalist movements with an Islamic base emerge in Central Asia, coupled with Mongol resurgence to the north? That development seems a genuine risk in light of the dissolution of the USSR. While China can take solace in the fact that the Han constitute some 92 percent of the total Chinese population, the potentially troublesome minorities occupy vast tracts of land on China's peripheries, including regions that border on Kazahkstan and Pakistan.

Naturally, Russian security policies have implications for many states other than China, and they are of special importance to the countries comprising the Northeast Asian region. It was the Russian hope to reestablish fully normal relations with Japan in 1991, signing a formal peace treaty and securing large-scale economic assistance in the form of both loans and investment. Those hopes were dashed, at least for the present. Gorbachev's trip to Tokyo in mid-April produced no agreement on the Northern Territories issue, and the Japanese private sector indicated to the Soviet leader that extensive trade and investment must await major structural changes in the Soviet economy. Given the tragic condition of the Soviet economic situation and the progressive political weakness of Gorbachev at home, together with the problems of the Kaifu government, the visit could scarcely have come at a less propitious time. Even after the political upheavals that occurred in 1991, both in Moscow and Tokyo, fragility of the political summits of the two nations continue to make a compromise on the territorial issue out of reach.[26]

Without greater accord between Russia and Japan, a broad security agreement pertaining to East Asia, or even Northeast Asia, will be extremely difficult. Another thorny issue has been presented by the situation on the Korean peninsula. Here the recent trends, at least up to mid-1992, have been promising if still subject to uncertainties. A combination of internal and external pressures has caused the North (DPRK) to make significant changes in its earlier policies, with the South reciprocating. The 25-point Accord of December 13, 1991, and the subsequent agreement on a nuclear-free Korea, were followed by the DPRK's acceptance of IAEA (International Atomic Energy Agency) inspection of the Yongbyon nuclear facilities, and a series of North–South agreements relating to economic and cultural issues, including limited exchange visits by divided families.

The role of the major states in encouraging these developments can scarcely be overestimated. Russia, faced with its deepening economic crisis, drastically revised its economic relations with the North, insisting on hard currency payments for its goods and international, not "friendship," prices. The result was a serious blow to an already weak DPRK economy, requiring Pyongyang to consider significant domestic as well as foreign policy alterations. Moreover, the establishment of Russian–South Korean diplomatic recognition dealt a fatal blow to the North's opposition to cross-recognition by the major powers and caused it to seek negotiations with Japan.

Meanwhile, by making it clear to Pyongyang leaders that it could not veto the ROK application for UN membership, China forced the North to shift its policy on this issue, and accept dual UN membership. Japan, in its negotiations with the DPRK, insisted that the nuclear issue be satisfactorily resolved prior to normalization, thereby adding to the pressure on that front. And most importantly, the United States removed the North's excuses for foot-dragging on nuclear inspection by removing nuclear weapons from the South and, in cooperation with the ROK, suspending the Team Spirit military exercises.

The future of ROK–DPRK relations may still be subject to twists and turns. Deep suspicions and bitter rivalry continue. Moreover, some 1.4 million military forces, North and South, still face each other under conditions of continuing tension. The recent trends, however, have been encouraging, and for this, Russia, along with the other large states concerned with Korea, should be given credit.[27]

Progress on the Korean and Northern Territories issues could lead to a reduction of tension in Northeast Asia sufficient to provide a firm foundation for major regional arms agreements. For understandable reasons, Russia would like to enter into naval arms limitation discussions with the United States, as noted earlier. At some point, this is certainly desirable from the standpoint of both parties, as are broader agreements about nuclear weapons, now more possible than at any time in the past. It would be extremely helpful, however, if the security obligations of the United States could meanwhile be reduced by alleviating or removing the remaining regional tensions. Until that time, unilateral adjustments by both major naval powers motivated by economic considerations and new military strategies are the most likely moves.[28]

Meanwhile, a number of states in the region have proposed multilateral approaches to security matters. The Russian proposals, first advanced in 1985, have been reiterated several times, including in Gorbachev's September 1988 Krasnoyarsk speech. His seven-point proposal included discussions relating to a freeze on nuclear weapons in the region; a balanced reduction of naval and air forces in the area and limits on their activities; further actions to reduce the risk of incidents at sea and in the air; and the opening of security talks pertaining to the Asia-Pacific region among three Security Council members, the USSR, the PRC, and the United States.[29] Subsequently, proposals for a multilateral conference have been put forth by Mongolia and, most recently, by Canada. Nonofficial discussions have already begun among scholars and other interested parties hosted by institutes in the United States, Japan, Mongolia, and Canada. In various forms, multilateralism is en route in Asia in the security as well as the economic realm, and Northeast Asia is a logical focus of attention.

Naturally, the Russian-Chinese relationship will continue to be critical to the broader economic, political, and security trends affecting the Asia-Pacific region as a whole. Like other bilateral relations between major states in this era, the likelihood is that the relationship will be a complex one combining cooperation and competition, with the mix varying from time to time and issue to issue.

As indicated at the outset, the dominant factor driving the foreign policies of both nations will be elitist perceptions of national interests. These perceptions will be influenced by economics first of all, but also by a sense of minimal security requirements. In defining and integrating these two central factors, the leaders will consciously or unconsciously be influenced by other considerations: cultural proclivities, historical memories, geopolitical circumstances, and prevailing ideological-political orthodoxies.

The likelihood of a close Russian-Chinese alignment in the foreseeable future is remote. As has been noted, there is very little that will draw these two nations together. Moreover, two massive states that are caused to live cheek by jowl beside each other with few buffer states separating them, and under conditions of major differences in culture, stage of development, and degree of military power, can be closely aligned only when they have a common enemy. The United States will not play that role again.

On the other hand, conditions now and in the near future argue strongly against a state of militant Russian-Chinese hostility. The costs of such a condition to both parties were graphically illustrated in the 1960s and 1970s. Above all, these two societies desperately need relief from heavy military expenses and situations where they are cut off from some part—any part—of external sources that might provide incremental support to economic development. Whatever its limitations, Russia can gain from economic interaction with China, and vice versa. Moreover, their cooperation, first, in not allowing third parties to play one off against the other, and second, in working together to reduce the threats posed by regional crises, can be very important to their own stability as well as that of others.

Since the old Soviet Union has been dissolved and the precise relationship of the republics in the Commonwealth of Independent States has not yet taken final shape, China like other nations faces a new set of problems that cannot be clearly discerned now. Similarly, the division of China into warring regions as occurred in the 1920s and 1930s would pose the Russian Republic and all other states with very troublesome issues. Developments in one country can have an enormous bearing upon the policy options of other nations today, and nowhere is the domestic scene more volatile than in the old Leninist nations.

There is an alternative future for both Russia and China—one very different from that of stagnation or disintegration. It is possible that at some point in the twenty-first century, China will emerge as a major power, having harnessed its very considerable human resources to a successful economic strategy with political stability and military strength achieved in the course of development. In that event, all neighboring states might have to worry about the resurgence of the

"Central Kingdom" mentality—a state of mind that remains powerful in this extraordinary society, vigorous denials of any ambition for hegemony by current leaders notwithstanding.

As we have noted, moreover, the Russian Republic has extremely rich resources and the potential for sustained growth under proper economic, social, and political policies. Here, cultural changes of major proportions will also be necessary to bring a people into rapport with modernity who have known only minimalism in most fields for a very long time, and who went from traditionalism to Stalinism with a most limited interval.

Yet a society that has produced Tolstoy, Dostoevsky, Sakharov, and a multitude of other talented people in technical and scientific as well as artistic fields has enormous human resources to be tapped. And Russia is not hampered by the burdens of a huge population. It is entirely possible that at some point in the twenty-first century, this will be a center of power again, it is hoped with a different political and economic ethic.

A truly strong Russia and China would confront each other as well as the rest of the world with new issues, as would also be the case if one, but not the other, successfully negotiated the difficult road to advanced and balanced development. For the coming decades, however, both Russia and China must concentrate on making up for lost time—a loss caused by the errors of leaders now dead and the shortcomings of a system now being set aside. Engaged in such an enterprise, they cannot afford either to return to alliance or to expend resources upon hostility. Suspicions will remain on both sides, but accommodation cushioned by other more important relations is the logical course.

Notes

1. For Soviet perspectives, see M.S. Kapitsa, *The CPR: Two Decades—Two Policies* (1969), translated in Joint Publications Research Service (JPRS) 51425, September 22, 1970; O.B. Borisov and B.T. Koloskov, *Soviet-Chinese Relations, 1945–1970* (Moscow: MYSL Publishing House, 1971). Among American studies, see O. Edmund Clubb, *China and Russia: The Great Game* (New York: Columbia University Press, 1971); and A. Doak Barnett, *China and the Major Powers in East Asia* (Washington, D.C.: The Brookings Institution, 1977).

2. For a very insightful Chinese view, see Wang Jisi, "U.S. Perceptions of the Chinese Communist–Soviet Relationship and its China Policy—1947–1950," unpublished manuscript written for St. Antony's College, Oxford University.

3. This author and his research assistants have gone through many Chinese Communist publications of the wartime and early postwar periods without finding any evidence of a critical approach to Soviet leadership or policies, or significant deviations from the international communist positions. To be sure, these are official documents for the most part, not "in-house" memoranda.

4. For an official perspective of the Truman administration, see *United States Relations with China—With Special Reference to the Period 1944–1949* (Washington, D.C.: U.S. Government Printing Office). This work is often referred to as *The White Paper*.

5. See Kapitsa, *The CPR: Two Decades*.

6. Two classic works on the Sino-Soviet split are Donald S. Zagoria, *The Sino-Soviet Conflict—1956–1961* (Princeton, NJ: Princeton University Press, 1962); and William E. Griffith, *The Sino-Soviet Rift* (Cambridge, MA: MIT Press, 1964).

7. An accurate, succinct summary of the events in Sino-Soviet relations in the period after the initial cleavage can be found in the fine article by Steven M. Goldstein, "Diplomacy Amid Protest: The Sino-Soviet Summit," *Problems of Communism* (September–October 1989), pp. 49–71.

8. For works that provide details on this period, including American and Chinese views and foreign policymaking processes, see A. Doak Barnett, *The Making of Foreign Policy in China: Structure and Process* (Boulder, CO: Westview Press, 1985); Yufan Hao and Guocang Huan, eds., *The Chinese View of the World* (New York: Pantheon Press, 1989); Harry Harding, ed., *China's Foreign Relations in the 1980s* (New Haven, CT: Yale University Press, 1984); Samuel S. Kim, ed., *China and the World: Chinese Foreign Policy in the Post-Mao Era* (Boulder, CO: Westview Press, 1984); and Robert A. Scalapino, "China's Foreign Policy: Coming of Age," in Joyce K. Kallgren, ed., *Building a Nation-State—China after Forty Years* (Berkeley, CA: Institute of East Asian Studies, 1990).

9. For one extraordinarily interesting article on the situation in the Soviet Union in early 1991, see Aleksey Kiva, "Under the Spell of Maximalism—On the Political Situation in the Country after the Fourth Congress of USSR People's Deputies and the Events in the Baltic," *Izvestiya*, January 25, 1991, p. 3, translated in Foreign Broadcast Information Service, Soviet Union (hereafter *FBIS-SOV*), 91–68, January 28, 1991, pp. 28–31.

10. Developments in Soviet strategic thinking and the debate over key issues up to 1989 are set forth in a paper prepared by the staff of the American Committee on U.S.-Soviet Relations entitled, *The Soviet Defense Debate: A Review Essay*, no. 12, September 1989. The paper is edited and contains an introduction by Linton H. Bishop, and there are extensive translations of the writings of Alexei Arbatov and Major-General Y. Liubimov. For Western and Japanese perspectives, see Andrew Mack and Paul Keal, eds., *Security and Arms Control in the North Pacific* (Boston, MA: Allen and Unwin, 1988); Robert O'Neill, "The Balance of Power in the Pacific," *Pacific Review*, vol. 1, no. 2, 1988; Masahiko Asada, "Confidence-Building Measures in East Asia: A Japanese Perspective," *Asian Survey*, May 1988; and Banning Garrett and Bonnie Glaser, "U.S.-Soviet Military Competition in Northeast Asia: The Case for Confidence-Building Measures," a paper presented at a symposium sponsored by the National Defense University, March 10–13, 1989, in Honolulu.

11. For a detailed discussion of Sino-Soviet economic relations, see Yang Shouzheng, "Development of Sino-Soviet Economic and Trade Relations and Its Impacts on North East Asia and Asia-Pacific Region," *Foreign Affairs Journal* (December 1990), pp. 26–49.

12. Ibid., p. 27. See also R. Sean Randolph, "The Soviet Economic Role in Asia and the Pacific—A Business Perspective," *Asian Survey* (December 1990), pp. 1169–1185.

13. Yang, "Development of Sino-Soviet Economic and Trade Relations," p. 27.

14. Randolph, "The Soviet Economic Role in Asia and the Pacific," p. 1170.

15. For the details, see "Building Confidence with China," *Vestnik* (June 1990), pp. 18–23; and "The Long-term Programme for Economic and Scientific and Technological Cooperation between the USSR and the PRC," *Vestnik* (June 1990), pp. 23–26.

16. See Xu Kui, "The Prospects of Sino-Soviet Relations," *Foreign Affairs Journal*, no. 12 (June 1989), pp. 28–37; also Henry Trofimenko, "Long-Term Trends in the Asia-Pacific Region," *Asian Survey*, March 1989, pp. 237–251.

17. See Robert A. Scalapino, *The Last Leninists—The Uncertain Future of Asia's Communist States* (Washington, D.C.: Center for Strategic and International Studies, 1992).

18. In the *Izvestiya* article cited earlier, Kiva lashed out at the "extremists" on both the conservative side and the democratic Left. Alternatively using logic and sarcasm, he accused "the extreme Right" of having been servile in the Brezhnev era when the Russian people were being condemned to a pitiful existence and "criminal waste" was taking place in the arms race. But he also pilloried the "Left" for their total lack of sensitivity to the situation in the country. When they criticize Gorbachev, upon whom do they count to advance their cause? The army? The KGB? The MVD? Continuing, Kiva asserted, "I think the left has failed to comprehend the role of the center in the political life of any country. The totalitarian thinking we inherited from Bolshevism often prejudices us against centrists, who are supposedly unable to make up their minds and 'swing' between left and right, getting in the way of both sides." It is the center that will determine the fate of *perestroika*, Kiva asserted, and subsequently he outlined the two "dense knots of problems" that had to be unraveled: an empire must be turned into a "normal multinational state," and "the administrative edict system" must be dismantled, with the "building of a normal society in its place." Although events have overtaken Kiva in many respects, his article remains a superb political tract.

19. For excellent, detailed materials on the Chinese debate over economic policies, see the translations of articles, with editor's introduction, published in *Chinese Economic Studies*, a quarterly put out by M.E. Sharpe, Publishers, Armonk, New York.

20. For a more extensive discussion of the authoritarian-pluralist system, see Robert A. Scalapino, *The Politics of Development: Perspectives on Twentieth Century Asia* (Cambridge, MA: Harvard University Press, 1989).

21. For a perspective on Soviet-Chinese relations in the recent past from the former head of the Asian division of the USSR Foreign Ministry and the current director of the Institute of Oriental Studies, see Mikhail S. Kapitsa, "Yalta System and After: Stability and Change in Northeast Asia," *Korean Journal of International Studies* (Winter 1990), pp. 497–521.

22. For a detailed account of USSR arms reduction plans in East Asia, see Dmitry V. Petrov, "Perestroika and Changes in the USSR's Approaches to the Post-Yalta Situation in Northeast Asia," *Korean Journal of International Studies* (Winter 1990), pp. 497–521, specifically, pp. 505–506.

23. For a general discussion of Soviet policies, economic, political, and strategic, for the Asian-Pacific region, see the speech by Foreign Minister Eduard A. Shevardnadze, delivered at Vladivostok on September 4, 1990, in connection with the Second Vladivostok Conference.

24. Petrov, "Perestroika and Changes," p. 506. See also Alexander O. Bogomolov, "Implications of Political and Economic Changes in Northeast Asia on the USSR Policy in the Region," a paper prepared for the Conference on Economic and Security Affairs in Northeast Asia, sponsored by the Atlantic Council, Washington, D.C., May, 14–16, 1990; Alexei Bogaturov and Mikhail Nosov, "The Asian-Pacific Region and Soviet-American Relations," *International Affairs* (February 1990), pp. 109–117.

25. In *The Military Balance—1990–1991*, published by the International Institute for Strategic Studies, London, it is asserted that the old statistics on percentage of Soviet GNP spent on the military were based on incorrect evaluations of total GNP, and that with production much lower than previously estimated, military expenditures may have been running as high as 25- 30 percent of GNP (pp. 42–43).

26. For the background, see Yasue Katori, "Japanese-Soviet Relations: Past, Present, and Future," *Japan Review of International Affairs* (Fall/Winter 1990), pp. 127–140; Andrew Mack and Martin O'Hare, "Moscow, Tokyo and the Northern Territories Dispute," *Asian Survey*, vol. 30, no. 4 (April 1990), pp. 380–394.

27. On Soviet policy toward the Korean peninsula, see Vladimir I. Ivanov, "Soviet Policy and the Korean Peninsula: Is the Cold War Over?" a paper presented at the conference sponsored by the University of Hawaii at Manoa and the East–West Center, August 19–21, 1990. For the background relating to the North, see Robert A. Scalapino and Hongkoo Lee, eds., *North Korea in a Regional and Global Context* (Korea Research Monograph No. 11, Berkeley: Institute of East Asian Studies, 1986). Also, see Chongsik Lee and Se-Hee Yoo, eds., *North Korea in Transition* (Berkeley: Institute of East Asian Studies, 1991).

28. For opposing American views on naval arms control, see Richard Fieldhouse, "The Case for Naval Arms Control," *Arms Control Today* (February 1990), pp. 9–15; and James R. Blaker, "Naval Arms Control: The Opposition," in ibid., pp. 16–20. For a second opponent, see Kenneth L. Adelman, "Arms Control in Asia," unpublished paper, January 8, 1990.

29. In addition to the articles previously cited, see Rajan Menon, "New Thinking and Northeast Asian Security," *Problems of Communism* (March–June 1989), pp. 1–29; Vladilen Vorontsov, "Far East: The USSR and Its Neighbours," *Far Eastern Affairs*, vol. 1, no. 6 (1990), pp. 1–9; and R.A. Aliev, "National Interests of the USSR in the Asia-Pacific Region: From Security Policy to the Policy of Cooperation," September 1990, unpublished paper for the Second Vladivostok Conference.

8

"More Friends, Fewer Enemies": Vietnam's Policy toward Indochina–ASEAN Reconciliation

William S. Turley

For decades, the main line of division in Southeast Asia ran between Vietnam and its non-communist neighbors. That division narrowed slightly following the Second Indochina War, but it widened again when Vietnam intervened in Cambodia in December 1978. From that time onward the Cambodian conflict was the main stumbling block to reconciliation between Vietnam and its Indochinese allies on one side, and the Association of Southeast Asian Nations (ASEAN) on the other. Although that conflict was primarily a contest between China and Vietnam over the latter's hegemony in Indochina, ASEAN became involved because Vietnam's military presence in Cambodia jeopardized the security of a member, Thailand, and drew distrusted communist powers into regional affairs more deeply than ever before. Reconciliation was deferred while Vietnam and ASEAN sought incompatible objectives in Cambodia.

Then, in the late 1980s, superpower détente, the contraction of Soviet power, upheaval in Eastern Europe, and Sino-Soviet normalization reduced the importance of the Cambodian conflict in the priorities of all external parties, encouraging them to disengage from or circumvent it as they responded to challenges and opportunities presented by the Cold War's end. This trend could not alone end the fighting or bring about a comprehensive peace settlement of what had become a predominantly civil conflict, but at least it permitted regional powers to resume their search for reconciliation.

This chapter examines the "localization" of the Cambodian conflict as the Cold War subsides, Vietnam's foreign policy adjustments to a much changed international situation, and prospects for reconciliation between Indochina and the six members of ASEAN. For Vietnam, reconciliation with ASEAN and integration into the Pacific rim economy are necessary for the success of domestic reform (*doi moi*—"renovation"—in Vietnamese), but they come at the price of diminished political and military predominance in Indochina. To formulate an effective policy response to the new situation, Hanoi must somehow resolve the tension between its economic requirements and security needs. The way in which it does this will fix Vietnamese relations with regional neighbors as well as with the Soviet Union, China, and the United States for a long time to come.

The Path to War

The historical and geopolitical sources of a conflict situation in Cambodia are by now well known. Though the Vietnamese, Cambodian, and Laotian communist parties shared origins in the Indochinese Communist party, Vietnamese pretentions to lead the three communist revolutions clashed with Cambodian nationalism. Even before the Vietnam War ended, the Vietnamese and Khmer communist parties diverged over questions of ideology, territory, and postwar relations. Differences of doctrine and experience on the road to power, exacerbated by an ancient enmity and Khmer xenophobia, drove them apart. Local factors contributing to conflict included factionalism in the Khmer communist movement, a weakly integrated political system under Prince Norodom Sihanouk, and the Vietnamese Communists' use of Cambodian territory with Sihanouk's blessing for supply and sanctuary during their war for reunification.

In the late 1960s, Khmer communists, especially those loyal to Pol Pot, perceived Hanoi's conciliation of Prince Sihanouk as a betrayal of revolutionary solidarity and deeply resented what they saw as efforts by Hanoi to manipulate their internal affairs. As early as mid-1971, the Khmer Rouge began attacking communist Vietnamese armed forces then stationed in eastern Cambodia as part of an effort to purge their movement of Vietnamese and Sihanoukist influences.[1] At war's end in 1975, Vietnamese reluctance to discuss border issues and the slow pace of Vietnamese withdrawal from bases on Cambodian territory further aroused Khmer suspicions. When Hanoi proposed that all three countries of Indochina "preserve and develop" a "special relationship," the Khmer felt their fears of Vietnamese hegemony had been confirmed. For reasons that remain obscure, but most likely to impress upon Hanoi the seriousness of its territorial claims in the Mekong delta and determination to remain outside any Hanoi-led bloc, Phnom Penh launched commando raids into Vietnam, which provoked counterthrusts by Hanoi. Following a major incursion by Vietnamese forces in December 1977, Phnom Penh severed diplomatic relations.

Tensions between the Khmer and Vietnamese blended with the Sino-Soviet rivalry for power from the outset. In 1970, when General Lon Nol ousted Prince

Sihanouk, Moscow maintained diplomatic relations with the U.S.-supported Lon Nol government while Beijing arranged an alliance between Sihanouk and the Khmer Rouge. After 1975, China feared that the USSR might exploit Khmer-Vietnamese differences and attempted to mediate the conflict, but the open rupture between Phnom Penh and Hanoi forced Beijing to choose sides. In February 1978, China denounced "hegemony" in the region and began shipping heavy artillery and other arms to its Cambodian ally. This shift in the Chinese stance seemed to confirm, for the Vietnamese, that Cambodia was the instrument of Beijing's aim to dominate all of Indochina. The Soviet Union, for its part, apparently indicated approval if Vietnam chose to remove this threat by forcibly eliminating the Pol Pot regime.[2] Though Khmer depredations alone were sufficiently compelling reason for Hanoi to adopt this course, Moscow must have foreseen that if Hanoi thus defied China it would have to strengthen ties with the USSR as Moscow wished.

In early spring 1978, Vietnam began recruiting refugees to join a dissident Khmer army. In June 1978 it accepted Moscow's offer to join the Council for Mutual Economic Assistance (CMEA), provoking China to suspend all remaining aid, and in November Hanoi signed a Treaty of Friendship and Cooperation with Moscow. Thus both Phnom Penh and Hanoi had the reassurance of rival great powers when Vietnamese forces entered Cambodia on December 25, 1978.

The fighting initially pitted up to 200,000 conventionally organized and equipped men of the Vietnamese army against the dispersed irregular units of the Khmer Rouge. At the outset an interstate war, with each of the contestants heavily dependent on the material support of another power, the conflict gradually acquired a civil dimension as the Vietnamese created a new Khmer government in Phnom Penh, the People's Republic of Kampuchea (PRK), and a Khmer army, the Kampuchean People's Revolutionary Armed Force (KPRAF). Though as creations of the Vietnamese the PRK and KPRAF lacked nationalist credibility, they provided rallying points against the hated Khmer Rouge. To shore up domestic and international opposition to Vietnam (and by extension the PRK), ASEAN and China arranged in 1982 for the small non-communist resistance organizations headed by Prince Sihanouk and Son Sann to join with the Khmer Rouge in forming the Coalition Government of Democratic Kampuchea (CGDK). This fig leaf of respectability helped Democratic Kampuchea, as the Khmer Rouge regime was formally named, to retain Cambodia's seat at the United Nations.

From a numerical and material standpoint, Vietnam and the PRK had an overwhelming advantage. Though the Vietnamese force level slowly declined, the KPRAF (renamed the Cambodian People's Armed Force, or CPAF, in October 1989) gradually acquired some 80 Soviet T-54 and T-59 tanks, 350 pieces of towed artillery, and a squadron of Mig-21s—hardware that resistance forces lacked.[3] Moreover, with direct access to Cambodia's population centers, the CPAF was able by the end of the decade to build a regular army of around

50,000[4] and a village militia estimated by the U.S. Department of Defense at 100,000.[5] On the CGDK side, by far the most effective military element was the Khmer Rouge, whose numbers stabilized during the late 1980s at around 45,000, including porters. Of 25,000 men actually under arms, a significantly smaller number, perhaps only 7,000 to 8,000, could be considered hard-core troops.[6] The largest non-communist faction in the CGDK was the Khmer People's National Liberation Front (KPNLF) until factional quarreling and morale problems reduced its troop strength to about 10,000 or even fewer.[7] Originally pulled together from bands of thugs and smugglers infesting the border camps early in the war, many KPNLF commanders were more deeply engaged in the border black market than in fighting. Sihanouk's force, the Armée Nationale Sihanoukiste (ANS), claimed by fall of 1989 to have nearly 22,000 combatants but also had problems of cohesion and quality.[8]

Real capabilities, however, depended heavily on outside support. So long as Vietnamese units were involved, the resistance could do little more than make forays a short distance into Cambodia from a string of camps along the Thai border. But neither could Vietnam and Phnom Penh completely suppress the resistance so long as it received weapons and supplies from abroad and enjoyed sanctuary in Thailand. Involvement by external parties assured a stalemate. Were that involvement to end, the only certainty was that either the Khmer Rouge or Phnom Penh, not the non-communist factions, would prevail.

Immediately following the Vietnamese troop withdrawal on September 26, 1989, resistance forces escalated their attacks into a "General Offensive." The gem mining district of Pailin and the mountain redoubt of Phnom Malai soon fell to the Khmer Rouge, while non-communist forces successfully attacked a number of isolated outposts. Pailin was a strategic prize, as the licensing of gem miners gave the Khmer Rouge an independent source of income of up to $5 million a month.[9] But the nature of the fighting and conditions inside the country made it difficult to know accurately how well any faction was doing. During the dry seasons, Phnom Penh forces used their superior numbers, equipment, and artillery to good effect, but resistance forces, particularly the Khmer Rouge, gradually extended their range of operations. In early 1991, one knowledgable journalist described a "vast network of roads, which allows them [the Khmer Rouge] to send supplies deep inside the country."[10]

However, anticipating a political settlement and goaded by China, the Khmer Rouge apparently decided to suspend large-scale military operations and concentrate more on political agitation. By most accounts, the Khmer Rouge had enjoyed a political comeback thanks to their superior discipline, village-based organization, and absence of corruption compared with all other factions, while Phnom Penh had squandered much good will through sheer incompetence and forced conscription. Some analysts guessed that the Khmer Rouge could win 20 percent of the votes in an election.[11] But Phnom Penh still possessed the stronger conventional forces, and in March 1991 the CPAF mounted artillery-supported (and, apparently, Mig-21-supported) operations against several Khmer Rouge strongholds, forcing the Khmer Rouge to withdraw temporarily from Pailin in early April. Whether Phnom Penh had rolled back Khmer Rouge main units to the Thai border alone or with help from the 12,000 Vietnamese troops estimated by diplomatic sources to be secretly in the country,[12] another round of diplomacy began with neither side holding a decisive advantage.

Vietnamese Perceptions and Strategy

Whether defined as invasion or intervention, the swift advance of the Vietnamese army across a neighbor's boundary and destruction of a sovereign state provoked coordinated opposition from China, ASEAN, the United States, Japan, and Western Europe. Calculating that the world would not come to the defense of the genocidal Pol Pot regime, Hanoi underestimated the fear in ASEAN capitals and outrage in China that its action would provoke. ASEAN, China, the West, and Japan coordinated to impose diplomatic and economic sanctions on Vietnam. In addition, China launched a punitive attack across Vietnam's northern border in February–March 1979 and connived with Thailand to supply the Khmer Rouge.

These pressures exacted a high price for Vietnam's toppling of a neighboring government, but it is doubtful that Hanoi would have let events take their course in Cambodia had it gauged the cost of intervention more accurately. For Vietnamese leaders, certain lessons with implications for Vietnam's vital interests were as compelling as the Munich analogy for a generation of leaders in the West. The most important of these lessons, gained in wars with France and the United States, was that Vietnam's security, independence, and unity depended on Laos and Cambodia having stable governments friendly to Vietnam. The need to confront the French in all of Indochina had been apparent to Vietnamese leaders in the 1930s, and the lesson was driven home by French and American use of Laos and Cambodia to attack vital lines of supply and communication between northern and southern Vietnam. As early as 1950, the Vietnamese formulated the doctrine that Indochina comprised a "single strategic unit" because for geostrategic reasons Vietnam's enemies would always have to treat it as one. As General Vo Nguyen Giap put it, "we cannot consider Vietnam to be independent so long as Cambodia and Laos are under imperialist domination, just as we cannot consider Cambodia and Laos to be independent so long as Vietnam is under imperialist rule."[13] Over thirty years later, the commander of Vietnamese forces in Cambodia put it this way:

> Experience over more than half a century on the Indochinese peninsula shows that the aggressive plots of the Japanese fascists, French colonialists, and U.S. imperialists as well as the Chinese expansionists and hegemonists down to the present have always treated Indochina as a target of aggression and a unified

battleground. . . . In their plots to annex Indochina and expand into Southeast Asia, the Beijing reactionaries cannot help but follow this law.[14]

This "law" implied that Vietnam was not safe so long as Laos or Cambodia were under the influence of any power hostile to Vietnam, and that all three states of Indochina were interdependent in matters of security. In 1978 the Vietnamese could not but view Chinese support for the Khmer Rouge as the third attempt by a great power in modern times—if China is considered one in regional context—to encircle and attack Vietnam from the west.

Like statesmen and generals everywhere, Vietnamese leaders were arguably the victims of their own lessons. Perceiving hostile or potentially hostile powers treating Indochina as a single strategic unit, Hanoi treated it the same way, provoking Phnom Penh to seek safety in an alliance with China that increased the threat to Vietnam, driving Hanoi into the arms of Moscow, and so forth, in a spiral of progressively intensifying antagonism. But the fact remains that the Vietnamese entered Cambodia and were willing to pay any price to defend, as they saw it, their own national security.

Vietnam's strategy was to cement a "special relationship" with Cambodia, like the one Vietnam already had with Laos, in order to strengthen "security interdependence" among the three countries. Vietnamese leaders recognized that this objective could not be realized through permanent occupation and that Vietnam's security in the long term depended on the construction of governments in Laos and Cambodia that were self-reliant as well as aligned with Hanoi. Regarding Cambodia, Vietnam's foreign minister Nguyen Co Thach acknowledged two "traps": Khmer dependency that required interminable Vietnamese military involvement; and premature withdrawal that permitted the Khmer Rouge—and behind them the Chinese—to return.[15] It was partly to avert the first trap that Hanoi announced in February 1982 "annual partial withdrawals" of Vietnamese troops. Hanoi fully expected some deterioration of Phnom Penh's military position as its troops withdrew and counted on this to make the Cambodians defend themselves. And it was partly to avert the second trap that Vietnamese forces launched devastating attacks along the Thai border during the 1985–86 dry season to demolish all major encampments of the CGDK and thus pave the way for the total withdrawal that Hanoi announced would take place by the end of 1990. Following those attacks, Phnom Penh pushed to consolidate the PRK apparatus at all levels, particularly in the densely populated basin around the Great Lake. With control of the overwhelming bulk of Cambodia's resources in this "inland front," Vietnamese strategists calculated, Phnom Penh would be able to cope with continued small-scale fighting along the "border front" with reduced Vietnamese assistance.[16] Schemes for economic integration complemented this strategy, with a view to assuring the survival of the PRK in alliance with Vietnam.

Gradually, Hanoi reckoned, the world would come to accept its *fait accompli.*

Its troop withdrawals certainly did not signify preparedness to accept Phnom Penh's outright military defeat or dissolution in a negotiated settlement. Though official discourse substituted "special relations of solidarity and friendship" for "special relationship," Hanoi clearly expected to maintain privileged access to its neighbors.

This strategy staked its success on Phnom Penh forces' holding their ground, or most of it, once the Vietnamese had withdrawn. But even the Vietnamese lacked confidence in the ability of these forces to hold out for long unaided.[17] The strategy therefore counted on the troop withdrawal to trigger a shift in international attention away from the conflict altogether or to the problem of preventing a Khmer Rouge return to power. Either way, international support for the resistance was likely to weaken, thus facilitating if not Phnom Penh's supremacy, then the maintenance of a balance. If the conflict dragged on, then Vietnam's withdrawal would have met the principal condition for the improvement of relations with China, ASEAN, the West, and Japan. Over the long term, Hanoi expected to salvage most of its intervention goals.

Toward ASEAN, this strategy implied a waiting game in expectation that contradictory threat perceptions, particularly regarding China, or preoccupation with internal security eventually would crack the association's unity. At the same time, Hanoi played upon Indonesian and Malaysian fears regarding great power intrusions into regional affairs by declaring support for the Zone of Peace, Freedom, and Neutrality (ZOPFAN) and Nuclear Weapons Free Zone (NWFZ), "pending a solution to the Cambodian problem,"[18] when these proposals re-emerged as priority items on ASEAN's agenda in 1984. This stance was a complete reversal of Hanoi's position in the immediate postwar period (1975–76), when it excoriated ASEAN as an anti-Vietnamese alliance and tool of imperialism.

The "Strategic Triangle" and Indochina

The Cambodian conflict might not have attracted as much attention from the Soviet Union, China, and the United States as it did, and almost certainly not so much direct involvement, had it not begun at a time of intense rivalry between the two communist great powers.[19] To offset what it perceived as an expansionist drive by Moscow, Beijing in the early 1970s had ended over twenty years of estrangement from the United States and welcomed a continued American military presence in Asia. But the American withdrawal from Vietnam left Beijing and Moscow as competitors to fill the resulting vacuum in Indochina. Facing a half-million Soviet troops arrayed along its northern border, Beijing was intensely anxious to exclude Soviet influence from China's southern flank. In this context Vietnam could not develop close ties to the Soviet Union, or advance its own interests in Cambodia while aligned with Moscow, without provoking China's ire.

By the time China invaded Vietnam in February 1979, Beijing's anger focused on disputes over their common land border and overlapping claims in the Gulf of Tonkin and South China Sea, Vietnamese economic policies that caused the exodus of "Hoa" people, Vietnam's close relationship with the USSR, and Hanoi's pursuit of "regional hegemony," which Beijing later identified as the "fundamental cause for the deterioration of relations between the two countries."[20] But its most urgent concern in attacking Vietnam in 1979 was Soviet penetration of a traditional sphere of Chinese influence. Though certain specific issues acted as both catalysts and symptoms of conflict escalation, Chinese policy toward Vietnam was primarily a response to the latter's relations with China's "principal enemy" of the moment.[21]

The strategy China subsequently pursued focused on Vietnam's installation of a client regime in Phnom Penh, the presence of Vietnamese troops in Cambodia, and the challenges these actions plus Soviet involvement posed to China's security and prestige. For a long time after its attack in 1979, China applied military pressures on its border with Vietnam to tie down Vietnamese armed forces in the north and "bleed" the Vietnamese economy. In Cambodia, Beijing counseled the Khmer Rouge to wage a protracted guerrilla war that would bog down the Vietnamese in a costly war of indefinite duration and drain resources from the Soviet Union. Beijing's initial, uncompromising demand for complete and unconditional withdrawal of Vietnamese troops was crafted to delay settlement until Vietnam had been weakened and Soviet determination had diminished.[22] To implement this strategy, China had to suspend its support of insurgencies in the ASEAN countries in exchange for improved state-to-state relations, particularly with the "front-line state," Thailand. Chinese arms and equipment then moved across Thai territory to the Khmer Rouge and later, in smaller quantities, to the non-communist resistance factions as well. The conflict thus provided China with an unprecedented opportunity to overcome its isolation from the ASEAN states, to enlist these states in Beijing's effort to bring Vietnam to heel, to contain Soviet influence in Indochina, and to play the guarantor of peace and stability in the region.

The Soviet Union's orientation was an outgrowth of its competitive bidding with Beijing for Hanoi's loyalty in the Sino-Soviet dispute and the Brezhnev regime's belief after 1975 that the United States had lost the will to oppose the expansion of Soviet-supported socialism. In Indochina, Hanoi's sense of beleaguerment and security aims in Cambodia coincided with Soviet global strategic priorities vis-à-vis China and the West. Vietnam's need of support provided Moscow an opportunity to block Chinese access to Indochina and to exercise influence in a region from which it was otherwise excluded. In return for that support, Moscow in March 1979 obtained the use of base facilities at Cam Ranh Bay and, in 1980, an airfield at Danang, which extended the reach of Soviet naval and air reconnaissance into the Indian Ocean and Persian Gulf. Moscow and Hanoi's shared hostility toward China and China's friend, the United States, thus cemented the Soviet-Vietnamese alliance and gave the Soviet Union its most important strategic gain since the end of the Second World War.

Vietnam could not have built the world's fourth largest army and maintained as large an occupation force in Cambodia as it did without very significant Soviet (and East European) assistance. While China, Japan, and virtually all Western countries suspended aid and severed trade links with Vietnam, Soviet economic aid in the early 1980s averaged over U.S. $1 billion annually and supplied all of Vietnam's requirements of fuel and lubricants, 90 percent of its steel, 90 percent of its nitrogenous fertilizers, and large proportions of other crucial commodities.[23] The estimated current dollar value of total military assistance to Vietnam, overwhelmingly from the Soviet Union, shot up from $100 million in 1977 to $3.4 billion in 1979 and averaged nearly $1.7 billion a year from then until 1987.[24] Soviet economic and military aid together accounted for about 20 percent of the country's GNP.[25] The Soviet Union also granted non-refundable aid directly to the Phnom Penh regime, amounting to U.S. $134 million in 1979–80.[26] Diplomatically, too, Moscow gave unstinting support to Hanoi's proposals to negotiate, based on the assumption that the Vietnamese-installed regime in Phnom Penh eventually would gain acceptance as a legitimate alternative to the Khmer Rouge.

For the United States, the Cambodian conflict presented a threat to Thailand (a treaty ally), a challenge to American reliability in Southeast Asia, and an opportunity to consolidate a tacit alliance with China against the Soviet Union. Though constrained domestically from becoming directly involved on a large scale, the United States tightened the economic embargo on Vietnam, expanded its naval and air capabilities in the Pacific, and increased arms sales to the ASEAN countries as part of the larger United States strategic aim of containing Soviet expansionism. At first strongly supportive of China's intransigent position, Washington adjusted its stance (under congressional pressure) to avoid appearing to support the Khmer Rouge or facilitating the spread of Chinese influence into Southeast Asia. But United States support was vital in stiffening ASEAN resolve to maintain military, diplomatic, and economic pressures on Vietnam. After 1982, the United States channeled about $5 million in overt aid and up to $24 million in covert aid annually to the non-communist factions of the Khmer resistance through an ASEAN-sponsored Working Group to maintain a non–Khmer Rouge alternative to the Vietnamese occupation.[27] Shared concern for the Soviet threat thus united the United States and China against Vietnam and brought the United States back into the region as a guarantor for ASEAN.

Emphasis on the "strategic triangle," which makes the conflict seem a proxy war, is neither complete nor satisfactory, however. Khmer Rouge forces had attacked Vietnamese territory and civilian population even before Pol Pot was assured of China's support, and Hanoi was prepared to respond with or without a Soviet guarantee and regardless of Phnom Penh's ties to Beijing. Moreover, Sino-Vietnamese relations contained unresolved bilateral tensions quite apart from the issue of Cambodia. And while the Sino-Soviet dispute intensified Beijing's concern for security on its periphery, China had always sought to exercise paramount influence in Indochina, at odds with Vietnam's own preeminence in the Laotian and Cambodian revolutions. Finally, ASEAN's confrontation with Vietnam masked a Thai-Vietnamese struggle, as Bangkok sought to restore Cambodia to its historical role of neutral buffer. Among the non-Khmer parties, Bangkok and Hanoi had as much potential as any great power to shape the outcome through capitulation.[28]

Still, the "triangle" does point to two important implications. One is that the Sino-Soviet dispute was the major factor dividing Moscow from Beijing over Cambodia and determining the level of their commitment to opposed sides in Indochina. It also assured the United States and ASEAN, along with other Western countries and Japan, of Chinese cooperation in imposing a crippling isolation on Vietnam and, by extension, a heavy burden on the USSR. From this it followed that Sino-Soviet relations would have the central role in shaping the international structure of the conflict. Second, the triangular dynamic for a long time gave all three powers as much interest in continuing the conflict as in ending it. The Soviet Union was assured of military access to Vietnam so long as Vietnam was dependent on the USSR for vital support of its intervention in Cambodia. And protracting the war enabled China and the United States to make the Soviet Union pay a heavy price for its expansionism. Even Thailand, the supposedly threatened "front-line" state, could take satisfaction from the economic debilitation of Vietnam while it itself grew strong and prosperous. This configuration of interests contributed to a situation that one analyst aptly described as "the stable war"[29] and another noted was "moderately pleasing . . . to all the major powers."[30]

The Changing International Structure of Conflict

For a decade, the terms that most aptly described efforts to end the Cambodian conflict were impasse, stalemate, and deadlock. The sustained support of China and the Soviet Union for the Khmer Rouge and Vietnamese respectively prevented outright military victory by either side or movement toward compromise in a negotiated settlement. Shifts that would lead to talks, however, began with indications in 1982 of Soviet interest in repairing relations with China. China reciprocated the following year by expressing willingness to resume negotiations with Vietnam on the normalization of relations in step with Vietnamese troop withdrawals from Cambodia, an offer that linked Moscow's interest to pressure on Vietnam. But the sharpest turn in the Sino-Soviet relationship came after Mikhail Gorbachev's ascent to power in March 1985 and his Vladivostok speech in July of the following year. Gorbachev's "new thinking" raised the pursuit of economic benefit through cooperation, a peaceful international environment, and normalization with China in Soviet priorities. From then on, Moscow's aim was to "decouple the Cambodian conflict from the progressive transformation of Sino-Soviet relations" by encouraging Vietnam to withdraw from Cambodia without damaging the Soviet reputation as a reliable security partner.[31]

Moscow appears not to have pushed Hanoi against its will into withdrawal or negotiations, and in fact Soviet economic assistance to Vietnam significantly increased for 1986–90. Pressure was not needed because Hanoi was almost certainly receptive to Moscow's urging when it came. As noted above, Vietnam recognized early on the "trap" of Phnom Penh's dependence, and the 1984–85 dry season attacks set the scene for withdrawal by a publicly announced date— before Gorbachev came to power. Moreover, Vietnamese leaders had reached a consensus by the mid-1980s on the need for radical domestic reforms. These reforms, formally adopted at the 6th Party Congress in December 1986, grew out of the manifest failure of central planning and were not simply a response to the international embargo or to *perestroika* in the Soviet Union. Market-oriented and outward-looking, the reforms gave Hanoi a shared interest with the Soviet Union in the creation of a stable, peaceful international environment in the western Pacific. As Foreign Minister Thach later put it, "Military adventures, especially military mires abroad, will pose a monumental danger to any country in the global economic and technological race." With economic growth possible only through participation in the international division of labor, Vietnam was "determined not to miss the opportunity again."[32] Finally, in nearly twelve years of the Cambodian conflict, Vietnam was to suffer 221,300 casualties, including 55,300 dead.[33] Hanoi had good reasons to seek a way out of direct, interminable involvement in Cambodia without Soviet prompting.

However, Moscow's mute response to a Chinese naval attack on the Vietnamese in the Spratly Islands in March 1988, its decision to withdraw gradually from Cam Ranh Bay, unveiled in January 1990, and a parallel one-third reduction in Soviet military assistance to Vietnam put Hanoi on notice that in the future it could not count on Soviet reassurance in the event of a major confrontation with China. Though Moscow continued a small development assistance program for Cambodia, its suspension of military aid to Phnom Penh at the end of 1990 underscored Hanoi's isolation.

Chinks also developed in the facade of ASEAN unity. ASEAN's official position was that negotiations had to take place in a framework that represented the conflict as a result of external aggression, flatly contradicting Vietnam's depiction of its intervention as defensive and humanitarian. But Indonesia and to a lesser extent Malaysia never wholeheartedly supported a stance that tolerated competitive intrusion by great powers in regional affairs and gave China an opportunity to expand its influence. Indonesia, ASEAN's largest member and self-presumed leader, also chafed at Thailand's setting the association's agenda. The gathering dissidence produced an abortive Malaysian proposal in 1985 to organize proximity talks between the PRK and CGDK, and an intensive effort by Indonesia's foreign minister, Mochtar Kusumaatmadja, to organize informal talks in 1987. Though ASEAN remained outwardly unified, growing unease in Indonesia and Malaysia regarding intrusion by extra-regional powers conflicted with the Thai interest in security through cooperation with China and the United States.

The ASEAN front collapsed, therefore, when Thai prime minister Chatichai Choonhaven proclaimed his desire in August 1988 to "turn Indochina from a battlefield into a marketplace." The slogan reflected the wish of a restive Thai business community to expand trade with neighbors and attract foreign investment. At a deeper level, it expressed growing confidence in Thailand's ability to cope with a receding threat from Vietnam. Chatichai's most dramatic move was to invite Hun Sen, premier and foreign minister of the Phnom Penh regime, for a three-day visit to Bangkok in January 1989. Intended to force the CGDK factions to participate in informal talks with Phnom Penh, the visit implicitly conceded legitimacy to the PRK regime and announced Bangkok's intention to deal directly and flexibly with all parties. Though Thailand continued to serve as the conduit both for Chinese supplies to the Khmer Rouge, and for United States, ASEAN, and Chinese supplies to the non-communist resistance, it ceased to confront Vietnam and reciprocated Hanoi's wish for improved relations even while the Cambodian conflict remained unresolved.

The Negotiating Track

The first step toward negotiations came in a July 1987 agreement between Vietnam and Indonesia, as representatives of their respective "blocs," on a format for informal talks. Talks were to take place in two phases, the first one among the Cambodians to discuss national reconciliation, the second to include Vietnam, Laos, and the ASEAN states to discuss the international aspects of settlement. The two-phase format broke the deadlock over how to represent the conflict by providing separate frameworks for discussion of internal and external dimensions. This compromise nearly foundered on Khmer Rouge obstinacy, however, until Prince Sihanouk took leave from the CGDK presidency to hold private talks with the PRK's Hun Sen in December 1987 and January 1988. Though the Sihanouk–Hun Sen talks produced no agreement, Sihanouk's apparent willingness to strike a separate deal, which would have collapsed the CGDK and removed the prince's protective legitimacy from the Khmer Rouge, jarred ASEAN, China, and the United States into adopting more flexible positions.

From these beginnings, two-phase talks began with the first Jakarta Informal Meeting (JIM-I) in late July 1988. JIM-I produced a "consensus," articulated by Indonesian foreign minister Ali Alatas, to link the withdrawal of Vietnamese forces with cessation of external assistance to the Cambodian parties, in line with Hanoi and Phnom Penh's wish. In February 1989, JIM-II reaffirmed that linkage but emphasized, as ASEAN demanded, that its execution was contingent upon a comprehensive solution including an internal settlement. However, the Jakarta meetings highlighted fundamental differences concerning the future role of the Khmer Rouge, power-sharing, and postwar governance, particularly among the Cambodians.

Meanwhile, China had agreed to direct negotiations with Vietnam, and the first official Sino-Vietnamese talks in nine years had taken place in Beijing at the vice-ministerial level in January 1989. On the understanding that the complete withdrawal of Vietnamese troops from Cambodia would remove China's chief objection to normalization, Hanoi announced at the Indochina foreign ministers' meeting on February 17 that all of its remaining troops would be withdrawn not later than the end of September of 1989 "within the framework of a political solution."[34] The two held a second round of talks on May 8–10, which resulted in "basic agreement" between them on the "international aspect" of the conflict and early convening of an international conference, though they remained far apart on the "internal aspect." That step helped Gorbachev to achieve normalization with China a week later without meeting China's previous adamant requirement that Moscow first terminate its support of Vietnam in Cambodia. For this, Hanoi was greatly relieved.[35] Sino-Soviet agreement to disagree raised hope in Hanoi that Sino-Vietnamese normalization also could be delinked from the Cambodian issue.[36]

By September 1989, Vietnamese leaders had concluded that détente among the great powers, ASEAN interest in development and regional stability, and Vietnam's imminent troop withdrawal had set the scene for a Cambodian settlement more or less on Hanoi's terms. As Foreign Minister Nguyen Co Thach put it:

> Peace, national independence, and development have become a major trend as shown in the ZOPFAN . . . concept. . . . This aspiration has been expressed in a most vehement and concrete fashion through Thai Prime Minister Chatchai's policy of "turning Indochina from a battlefield into a marketplace." Together with Indonesia's efforts for peace and with the new policy of Thailand, the struggle of the peoples of Vietnam, Laos, and Cambodia has reached a turning point in the search for a political solution to the Cambodian problem. At present, the Southeast Asian situation is very promising. Chances are that a political solution to the Cambodian problem will be achieved on the basis of a complete withdrawal of the Vietnamese volunteer army from Cambodia by September 1989 and the elimination of the genocidal Pol Pot clique in conjunction with the establishment of a zone of peace and cooperation in Southeast Asia for all countries in the region.[37]

Neither a comprehensive settlement on these terms nor delinking were to occur, however, as China along with the United States made Vietnam's assent to a "just and reasonable" Cambodian settlement a condition of normalization. While Hanoi apparently had agreed in May 1990 to Khmer Rouge participation in interim arrangements and to drop references to "genocide,"[38] talks in June 1990 broke down over details of a settlement's implementation.[39]

Efforts to get negotiations started revealed a growing tension between international interest in ending the conflict and the inability of the Khmer parties to reach any kind of agreement. This tension came out into the open at the nineteen-nation Paris International Conference on Cambodia (PICC) during July 1989. To be sure, the great powers, Vietnam, and ASEAN were not yet ready to abandon their respective Khmer allies in return for peace. Hanoi, with Soviet concurrence, held out for resolving the conflict's external aspects first, calculating that suspension of arms supplies to the Khmer Rouge in return for Vietnam's troop withdrawal would leave Phnom Penh in a position to prevail internally. And ASEAN, supported by the United States and China, insisted on linking the external and internal aspects in order to keep pressure on Hanoi to settle the latter on terms favorable to the resistance.

But the core stumbling block was the fundamental irreconcilability among the Cambodians. Following the meeting in Paris, growing consensus among the great powers contrasted with the intractability of the local parties. Beginning in January 1990, the UN Security Council "Perm-Five" held six meetings culminating on August 28, 1990, with the issuance of a five-part document outlining a framework for peace including transitional UN administration of five key ministries in Phnom Penh; military arrangements to supervise disarmament, cease-fire, and peace-keeping; elections; human rights; and international guarantees. Besides committing the great powers to a significant UN role, the Perm-Five process helped China back away from supporting a Khmer Rouge return to power by force. Ostracized for the Tiananmen incident and left behind by United States and European Community decisions to change votes on Cambodian representation at the UN, Beijing was anxious to avoid worse isolation as sole supporter of the Khmer Rouge. During a visit to Jakarta in August 1990, Chinese premier Li Peng said Beijing "will never support the Khmer Rouge to pursue power through the battlefield" and would suspend aid to all Cambodian resistance forces when the UN had confirmed Vietnam's troop withdrawal.[40] Li apparently told Thailand's Chatichai that Beijing also would not support the Khmer Rouge in a dominant role, evidently to placate the United States.[41] While not abandoning the Khmer Rouge, China thus agreed conditionally not to facilitate its outright military victory.

Among the Cambodians, Sihanouk and Hun Sen resumed their talks under Thai auspices in February 1990 and agreed on the establishment of a Supreme National Council (SNC) to embody Cambodia's sovereignty in an interim period before elections. In April, Sihanouk proposed that the SNC be composed of six representatives from each of the "two existing Cambodian governments,"[42] conceding parity between the CGDK and State of Cambodia (as the Phnom Penh regime now called itself). On this basis Sihanouk and Hun Sen met in Tokyo in early June to sign a cease-fire agreement, though without Khmer Rouge participation the gesture was meaningless. Finally, on September 9, all four factions agreed in principle to a UN framework for settlement and to the establishment of the SNC and named delegates to this body. Meeting in Paris on December 21–22 to respond to the Perm-Five "framework document," the SNC produced "agreement on most of its fundamental points,"[43] and even the Khmer Rouge declared "readiness to give our full cooperation to the UN Transitional Authority in Cambodia [UNTAC] in implementing these documents."[44]

In fact, however, the Cambodians remained deeply divided over such key issues as disarmament and demobilization in the transitional period.[45] Moreover, Phnom Penh had indicated all along that it would not accept arrangements that required it to dismantle or turn control of its administrative apparatus over to the UN. Nor did it ever cease demanding the exclusion of the top-ranked Khmer Rouge leaders from the postwar scene. In November, Hun Sen listed four "principles" by which the SOC would judge any draft agreement: (1) non-return of the genocidal regime; (2) non-dissolution of the government of the State of Cambodia; (3) non-dissolution of the Cambodian Armed Forces; and (4) non-violation of the Cambodian sovereignty by any country or international organization.[46]

On these issues Phnom Penh had Hanoi's fervent support. While it officially "welcomed" the Perm-Five document, Hanoi criticized it both for interfering in "internal questions" that were properly matters for the Cambodians themselves to decide and, somewhat contradictorily, for saying nothing, as Foreign Minister Thach put it, about the "definitive elimination of the genocidal regime."[47] Hanoi still demanded that the peace process maintain a rigid distinction between "internal" and "external aspects" of the conflict yet assure the extinction of the Khmer Rouge. Intriguingly, statements from Hanoi sometimes seemed to oppose Khmer Rouge participation more strongly than ones from Phnom Penh. In June 1990, for example, Hun Sen denied that his government had demanded the exclusion of all Khmer Rouge from a political solution and said that the fate of the "eight undesirables" (top-ranked "Polpotists") could be left for the people to decide in elections: "[S]hould they be recognized and elected by the people, it would be the people's choice and we would respect it."[48] Whatever the shades of difference between Hanoi and Phnom Penh, if any, Hanoi clearly had decided for the time being not to pressure Phnom Penh into accepting a settlement that might gain, for Hanoi, normalization of relations with China and the United States, an end to the embargo, and full access to the markets and investment of the West and Japan.

Just why Hanoi should have held back at this late date from fully approving a plan that would have permitted it to achieve such important objectives is unclear. The theory that Hanoi feared the potential of free competitive elections in Cambodia to fuel demand for the same right in Vietnam lacked plausibility considering the Vietnamese leadership's firm domestic grip and commitment to reform. If there was a domestic determinant of Hanoi's stance, it was most likely a policy rigidity arising from factional strife related to relations with China and preparations for the 7th Party Congress scheduled for June 1991. Internationally, Hanoi could not abandon Phnom Penh without sacrificing the "security interdependence" of all three Indochinese states. Vietnam's security interests in Cambodia required it to hold out for guarantees of these interests in a settlement.

Moreover, Hanoi shared Phnom Penh's deep fear and loathing of the Khmer Rouge and genuinely perceived the State of Cambodia's (SOC) administration and army as the only effective blocks to a Khmer Rouge return to power. Not unreasonably, the two allies suspected that the resistance—which after all had held Cambodia's seat in the UN and manipulated the UN with ASEAN, U.S., and Chinese help for years—would use a UN solution to undermine the SOC, paving the way for the Khmer Rouge to return behind a Sihanouk electoral victory.[49] Given Khmer Rouge military gains and Phnom Penh's gradual decay over preceding months, could even the Perm-Five provide reliable assurances that their proposed settlement would not have this dreaded outcome? Hanoi felt its only option was a solution that guaranteed the demise of the Khmer Rouge separately from elections. Elections without this guarantee involved, for Hanoi, the risk of legitimating a government presided over by Sihanouk but controlled by the Khmer Rouge.

On April 22, 1991, France and Indonesia as co-chairs of the Paris Conference, joined by UN Secretary General Javier Pérez de Cueller, appealed for a temporary cease-fire beginning May 1. Hanoi and Phnom Penh immediately "welcomed" this overture. The resistance factions also responded favorably, though four days later and with less enthusiasm, charging that Vietnam continued to station over 50,000 troops in Cambodia and could not be trusted to respect the call.[50] A very shaky truce ensued. Another meeting of the warring parties in Jakarta on June 2–4 ended inconclusively, with Phnom Penh still demanding concrete measures to prevent a Khmer Rouge return to power and a war crimes tribunal to try Khmer Rouge leaders for genocide.

Hanoi's Predicament

The importance to Hanoi of excluding the Khmer Rouge was evident in its steadfastness despite unfavorable international trends. Vietnam's economy had stagnated under the combined effects of the embargo and central planning while economies of ASEAN neighbors had boomed, widening the income gap between the region's socialists and capitalists to embarrassing proportions. At decade's end, Vietnam found itself further beleaguered by events in the socialist world. Vietnamese leaders reacted with horror to the overthrow of Eastern European regimes and disarray in the Soviet Union, which foretold an end to essential political and economic support. The shift by socialist and former socialist countries to trade in hard currencies at world market prices after January 1991 and cutbacks in assistance effectively terminated CMEA subsidization of the Vietnamese economy. Soviet aid, which had run between one and two billion dollars a year for a decade, was reduced in 1991 to $110 million.[51] Vietnamese leaders began routinely acknowledging that "complicated developments in the political and economic situation in the Soviet Union and Eastern Europe" had exacerbated Vietnam's economic difficulties.[52]

Facing the prospect of sharply declining CMEA trade and assistance while the American embargo remained in effect, Vietnam launched an almost desperate courtship of new economic partners. However, Hanoi's interest implicitly conceded leverage to the carrot-and-stick diplomacy of the United States and China. The carrot consisted of economic ties and suspension of the embargo in return for Hanoi's help in obtaining Phnom Penh's agreement to an interim UN administration and free elections; the stick was China's continued armament of the Khmer Rouge if Hanoi did not comply.

Hanoi's obvious strategy, therefore, was to delink the Cambodian issue from its drive to expand economic relations with partners wherever they could be found. In this regard Vietnam made some headway even with China after the Sino-Soviet rapprochement in May 1989. By reducing military assistance to Vietnam and reducing its presence in Cam Ranh Bay, the Soviet Union alleviated the threat that had been China's main concern in Southeast Asia since 1979 and removed much of Beijing's incentive to go on punishing Vietnam. Following the upheaval in the socialist world during 1989, Chinese leaders also began to see Vietnam as potentially sharing their interest in the preservation of socialist orthodoxy. From September 3 to 7, 1990, Vietnamese and Chinese party secretaries and prime ministers met secretly in Chengdu in an attempt to resolve differences over Cambodia, and the Chinese apparently tried to bait the Vietnamese with an aid offer.[53] A couple of weeks later, General Vo Nguyen Giap led a Vietnamese delegation to the Asiad '90 games in Beijing as a distinguished guest of the Chinese government. Informal trade between China and Vietnam, which had bloomed following the withdrawal of Vietnamese troops from Cambodia, flourished. Though the trade was in China's favor and displaced Vietnamese goods in their home market, Hanoi claimed to see a "remarkable reduction of tension in the border areas, . . . laying the premise for the normalization of tensions between the two countries."[54] Moreover, China normalized relations with Hanoi's ally, Laos. In mid-December 1990, Li Peng headed a forty-member delegation to Vientiane, signed an agreement on economic and technical cooperation, and initiated a small aid program. Sino-Lao normalization, like Sino-Soviet normalization, held out hope to Hanoi that Beijing might someday agree to disagree on Cambodia while improving relations in other spheres. However, trade and informal interaction aside, China continued to insist that a Cambodian settlement come before it would negotiate formally with Vietnam on bilateral issues.[55]

End Run through ASEAN

Much better prospects for Vietnam to break out of its isolation and obtain economic help, with or without a Cambodian settlement, existed in developing relations with the ASEAN states, particularly Indonesia, Malaysia, and Thailand.

In November 1990, President Suharto made the first visit to Hanoi by a top-ranked Indonesian leader in thirty-three years and the first by the head of state of a non-socialist country since 1979.[56] During the visit, the Indonesian and Vietnamese foreign ministers jointly warned that they would not let relations between their two countries remain forever "hostage" to the Cambodian problem.[57] Suharto's delegation was heavily weighted with economics experts, and the two sides signed an accord on economic, scientific, and technical cooperation. They also agreed to expedite negotiations on the continental shelf boundary. The Vietnamese reiterated their wish to accede to ASEAN's Treaty of Amity and Cooperation and later to join ASEAN, a wish Suharto welcomed.[58]

In Malaysia (as in South Korea and Taiwan), Hanoi perceived a successful model of export-oriented industrialization that it wished to emulate. Hanoi also valued Kuala Lumpur's role as ASEAN's leading advocate of the ZOPFAN and NWFZ concepts. During a visit to Kuala Lumpur in early February 1991, the first vice-chair of Vietnam's Council of Ministers, Vo Van Kiet, participated in a symposium under World Bank auspices to "exchange experiences in market-oriented macro-economic management" and agreed with Malaysia to work on plans for trade expansion and joint ventures.[59] In March 1991, Malaysia became the first ASEAN country to set up a consulate in Ho Chi Minh City, resumed grant aid that had been suspended since December 1978, and agreed to help Vietnam develop its oil industry.

Hanoi courted Bangkok even more aggressively than Jakarta and Kuala Lumpur, and its courtship was warmly reciprocated. In late October 1990, Foreign Minister Thach called for a "summit meeting" between Premier Do Muoi and Prime Minister Chatichai, to which the Thai agreed. Thach was explicit about seeking this meeting to revive the Thai-Vietnamese Cooperation Commission, set up in 1978 but never activated, along the lines of one agreed to between Indonesia and Vietnam during Suharto's visit.[60] The Thai and Vietnamese also agreed to set up a working group to revise, amend, and write new treaties, particularly ones pertaining to trade and investment, and Thai foreign minister Subin Pinkhayan proposed cooperation to control fluctuations in the price of rice in international markets.[61] Other agreements to cooperate in such areas as petroleum exploration in overlapping territorial claims followed.

The intensity of Bangkok's interest fully matched that of Hanoi because of Thailand's growing need to export consumer products, food, processed and semi-processed products in return for raw materials, and primary products that Vietnam has in abundance. The Thai also saw prospects in serving as a channel for finance and investment and even in providing reconstruction assistance to the Indochinese countries.[62] The generals who overthrew the Chatchai government on February 23, 1991, ended Bangkok's unilateral attempts to accelerate the Cambodian peace process and postponed Do Muoi's visit. But in most other respects they left Chatchai's Indochina policy unchanged, including a Chatchai proposal to secure the cooperation of all four Cambodian factions in rehabilitating

Cambodia's infrastructure under Thai guidance before a settlement.[63] The generals also maintained the commitment to economic cooperation with Vietnam, and in March, coup leader General Suchinda Khongsomphong announced plans to visit Hanoi.

Vietnam's immediate post–Cold War policy toward the ASEAN countries, individually and collectively, was simple and clear. It was, as a review of 1990 in the party newspaper *Nhan Dan* (The People) put it, "to leave the Cambodia issue behind and put aside the difference of . . . political systems to move closer together," even if that meant leaving the Cambodian conflict unresolved. While Hanoi asserted that the Phnom Penh government should survive more or less in its present form because it "continues to run all affairs" of Cambodia and is a reality "nobody can deny," it anticipated that the Indochinese and ASEAN countries would continue to improve relations, particularly in the economic field.[64]

This policy aimed to vault across a "bridge" of cooperation with Indonesia, Malaysia, and Thailand to economic integration with ASEAN, thus helping to offset the effects of the United States–imposed embargo.[65] Over the long term, Hanoi hoped that such ties (including ones with South Korea, Taiwan, the European Community, and eventually the United States), would compensate for the loss of Soviet and Eastern European inputs while they counterbalanced Chinese military-political influence and Japanese economic penetration. Promoting cooperation within the region and striving for membership in ASEAN were but parts of a larger strategy to avoid excessive dependence on, or interference by, any one great power.

Thus Vietnam's diplomacy came to be a very high priority on the development of broad-gauged cooperative relations with ASEAN members. Where it once had sought to deal with ASEAN members bilaterally in order to divide the association, it now did so to sidestep the Cambodian issue and end Vietnam's economic isolation. Besides, in the absence of concrete, plausible schemes for the creation of a common market or for security cooperation among existing ASEAN members, there was no reason for Vietnam to seek its ends through a multilateral rather than bilateral framework.

However, Hanoi sought acceptance from ASEAN countries with a view to becoming a member of the association as well. In 1986, Laos had proposed supplanting ASEAN with a larger organization to which the Indochinese countries could adhere, but during Suharto's visit to Hanoi in fall 1990 the Vietnamese expressed for the first time a strong preference to join the existing regional framework.[66] Although Suharto made clear that the Cambodian issue remained a stumbling block, the exploration of mutual interests with other Southeast Asian nations was useful and probably comforting to Hanoi. In the long run, Hanoi looked forward to sharing in whatever success ASEAN enjoyed as a lobby for Southeast Asian interests in other international fora, to participating in the association's discussions of regional security issues, and to coordinating with Indonesia through ASEAN to limit great power, particularly Chinese, influence in the region.

The priorities of both Vietnam and ASEAN shifted toward the end of the 1980s, as the perception of a threat to regional stability in Cambodia gave way to economic preoccupations. This was partly an effect of the global relaxation of tensions, which helped to soften threat perceptions in the region, and partly of Vietnam's reform drive combined with export-oriented industrialization in the ASEAN countries. With Vietnamese troops withdrawn from Cambodia, ASEAN increasingly viewed the Khmer squabble as an obstacle to regional prosperity, to be resolved if possible or ignored if necessary. The determination of Indonesia, Malaysia, and Thailand to nurture the economic boom on a regional scale no doubt played into the hands of Hanoi, which hoped that by courting ASEAN it could still obtain its preferred outcome in Cambodia. But Hanoi also genuinely wished to redirect its economic relations from a moribund socialist world to a vibrant capitalist one and to cooperate with ASEAN in meeting security needs it could no longer meet with Soviet support or maintenance of its own large military establishment.

Against this background, the treaty signed in Paris on October 22, 1991, by eighteen nations plus Cambodia's Supreme National Council was an anticlimax to the consensus among the Perm-Five and everyone else but the Cambodians to move the Cambodian conflict offstage. Under the terms of this treaty, a UN Transitional Authority in Cambodia (UNTAC) was to have 15,900 peace-keeping soldiers, 3,600 police, and 2,400 civilian administrators in place by summer 1992. The numbers of personnel and the cost—over U.S. $2 billion—make this the biggest peace-keeping operation in the UN's history. Until elections could be held in spring 1993, UNTAC's principal duties were to disarm and demobilize 70 percent of the Cambodian combatants, supervise mine clearing, repatriate up to 350,000 refugees from camps on the Thai border, supervise key ministries, and make arrangements to guarantee that the elections are free and fair. Meanwhile, Hun Sen's State of Cambodia remained the country's principal administrative structure while the Supreme National Council embodied the country's sovereignty.

These arrangements might seem to keep Cambodia on the agenda. UNTAC is sure to weigh heavily in the UN's perpetual budget crisis. But this misses the point: the UN plan afforded the involved external parties an opportunity to withdraw from direct participation in the Cambodian conflict, face and interests intact. It became a reality because in the post–Cold War climate, the incentive for great powers to support opposed factions in local contests for power declined while the incentive to remove frictions that impeded progress in other issue areas increased. In this climate, no Southeast Asian country can afford to remain mired in a backyard conflict when great power support waned and new opportunities for trade and investment opened up. The plan's priority of disengaging external powers without sacrificing their interests—or guaranteeing those of the Cambodian people—was evident in its legitimation of all four Cambodian factions without effective guarantee that new parties could emerge before elections took place.[67] Within this framework, the only real choice open to Cambodians in elections seemed likely to be between a Hun Sen–Sihanouk alliance steeped in corruption and nepotism, on the one hand, and the Khmer Rouge, who had changed neither leaders nor tactics, on the other. But neighboring states saw in the framework a green light to move ahead swiftly with deferred plans.

For Vietnam, the treaty, as Hanoi's new foreign minister Nguyen Manh Cam described it, was an opportunity to "remove the last obstacles to the establishment of our foreign policy of normalization and diversification of our relations with all countries, firstly among the countries of Southeast Asia, and more widely with countries of Asia and the Pacific on the basis of the principle of equality and mutual benefits."[68] In this hope, Hanoi was not disappointed. The ink was hardly dry when Council of Ministers Chair Vo Van Kiet made a grand tour in late October of Indonesia, Thailand, and Singapore. In each capital Kiet reiterated Vietnam's wish to sign the 1976 Bali Treaty of Amity and Cooperation and received assurance of support for Vietnam's participation; in Bangkok the two sides initiated talks on long-standing irritants concerning Vietnamese residents of Thailand, Thai fishermen detained in Vietnam, and sea boundaries; and Singapore promised to lift its long-standing ban on investment in Vietnam and to exchange embassies. The timing underscored the high priority Hanoi attached to relations with the ASEAN states as it came just before, and partly to counterbalance, Kiet and Party Secretary General Do Muoi's trip to Beijing, planned since September.[69] That trip ended on November 10 with the announcement that Beijing and Hanoi would restore full normal relations. Although normalization between Vietnam and the United States remained tied up in the MIA/POW issue, the way was clear to tear down all remaining divisions left by colonial rule and the Cold War in Southeast Asia, permitting more integrated patterns of regional politics and economy to emerge.

More pulls Vietnam and ASEAN together than drives them apart. With Hanoi's agreement to take back refugees under UN surveillance, a long-standing source of friction has been removed. Overlapping territorial claims in the South China Sea are an emerging source of dispute among all Southeast Asian nations, but China's claim to the entire sea helps to unite them. Despite widely different levels of economic performance, Vietnam and the ASEAN states are preoccupied with development and have similar concerns for market access, foreign investment, global environmental policy, population policy, and the like. Among the ASEAN states, Vietnam finds acceptance without the kind of concern for democracy and human rights that it faces in the West. ASEAN states see in Vietnam a country that shares their wariness toward China, and that might help the organization to counterbalance China.

The ASEAN heads of state discussed membership in ASEAN for Vietnam and Laos (Cambodia and Burma had yet to indicate an intention to join) at their fourth meeting in January 1992, and their joint declaration welcomed all Southeast Asian states to accede to the 1976 treaty, which binds signatories to resolve disputes peacefully, as a first step. Although Vietnam wished to join immediately, reservations about potential impact on the character of the organization and on economic disparities among member states remained obstacles. The ASEAN states were divided on how soon Vietnam should attain membership, with the consensus demanding delay until Vietnam's market-oriented reforms had time to establish their viability. An influential Indonesian analyst suggested that the modalities and timing of membership could be considered at the next ASEAN summit in 1995.[70]

The Demise of "Indochina"

In ASEAN's agenda, preoccupied with obstacles to export-oriented development and the emergence of trade blocs in Europe and North America, the Cambodian issue has slid from first to last place. It is not obvious, however, that all differences of interest between Vietnam and ASEAN with respect to Indochina can be so easily and permanently papered over. While direct intervention in Cambodia by any outside party is unlikely so long as the great power consensus holds, settlement there does not remove all potential for friction. The Vietnamese have not completely forsaken hope of preserving special access to both Laos and Cambodia, which the Thai and Chinese would deny them.

Hanoi must remain concerned, too, about the resurrection of the Khmer Rouge, which could become a real possibility should the UN peace-keeping effort collapse or the supervised election produce an unstable, corrupt, and incompetent government in Phnom Penh. At the time of this writing (June 1992), Khmer Rouge refusal to let UNTAC observers into zones under their control, and the continuing failure of the other three factions to offer an attractive alternative provided little basis for confidence that the elections, if held at all, would result in the installation of an effective, popular government and the withering away of the Khmer Rouge. Although Hanoi is heavily constrained by its strong desire to preserve carefully nurtured relations with China and ASEAN and to concentrate on domestic reform, its response to political disintegration and renewed conflict in Cambodia would be hard to predict. Much would depend on the response of the world community.

Attempting some months before the Cambodian peace treaty was signed to define the relationship among all three Indochinese countries, an article in a Vietnamese military journal cited "voluntariness, equality, mutual respect for independence and sovereignty, non-interference in internal affairs," but also noted that "we cannot agree with the few people who want to lower and shift this relationship . . . to the level of an ordinary international relationship of the type shared by many countries." This meant retaining elements of "collective responsibility and solidarity and mutual aid depending on the realistic capacity of each party and each country."[71] The author of the article cannot have welcomed the less certain guarantees of UNTAC or have had much confidence that normalization with former adversaries could substitute for special ties with Laos and Cambodia.

Officially, Hanoi has narrowed the scope of its interest in Laos and Cambodia to security, leaving each country to "choose its own way" in other areas.[72] It remains unclear, however, how the Vietnamese define their security needs relative to their two neighbors, or if they agree upon them among themselves. These needs could range from simple assurance that Laos and Cambodia will not let foreign powers use their territory for aggression against Vietnam, to the reality of stable regimes capable of minimizing foreign influence and remaining sympathetic to Vietnam. Normalization and reconciliation with neighbors encourage Hanoi to settle for the first, more restrictive definition.

Meanwhile, a Vietnam hell-bent on market-oriented reforms and attracting foreign investors can hardly deny Laos and Cambodia the right to adopt "open door" policies of their own. Nor does Vietnam have the means to bind them into its own feeble economy. Ideology, inter-elite ties, educational exchange, a Vietnamese advisory presence, and small aid projects may count for something in Laos, and less as time passes in Cambodia, but Vietnam's economic magnetism is near zero. Unwilling and unable to impose "solidarity" by military means, Hanoi must let its two small neighbors forge whatever economic links they wish with the rest of the world. With these links must come foreign economic penetration and a counterbalance to Vietnamese influence.

Laos may portend the future. As mentioned earlier, China initiated an aid program and laid the basis for expanded commercial contacts with Laos at the time of their normalization in December 1990. China's presence in an "open" Laos is certain to increase if only because of its sheer size and geographical location. More striking considering relative size, however, has been Laos's economic penetration by Thailand, Vietnam's traditional rival for influence in the "buffer states" between them. Bangkok officially sanctioned trade with all three Indochinese countries in fall 1988, partly to regularize informal trade that was already rapidly expanding and in deficit. A year later, each country set up a cooperation committee to promote economic, trade, cultural, scientific, and technical cooperation with the other. This was a prelude to a week-long ceremonial visit to Laos by Thai crown princess Maha Chakkri Sirinthon in March 1990, the first such visit by a member of the Thai royal family in modern times. By November 1989, Thai companies were the largest foreign investors in Laos, ahead of France, the United States, and China.[73] In early 1991, upward of 600 Thai companies were engaged in trade with Laos, capitalizing on a Lao thirst for imported goods and arousing concern in some quarters of the Lao government that trade might facilitate subversion by "exiled Lao reactionaries."[74] Thai trade with all of Indochina had increased fivefold in five years to U.S. $194 million in 1990, not counting smuggling and black marketeering.[75] In March 1991, Thailand's Ministry of Foreign Affairs unveiled a proposal to upgrade relations with Laos still further by allocating it baht 100 million (U.S. $3.7 million) from Bangkok's new baht 200 million aid program. The purpose, said a well-placed ministry source, was to "reduce Laos's security dependence and ideological attachment to Vietnam."[76] Bangkok subsequently lowered import duties on Lao goods and agricultural products by 20 percent and offered scholarships for 230 Lao students.[77]

Considering Thai economic dynamism and the far more efficient access to world markets that Thailand can offer to Laos, not to mention the cultural affinity between the two nations, Thailand's economic importance for Laos is bound to overshadow that of Vietnam. As if to signal readiness for its impending absorption via Thailand into the world capitalist economy, the Lao People's Revolutionary Party at its 5th National Congress in March 1991 resolved that the word "socialism" be dropped from the state's motto and the hammer and sickle removed from the national insignia. Cambodia's Communists also felt the need in October 1991 to change the party's name, deleting the word "Communist," and in June 1991 Thailand's Siam Commercial Bank became the first foreign non-socialist financial institution to sign a joint venture agreement with the Phnom Penh government.

This is not to suggest that China, Thailand, or all the ASEAN countries together are about to turn Laos and Cambodia into their economic provinces, or that Hanoi is likely never to try reversing the economic tide by non-economic means. It is only to point out that economic interaction between booming ASEAN (and China and Japan) on one side, and chronically aid-dependent Laos and Cambodia on the other, has already altered the distribution of power and influence on the Southeast Asian mainland, undermined Vietnam's predominance in Laos and Cambodia, and weakened the unity of the three Indochinese states. Hanoi has no reason to feel threatened by these trends so long as great power rivalries remain in abatement and Vietnam maintains good relations with China and ASEAN. Viewed in retrospect, its diligent diplomacy of reconciliation with ASEAN has involved an exchange of the security interdependence of the Indochinese states for the greater rewards of cooperation in maintaining the peaceful environment it so desperately needs for its development.

Notes

1. Kenneth M. Quinn, "The Origins and Development of Radical Cambodian Communism," Ph.D. diss., University of Maryland, 1982, pp. 80–84.

2. Nayan Chanda, *Brother Enemy: The War after the War* (New York: Harcourt Brace Jovanovich, 1986), p. 216.

3. International Institute for Strategic Studies (London), *The Military Balance 1989–1990* (London: Brassey's for IISS, 1989), p. 157. It is doubtful that the CPAF was able to keep all of this equipment in working order, however. In spring 1991, only five of Phnom Penh's eighteen MiG-21s were reported to be operational. Agence France Presse (Hong Kong), 6 April 1991, in Foreign Broadcast Information Service, *Daily Report: East Asia* (hereinafter *FBIS-EAS*), 8 April 1991.

4. *The Nation* (Bangkok), 23 October 1989, in *FBIS-EAS*, 24 October 1989.

5. *The Nation*, 23 October 1989, in *FBIS-EAS*, 24 October 1989.

6. Nayan Chanda, "Cambodia 1989: The Search for an Exit," The Asia Society, Asian Update Series, June 1989, p. 21. In late 1990, a private American fact-finding group estimated total Khmer Rouge combat strength at 30,000, *The Nation*, 17 December 1990, in *FBIS-EAS*, 18 December 1990.

7. Agence France Presse (Hong Kong), 30 September 1989, in *FBIS-EAS*, 2 October 1989.

8. Voice of the Khmer radio, 5 September 1989, in *FBIS-EAS*, 5 September 1989.

9. *The Economist*, 11 May 1991, p. 32.

10. Jacques Bekaert, article in *Bangkok Post*, 1 February 1991, in *FBIS-EAS*, 1 February 1991.

11. Nate Thayer, "A Khmer Ruse," *Far Eastern Economic Review*, 7 March 1991, pp. 25–26.

12. *The Economist*, 11 May 1991, p. 34.

13. Vo Nguyen Giap, "Nhiem vu quan su truoc mat chuyen sang Tong phan cong" [The military mission in transition to the general offensive and uprising] (Ha Dong Committee for Resistance and Administration, 1950), p. 14, in the Library of Congress, Orientalia/South Asia 4 microfilm collection, *Vietnamese Communist Publications*, P.T. Chau, ed., item 40.

14. General Le Duc Anh, "Quan doi nhan dan va nhiem vu quoc te cao ca tren dat ban Cam-Pu-Chia" [The People's Army and its lofty internationalist mission in friendly Kampuchea], *Tap chi Quan doi nhan dan* [People's Army Journal], December 1984, p. 32.

15. Nguyen Co Thach, interview with the author, Hanoi, 25 April 1984. For more detailed discussion of Vietnamese strategy, see William S. Turley, "Vietnam's Strategy for Indochina and the Security of Southeast Asia," in Young Whan Kihl and Lawrence E. Grinter, eds., *Security, Strategy, and Policy Responses in the Pacific Rim* (Boulder: Lynne Rienner, 1989), pp. 163–188.

16. Le Duc Anh, "Quan doi nhan dan va nhiem vu quoc te . . ."

17. See article by Jacques Bekaert in *Bangkok Post*, 21 July 1989, in *FBIS-EAS*, 26 July 1989.

18. Communiqué, Radio Hanoi, 18 January 1985.

19. China is not a global superpower rivaling the United States or the former Soviet Union, but it behaved as a great power in the limited context discussed here and so I shall thus refer to it for the sake of convenience.

20. Xinhua, 6 March 1980, quoted in Charles McGregor, "China, Vietnam, and the Cambodian Conflict," *Asian Survey*, vol. 30, no. 3 (March 1990), p. 267.

21. This is the argument advanced in Robert S. Ross, *The Indochina Tangle: China's Vietnam Policy 1975–1979* (New York: Columbia University Press, 1988).

22. McGregor, "China, Vietnam, and the Cambodian Conflict," p. 269.

23. For details of Vietnam's economic dependency on the Soviet Union, see Adam Fforde, *Economic Aspects of the Soviet-Vietnamese Relationship: Their Role and Importance* (Birkbeck College Discussion Paper, no. 156, October 1984); and Derek Martin Da Cunha, "Aspects of Soviet-Vietnamese Economic Relations, 1979–84," *Contemporary Southeast Asia* (March 1986), pp. 306–319.

24. United States Arms Control and Disarmament Agency, *World Military Expenditures and Arms Transfers 1988* (Washington, D.C., June 1989), p. 108.

25. Da Cunha, "Aspects of Soviet-Vietnamese Economic Relations," p. 310.

26. Leszek Buszynski, "Indochina in Soviet Policy: Diverging Priorities under Gorbachev," paper presented to the Regional Security Conference organized by the International Institute for Strategic Studies (London) and the Institute of Security and International Studies (Bangkok), Chiang Mai, Thailand, July 1989, p. 7.

27. *New York Times*, 16 November 1989.

28. On Thai-Vietnamese relations, see William S. Turley, "Thai-Vietnamese Rivalry in the Indochina Conflict," in Lawrence E. Grinter and Young Whan Kihl, eds., *East Asian Conflict Zones* (New York: St. Martin's Press, 1987), pp. 149–176; and David W.P. Elliott, "Deadlock Diplomacy: Thai and Vietnamese Interests in Kampuchea," in David A. Ablin and Marlowe Hood, eds., *The Cambodian Agony* (Armonk, NY: M.E. Sharpe, 1987), pp. 65–92.

29. Donald K. Emmerson, "The Stable War: Cambodia and the Great Powers," *Indochina Issues*, no. 62 (December 1985).

30. David P. Chandler, "Strategies for Survival in Kampuchea," *Current History* (April 1983), p. 153.

31. Michael Leifer, "Cambodian Conflict—The Final Phase?" *Conflict Studies*, no. 221 (May 1989), p. 5.

32. Quoted in *Nhan dan* [The People] (1 January 1989), translated in *FBIS-EAS*, 19 January 1989.

33. Maj. Gen. Nguyen Van Thai, press conference in Ho Chi Minh City, in *The Nation* (20 September 1989), in *FBIS-EAS*, 21 February 1989.

34. Phnom Penh radio, 17 February 1989, in *FBIS-EAS*, 21 February 1989.

35. Interview with Nguyen Co Thach in *The Nation* (Bangkok), in *FBIS-EAS*, 25 May 1989.

36. Hanoi radio, 17 May 1989, in *FBIS-EAS*, 18 May 1989.

37. Article by Nguyen Co Thach in *Tap chi Cong san* [The Communist], August 1989, translated in *FBIS-EAS*, 12 September 1989.

38. *Bangkok Post*, 23 May 1990, in *FBIS-EAS*, 23 May 1990; also see Moscow radio, 23 May 1990, in *FBIS-EAS*, 24 May 1990.

39. Tran Quang Co interview, Vietnam News Agency (Hanoi), 22 June 1990, in *FBIS-EAS*, 22 June 1990; and *The Nation*, 15 August 1990, in *FBIS-EAS*, 16 August 1990.

40. BERNAMA, 8 August 1990, in *FBIS-EAS*, 8 August 1990; and ANTARA, 8 August 1990, in *FBIS-EAS*, 8 August 1990.

41. *The Nation*, 15 August 1990, in *FBIS-EAS*, 16 August 1990.

42. *The Nation*, 10 April 1990, in *FBIS-EAS*, 10 April 1990.

43. Commniqué of the meeting broadcast over Voice of the National Army of Democratic Kampuchea (VONADK), 25 December 1990, in *FBIS-EAS*, 26 December 1990.

44. Voice of the National Army of Democratic Kampuchea, 23 December 1990, in *FBIS-EAS*, 26 December 1990.

45. Agence France Presse (Hong Kong), 26 December 1990, in *FBIS-EAS*, 26 December 1990.

46. SPK (Phnom Penh), 4 December 1990, in *FBIS-EAS*, 4 December 1990.

47. Press release no. 19/BC, Viet Nam Permanent Mission to the UN, 19 December 1990.

48. Phnom Penh radio, 10 June 1990, in *FBIS-EAS*, 12 June 1990.

49. See Hun Sen speech, Phnom Penh radio, 25 November 1990, in *FBIS-EAS*, 28 November 1990; speech by Political Bureau member Sar Kheng, Phnom Penh radio, 1 December 1990, in *FBIS-EAS*, 3 December 1990; and Heng Samrin speech, Phnom Penh radio, 25 December 1990, in *FBIS-EAS*, 26 December 1990.

50. "Statement of the Cambodian National Resistance Forces," broadcast over Voice of Democratic Kampuchea radio, 26 April 1991, in *FBIS-EAS*, 29 April 1991.

51. Agence France Presse (Hong Kong), 22 April 1991, in *FBIS-EAS*, 24 April 1991.

52. Premier Do Muoi, Hanoi radio, 18 October 1990, in *FBIS-EAS*, 24 October 1990.

53. Agence France Presse (Hong Kong), 17 September 1990, in *FBIS-EAS*, 17 September 1990; and KYODO News Service (Tokyo), 17 September 1990, in *FBIS-EAS*, 18 September 1990.

54. Vietnam News Agency (Hanoi), 16 February 1991, in *FBIS-EAS*, 20 February 1991.

55. A Vietnamese party delegation visiting China for two weeks from 20 January 1991 to study China's economic reforms met Li Peng and held talks with Vice Foreign Minister Qi Huaiyuan. According to a Vietnamese source, the Vietnamese proposed setting up a committee to discuss security and trade across the border and to exchange delegations to study the socioeconomic situation in each country. However, the Chinese repeated that a Cambodian settlement had to come before bilateral issues could be negotiated. KYODO News Service, 31 January 1991, in *FBIS-EAS*, 31 January 1991.

56. Vietnam News Agency (Hanoi), 9 January 1991, in *FBIS-EAS*, 17 January 1991.

57. Agence France Press (Hong Kong), 21 November 1990, in *FBIS-EAS*, 21 November 1990.

58. Hanoi radio, 21 November 1990, in *FBIS-EAS*, 23 November 1990.

59. VNA interview with Vo Van Kiet, Hanoi radio, 2 March 1991, in *FBIS-EAS*, 5 March 1991.

60. *Bangkok Post*, 30 October 1990, in *FBIS-EAS*, 30 October 1990.

61. Hanoi radio, 30 October 1990, in *FBIS-EAS*, 31 October 1990.

62. See interview with Dr. Somchai Phakhaphatwiwat in *The Nation*, 23 February 1991, in *FBIS-EAS*, 27 February 1991.

63. *The Nation*, 14 March 1991, in *FBIS-EAS*, 14 March 1991.

64. Vietnam News Agency, 9 January 1991, in *FBIS-EAS*, 17 January 1991.

65. Vietnamese official cited in *The Nation*, 12 January 1991, in *FBIS-EAS*, 17 January 1991.

66. *The Nation*, 24 November 1990, in *FBIS-EAS*, 26 November 1990.

67. Attempts by individuals outside the elite circle of the four factions to form new parties in Phnom Penh have been unsuccessful. In October 1991, a Cambodian-American gave up such an attempt, citing intimidation by government agents, acting with the approval of SOC prime minister Hun Sen. Agence France Press (Hong Kong), 11 November 1991, in *FBIS-EAS*, 12 November 1991. In January 1992, former SOC minister of communciations Ung Phan announced the formation of a Free Democratic Society Party and was shot and wounded eleven days later. One of Phan's associates was severely beaten in March. SOC agencies outside Hun Sen's control apparently were responsible for Phan's shooting. See Stan Sesser, "Report from Cambodia," *The New Yorker* (18 May 1992), pp. 60–61. Individual and group protests against SOC corruption, such as by students in December 1991, also have provoked lethal responses.

68. Agence France Presse (Hong Kong), 23 October 1991, in *FBIS-EAS*, 24 October 1991.

69. Agence France Press (Hong Kong), 29 October 1991, in *FBIS-EAS*, 29 October 1991.

70. Jusuf Wanandi in *The Nation*, 30 January 1992, in *FBIS-EAS*, 5 February 1992.

71. Pham Xuan Que, "Some Reflections on the Relations between Vietnam, Laos, and Cambodia in the New Situation," *Tap chi Quoc phong Toan dan* [All People's Defense Journal], February 1991, in *FBIS-EAS*, 24 April 1991.

72. Author's interview with Chau Phong, Director of the Institute of International Relations, Hanoi, 12 June 1989.

73. *The Nation*, 11 January 1991, in *FBIS-EAS*, 1 February 1991.

74. Vientiane radio, 4 January 1991, in *FBIS-EAS*, 9 January 1991.

75. *The Nation*, 26 January 1991, in *FBIS-EAS*, 1 February 1991.

76. *The Nation*, 25 March 1991, in *FBIS-EAS*, 26 March 1991.

77. Vientiane radio, 8 May 1991, in *FBIS-EAS*, 9 May 1991.

9

ASEAN and Indochina: The "ASEANization" of Vietnam

Donald E. Weatherbee

Introduction: Two Southeast Asias

In 1975, the victories of communist armies in Vietnam, Cambodia, and Laos brought all of Indochina into a Hanoi-centric, Marxist-Leninist subregion of Southeast Asia. Since then the central problem of regional peace and security has been to decide the nature of the relations to be established between the Indochinese states and the non-communist, market-oriented states of the Association of Southeast Asian Nations (ASEAN). This task has been immensely complicated by the external political and security linkages of the competitive systems, making Southeast Asia a theater of the wider triangular confrontations between the United States and China and the former Soviet Union. As the ASEAN economies grew rapidly, firmly embedded in the global marketplace, Vietnam's economy, mired in the socialist camp, has only belatedly turned to market-oriented practices but has remained internationally frustrated by the consequences of its invasion and occupation of Cambodia. Attention since December 1978 has concentrated on the Cambodian conflict, the so-called "Third Indochina War," as the concrete manifestation of the problem of ASEAN–Indochina relations. Now with a paper settlement of that war[1]—at the least in its international and interregional dimensions—it is appropriate to take up again the adjourned agenda of building a security system in Southeast Asia that would allow for peaceful coexistence between the two subregions.

There were tentative prospects for some kinds of accommodative arrangements between ASEAN and Vietnam in the immediate post–Second Indochina War diplomacy. After an initial fear on the ASEAN side of an intensification of Vietnam-spurred revolution in the region, there was a two-year feeling-out period, hesitant and on the ASEAN side uncoordinated, which some leaders like Thailand's Prime Minister Kriangsak hoped would lead to a peaceful relationship between Indochina and ASEAN. Through bilateral contacts and the articulation by both sides of a regionwide notion of a Southeast Asian Zone of Peace, Freedom, and Neutrality (ASEAN's ZOPFAN)/Zone of Peace, Genuine Independence, and Neutrality (Vietnam's ZOPGIN), at the minimum the ASEAN states and Vietnam had by 1978 established the basis for dialogue, perhaps even for ASEAN's cooperation in Vietnam's economic recovery from the impacts of the First and Second Indochina Wars. But then came the Vietnamese invasion and occupation of Cambodia, which regardless of the motives of Vietnam, was viewed by ASEAN as aggressively expansionist, with Cambodia becoming Southeast Asia's first "domino."[2]

We do not know whether the aborted early ASEAN–Vietnam dialogue would have resulted in structures or instrumentalities to resolve the almost inherent differences of interest between the two Southeast Asias. Even so, despite a dozen years of bleeding stalemate on the ground inside Cambodia, both the ASEAN states and Vietnam continued to entertain in their public rhetoric a vision of a future stable, peaceful, and secure Southeast Asian region. It is our purpose here to examine both the process of building and the possible configurations of such an order, the great power parameters of which have been dramatically changed with the disappearance of the USSR and the termination of the American military base rights in the Philippines.

The Dialogue Resumed: The Cambodian Peace Process

On November 19, 1990, Indonesia's President Suharto stepped down from his Garuda Indonesian Airlines DC-10 onto the arrival red carpet at Hanoi's Noi Bai International Airport to begin a three-day official visit, the first visit to Vietnam of an Indonesian head of government (who in the Indonesian system is also head of state) since President Sukarno's exchange of visits with Ho Chi Minh in 1959. More significantly for the region, it was the first meeting between an ASEAN leader and his Vietnamese counterpart since Pham Van Dong visited Thai prime minister Kriangsak in 1977. With the retirement of Singapore's Lee Kuan Yew, Suharto has become ASEAN's senior head of government. The dual bilateral and regional importance of the Indonesian president's presence in Hanoi was remarked upon in the speeches and commentary surrounding the occasion.[3]

At the bilateral level, the Suharto visit represented the picking up of the threads of a relationship colored by a common emotive nationalism not shared between Indonesia and any other Southeast Asian state. The Vietnamese hosts in particular unabashedly praised the continuity of the two countries' common anticolonial struggle that had been lifted to new heights by Sukarno and Ho Chi Minh. Indonesian foreign minister Ali Alatas called the event, "a very important milestone which opened the prospect of greatly enhanced cooperation between Indonesia and Vietnam." It also opened the prospect of greatly enhanced cooperation between Vietnam and the ASEAN regional grouping, being, in Suharto's words, "a manifestation of the heartening developments" in the region.[4]

Not the least of these developments has been the progress of the international political process in establishing a framework for peace in Cambodia. We must distinguish very carefully here between the internationally agreed-upon terms of political settlement contained in the October 23, 1991, Final Act of the Paris Conference and the possible perpetuation of the domestic Cambodian civil war because of its ultimate rejection by the armed Khmer parties. The former is the product of the superimposition of the will of the Permanent Five members of the United Nations Security Council on their regional friends and allies on both sides of the issue. In the Permanent Five's comprehensive agreement, which is now the charter for the United Nations Transitional Authority in Cambodia (UNTAC), the political burden of implementation is on the Khmer factions, not on ASEAN or Vietnam.

In terms of Vietnam's role in Cambodia—the bottom line for more than a decade in ASEAN–Vietnam relations—the Paris settlement imposes no new obligations on Vietnam that have not already been met in ASEAN eyes. ASEAN leaders seem satisfied that the bulk of Vietnamese armed forces have been withdrawn from Cambodia. While there are still voices in ASEAN capitals cautioning about a residual Vietnamese military presence in Cambodia and the large number of Vietnamese civilians engaged there, the problem of "invasion and occupation" is no longer the albatross weighing down Vietnam–ASEAN relations. Even though it is far from clear that UNTAC can work the international community's will, this is not attributed by ASEAN leaders to Vietnamese sabotage but to a Khmer bloody-mindedness. ASEAN leaderships have accepted at face value Vietnam's declaratory support for a settlement in the real international context of the collapse of Vietnam's relationship with the former USSR and its desire to normalize fully its relations with the PRC. On the other hand, Vietnam seemed reluctant to use its crucial influence with Phnom Penh to persuade it to accept a plan that called for the virtual dismantling and disarming of the State of Cambodia without dealing with the Khmer Rouge's genocide. Vietnamese ambivalence in this respect was evident in the February 1991 Hanoi meetings with the Indonesian and French co-conveners of PICC and the failure to break the impasse that had developed in the peace process before the decisive intervention of the Permanent Five.[5] Nevertheless, with Vietnam and Cambodia reeling from the economic fallout of the upheavals in the USSR and East Europe, there seems from ASEAN's vantage little incentive for Hanoi to renew a cold war with ASEAN over the future of Cambodia as long as minimum Vietnamese security interests seem assured. This minimum can be now stated as the exclusion from power in Cambodia of the Khmer Rouge, a retreat in objective from the more politically expansive goals of the original invasion of Cambodia in December 1978. Even this minimum may not be achievable by Hanoi if UNTAC's mission fails.

The fact that both ASEAN and Vietnam have signed off on the UNTAC formula, although differing over implementation, symbolically capped what was already politically real in the Jakarta Informal Meeting (JIM) process initiated in the August 1987 Mochtar–Nguyen Co Thach communiqué that effectively decoupled the ASEAN–Vietnam, or external, dimension of the Cambodian political conflict from the Khmer, or internal, military conflict.[6] Once ASEAN admitted Phnom Penh as an autonomous actor in the negotiating framework, the entire structure of the peace process changed. This meant for ASEAN that peace was both functionally and geographically divisible. ASEAN as a group was on the threshold of political peace with Vietnam, and some ASEAN states had already crossed the threshold well before the signing of the final peace accords. Unlike the United States, ASEAN is building its new relationship with Vietnam without demanding that real peace be in place in Cambodia.[7]

ASEAN's Road to Reconciliation

Although important, the Suharto visit to Hanoi did not mark any great discontinuity in ASEAN–Vietnam relations. It was part of a continuing Indonesian diplomatic engagement that has sought to find bridges across the political abyss that has divided Southeast Asia for so long. That it was Suharto who became the first ASEAN head of state to go to Hanoi is a little surprising since former Thai prime minister Chatichai Choonhaven had been the most visible ASEAN proponent of a quick normalizing of relations with Vietnam. It may well be that the timing of the Indonesian leader's visit had more to do with the resumption of diplomatic relations between Indonesia and China than the problem of Cambodia. After more than twenty years of suspension, Jakarta and Beijing officially normalized their relations in August 1990 during a state visit by Chinese premier Li Peng to Indonesia. The Sino-Indonesian rapprochement was given its final blessing by Suharto's own state visit to China in November after his attendance at the enthronement of the new Japanese emperor. The flight that brought the Indonesian president to Hanoi was coming from Beijing. This seems to have been intended as a clear sign of balance for the Vietnamese.

Indonesia served as ASEAN's official diplomatic conduit to Vietnam on the Cambodian issue; since 1985, it has been ASEAN's "designated interlocutor" with Hanoi. This multilateralized what was already occurring in Indonesia's bilateral dialogue with Vietnam, which in the Indonesian conception of "dual track" diplomacy dealt with issues of the Cambodian war as well as bilateral relations. Indonesia's desire to break the diplomatic stalemate caused by what seemed in Jakarta to be inflexible postures on both sides was dramatically signaled by Armed Forces chief Benny Murdani's February 1984 official visit to Vietnam, the first visit by a senior member of an ASEAN government to Hanoi since 1980. In March 1984, Foreign Minister Nguyen Co Thach visited Jakarta. This visit was reciprocated by Indonesia's Mochtar in March 1985. A month later Vietnam's defense minister returned General Murdani's visit. In August 1985, Nguyen Co Thach was again in Jakarta, meeting this time with President Suharto as well as his own Indonesian counterpart. At that time the Vietnamese leader noted that "progress towards a settlement in Cambodia was very encouraging" and that common ground had been found between ASEAN and Vietnam. Mochtar agreed that the Vietnamese pledge of total withdrawal of their troops (a conditional one at that point) had improved the atmosphere.[8]

At that point in the diplomatic waltz the stumbling block was the structure of a negotiating forum and agenda. Vietnam had been insisting on a limited international conference to discuss all problems of peace and stability in Southeast Asia, while ASEAN's format was direct negotiations between the Khmer Resistance's Coalition Government of Democratic Kampuchea (CGDK) and Vietnam on the terms of implementing the UN's 1981 International Conference on Kampuchea (ICK) resolutions. In 1985, the latest version of the official ASEAN position was Malaysia's "proximity talks" proposal for indirect negotiations between the CGDK and Vietnam with the representatives of the "Heng Samrin regime" attending as part of the Vietnamese delegation.[9] For Vietnam, however, ASEAN had to deal with Phnom Penh. In what was perhaps his most constructive contribution to breaking the diplomatic logjam, Prince Sihanouk (apparently in consultation with the French) in September 1985 came up with the idea of the "cocktail party," an informal, non-official get-together of all interested parties from the Khmer factions to the great powers as a prelude to formal talks.[10]

It was Indonesia's Mochtar who turned the "cocktail party" idea, which included the Phnom Penh regime as an invited guest, into the *démarche* that led directly, if politically tortuously, to the Paris International Conference on Cambodia. In November 1985, Indonesia offered to host a "cocktail party," but with a much smaller guest list. In Mochtar's view it should be limited to the Cambodian factions and the theme should be national reconciliation.[11] While the name was changed from the frivolous "cocktail party" to "informal meeting," ASEAN diplomacy, driven by Indonesian-Vietnamese diplomacy, was geared to the establishment of the modalities of a negotiating format that would include the Phnom Penh regime, now represented by Premier Hun Sen, and that put Vietnam on the same footing vis-à-vis the Hun Sen government as ASEAN had vis-à-vis the CGDK. Vigorously massaged by Indonesian-Vietnamese senior officials' meetings and worried at the edges in various ASEAN forums, the core element of Foreign Minister Mochtar's "cocktail party" proposal prevailed in ASEAN's eventual acceptance of the formula outlined in the Mochtar–Nguyen Co Thach communiqué of July 1987. The Hun Sen government was accepted as a legitimate actor in an internal Cambodian negotiation that was connected to and conducted parallel to a semi-autonomous ASEAN–Vietnam, and behind that, China–Soviet Union, negotiation over the quality and material component of their links to the various Cambodian factions. A minimally satisfactory outcome of this second and third level of diplomacy was not dependent on the final position of the Cambodians themselves. Only the United States required that.

In terms of immediate concessions in 1987, it is clear that Foreign Minister Mochtar, on the surface at least, gave the most in his acceptance of Hun Sen's regime as a party to what was being redefined as a Cambodian civil war with foreign intervention. Through 1986 and up to and beyond the Mochtar–Nguyen Co Thach communiqué in 1987, the appearance of one-sided concessions bedeviled intra-ASEAN consultations. In the longer run, however, an examination of the framework for comprehensive peace in Cambodia reveals that with the exception of an internationally supervised and verified Vietnamese withdrawal from Cambodia, which will have to be ratified by UNTAC ex post facto, the goals stated in the ICK "Declaration" have been accepted implicitly by Vietnam through the JIM, PICC, and UN Permanent Five's proposals.[12] There remains the problem of implementation, but, as we have mentioned above, this is seen by ASEAN as essentially a Khmer question.

Why did Indonesia take the lead in the mid-1980s in the search for ASEAN reconciliation with Vietnam? In the first place, Indonesia never accepted the proposition that the Vietnamese invasion and occupation of Cambodia was the major security threat in Southeast Asia. From the outset, Indonesia was empathetic with Vietnam's concerns about great power (i.e., the People's Republic of China) intervention and the operation of the Sino-Soviet rivalry in Southeast Asia. This was behind Jakarta's floating in March 1980 of the "Kuantan formula," which sought to regionalize in Indochina the general principles of the ZOPFAN, calling for an end to the Soviet-Vietnamese alliance while recognizing Vietnam's legitimate concerns about a Chinese security threat.[13] As the PRC became through the Khmer Rouge the Khmer resistance's major military backer, Indonesia became increasingly concerned that prolongation of the crisis was serving to open a strategic window on Southeast Asia for China. The Thai-Chinese military embrace only heightened Indonesian apprehensions about the long-term regional security environment. Jakarta suspected that China through Thailand simply sought a bleeding endless war for Vietnam, not a peaceful resolution of it. Indonesian policymakers suspected that it was at Chinese insistence that Bangkok as ASEAN's "front-line state" (seconded by Singapore for its own reasons) had scuttled promising openings that would admittedly have required compromise on ASEAN's part. The Indonesian dilemma was sharpened by its military's perception that rather than having Vietnam as an enemy, Vietnam should be supported as a bulwark against possible PRC expansionism. Although Indonesia's commitment to ASEAN as such was so strong that it would not break ASEAN solidarity and make a separate peace with Vietnam, it nevertheless sought to move ASEAN away from simply uncritical adoption of the "front-line state" policy. In a sense, the brokering of peace in Cambodia became an Indonesian security policy.

Ironically, it was the "front-line state" that made the most abruptly dramatic shift of policy in ASEAN in the direction of reconciliation with the Indochinese states. When the Chatichai government assumed office in August 1988, one month after JIM-I, the prime minister announced his intention to turn the battle-field of Indochina into a marketplace. To the despair of the foreign policy elite that had been in charge of policy for a decade, this has meant essentially the full normalization of relations with Vietnam, including abandoning any pretense of economic embargo, and an intervention into the politics of the four Khmer factions that has tended to enhance the status and negotiating stance of the Hun Sen government.[14] In what one well-known analyst of Thai affairs described as a "stunning series of innovative policy proposals," the Chatichai government over-turned Thailand's decade-long strategy toward Vietnam.[15] Perhaps the most stunning move was the January 1989 reception of Hun Sen in Bangkok with the political status—but certainly without the protocol—of a head of government. In terms of the actual mechanics of the peace process in Cambodia itself, the Chatichai government assumed the task of attempting to broker informal agree-ment among the four factions to facilitate the structurally larger comprehensive peace process that was being orchestrated by Indonesia, and then Indonesia and France. In doing this, of course, Bangkok sought to position itself to the advan-tage of its postwar economic interests.

The altered Thai policy injected a new sense of urgency into the diplomatic process. While cynical wags might speak of the Indonesianization of Thai policy, there were marked differences between the two approaches. In the first place, the Indonesians were constrained by their consciousness of the need for consultation with their ASEAN partners. Bangkok did not feel the same imperative. In the context of ASEAN consensus, Indonesia pursued a multilateral "dual track," while Thailand unilaterally free-lanced. Furthermore, Bangkok's willingness to rush to reconciliation with Hanoi and Phnom Penh was seen in Jakarta as under-cutting the Indonesian-sponsored diplomatic effort by prematurely granting to Vietnam without reciprocal gestures the rewards of a successful negotiation. What were the motives for Thailand's rush to reconciliation? It is at once more complex but simpler to explain than Indonesia's more leisurely pace.

At one level of analysis, the shift in policy reflected the views of a group of personal advisers to the new prime minister who had long opposed what they saw as the sterile inflexibility of the Foreign Ministry–directed "front-line state" policy. Caustic in their criticism, witty in their retorts, and sometimes brilliant in their analyses, the policy advisers had the ear and confidence of the prime minister. Although the "advisers" functioned in a somewhat ambiguous bureau-cratic setting, they did not limit their role to counsel. When obstructed by the Foreign Ministry, they would become operators themselves in direct dealings with the Cambodian factions. Their policy premise was that Thai national interest was not promoted by a permanent war on its eastern border. A perpetuation of a vague state of insecurity in the country because of a proximate threat of warfare on the Thai-Cambodian border only had domestic payoffs for the Thai military, whose budgets and pretensions remained a menace to fragile parliamentary institutions. Finally, because of previous inflexibility, Thailand was becoming marginalized in a diplomatic process that was inevitably leading to some kind of settlement on less than Thailand's maximum terms.

At another level of analysis, the Thai rush to reconciliation was spurred by anticipation by Thai business interests behind the coalition government of huge economic rewards from an opening to the east. With almost unseemly haste, Thai entrepreneurs vied for contracts and concessions in Indochina. What the Thais called "*baht* fellowship" was a scramble for advantage in largely resource-oriented areas of economic activity: forests, fisheries, minerals, and tourism. In January 1989, Thailand lifted the ban on the export of strategic goods to Indochina that had been imposed by the previous Prem government. It should be quickly pointed out, however, that the Thais were not alone in their efforts to forge postwar (before the "post") economic ties to Vietnam. Indonesian, Singaporean, and Japanese business interests were already positioning themselves in Vietnam, as were the British, the Dutch, and the French, to mention only the most prominent. And, without fanfare or visibility, Philippine commercial interests were also present in Vietnam. It is fair to say that the "marketplace" was already there in Indochina before the Chatichai government overtly supported full economic normalization with Indochina. The "carrot" was preferred without a "stick."

A number of questions remain with respect to the changed Thai policy toward the Cambodian settlement. They can only be raised here, not answered, since there is not sufficient information—only gossip and guesses. The first has to do with the role of the army in the shaping of Thai policy toward Indochina in the Chatichai government. There is no question but that the Government House coordinated its policy with the army leadership, then under General Chavalit. An uneasy alliance between Chavalit and the prime minister's men facilitated the latter's contacts within Cambodia. Nor is there any doubt but that army-related enterprises have enjoyed some of the economic rewards of the Indochina "marketplace." The *Suwannaphume* or "golden peninsula" concept of a Thai-centered continental political economy had its origins in army forums.[16] There is some reason to think, however, that the army acted as a brake on the speed with which the prime minister's people moved to engage Vietnam and the Hun Sen regime in fellowship. A second question is where Thai policy toward the PRC fits into the picture. Beijing was originally depicted as being somewhat censorious of Chatichai's initiatives. If China conforms to the UNTAC framework, differences between Thailand and China on Phnom Penh are fewer. On the other hand, China's ability to continue to intervene directly in Khmer affairs depends on Thai military facilities. The military's connection to the Khmer Rouge was one of the structural contradictions of policy in the Chatichai government. At the same time that the prime minister's policy advisers railed against the suggestion of U.S. lethal assistance to the Khmer resistance, the Thai army was the conduit for lethal assistance to the Khmer Rouge.

Concerns about the Thai army's role in Indochina politics became more salient after the February 1991 military coup in Thailand that overturned the Chatichai government and imposed a non-constitutional military junta calling itself the National Peace-keeping Council (NPKC). Although NPKC spokesmen insisted that there would be no change in Thai policy on Indochina, initial indicators suggested some modification. Some economic overtures toward Phnom Penh were canceled. A visit to Bangkok by Vietnamese premier Do Muoi was postponed. The senior officers of Chulamklao Military Academy Class 5 who made the coup were heavily involved in the forging of the Sino-Thai military relationship. During the year-long technocratic administration of interim prime minister Anand Panyarachun, however, Thailand and Vietnam moved ever closer. In September 1991, Foreign Minister Arsa Sarasin visited Hanoi and a Joint Economic Commission was established.[17] In October, Vietnamese prime minister Vo Van Kiet arrived in Bangkok for a three-day visit aimed at consolidating a long-term cooperative relationship.[18] In January 1992, Anand made the first ever visit by a Thai prime minister to Hanoi, following by a week Thai military chief General Suchinda Kraprayoon's reception in Hanoi.[19]

The short-lived assumption of the premiership by General Suchinda in April–May 1992 gave some indication that a fully military-dictated policy toward Thailand's eastern neighbors would not be wholly congenial to Thai–Vietnamese reconciliation. Vietnam criticized Suchinda's government through the columns of *Nhan Dan,* describing his appointment as "nothing other than a second coup d'etat."[20] A perceived slight by General Suchinda to Khmer Prince Sihanouk raised questions about Thai intentions in western Cambodia, already thoroughly penetrated by Thai military enterprises.[21] Suchinda's foreign minister, Pongpol Adireksarn, a long-time director of Express Transport Organization (ETO), which monopolized at high rates road transport to Laos, said he wanted to visit Vientiane to set the record straight after a Lao textbook accused ETO of exploiting Laos.[22]

Toward the Normalization of ASEAN–Vietnam Economic Relations

The converging policies of Indonesia and Thailand positioned ASEAN for reconciliation with Vietnam. ASEAN diplomacy became single-tracked without "front line" or "rear." The next problem was how to make the transition from a special diplomatic structure to solve the particular conflict question in Cambodia to a regional international order that would provide stability and security in a unified Southeast Asia. Even while the multilateral process was disengaging the great powers from the Cambodian conflict and the Khmer factions continued their political and military efforts at one-upmanship, the ASEAN and Indochinese states began seriously to consider the structures and processes that will regulate their international interactions in the postsettlement Southeast Asian political economy. With respect to Cambodia itself, if there is full implementation of the comprehensive settlement, the security of its political identity will be a matter of international guarantee as provided for by the comprehensive settlement. Vietnam will have the same obligations as Thailand and other countries to safeguard Cambodia's independence and neutrality and refrain from any interference in Cambodia's internal affairs. Certainly more determinative than Cambodia's future status in shaping the regional international order will be the quality of the relations beginning now to be forged among Vietnam and, in an only partially derivative manner, Laos and the ASEAN states collectively and bilaterally.

Laos is a special case that cannot simply be paired with Cambodia or Vietnam in any discussion of the relations of the Indochinese states with ASEAN or other regional groupings. There is little reason to expect that the formerly existing "special relationship" between Laos and Vietnam will endure. In its place we see the reassertion of the "traditional" relationship between Thailand and Laos in which Thai economic influence is buttressed by cultural affinities. From the low point of winter 1987–88 military confrontation over the disputed Mekong border area of Ban Rom Klao that began with General Chavalit's November 1988 visit to Vientiane, Thailand and Laos have created a variety of institutional structures for economic cooperation between the two states; a joint Thai-Lao Border Committee acts to reduce security tensions. In November 1990, Prime Minister Chatichai made an official visit to Laos, marking the great improvement over two years in the relationship between the two countries.[23] Thai economic activity in Laos, where by the end of 1990 some 600 Thai companies were registered to do business, has led to an essentially unequal economic relationship with Thailand winning, as one Lao commentary put it, through the strategy of the marketplace what it could not win on the battlefield.[24] The integration of Laos in *Suwannaphume* gave it special priority in Thai policy ahead of the rest of Indochina and Burma.[25] On February 19, 1992, Thailand and Laos signed the Treaty of Amity and Cooperation, the first such treaty ever signed by Laos.[26] The concrete symbol of the new relationship was the inauguration on November 24, 1991, of the construction of the first bridge across the Mekong linking the two countries, appropriately named the Mittraphap (Friendship) Bridge.[27]

Contrary to the Thai *Suwannaphume* or center–periphery model of its relationships with the Indochina states, the bilateral model Vietnam appears to be seeking with its former ASEAN rivals seems to be patterned on its emerging relations with Indonesia. At the end of Suharto's visit, the two countries signed an agreement on economic, trade, scientific, and technological cooperation. In addition, they agreed to set up a joint ministerial level commission to further promote ties between them.[28] Referring to the newly established Vietnam-

Indonesian Commission, Foreign Minister Nguyen Co Thach proposed that Thailand and Vietnam revive their joint commission established in 1978 (before the invasion of Cambodia) to pursue ties ranging from trade and investment to culture and sport.[29] In January 1991, during Vietnamese deputy prime minister Vo Van Kiet's visit to Kuala Lumpur, his Malaysian counterpart Ghafar Baba announced the setting up of a Vietnam-Malaysian joint commission to expand bilateral functional ties between the two states.[30] This followed up an official visit to Hanoi in February 1990 by a delegation headed by the Malaysian Foreign Ministry's secretary general at which expanded bilateral trade and economic ties had been discussed.[31] A Thai-Vietnamese Joint Economic Commission was finally established in September 1991.[32] The establishment of bilateral joint commissions provides a planning framework within which Vietnam can seek to direct strategic investment. It also provides a structure through which the operation of the relatively open market economies of the ASEAN states can be articulated with the command-directed Vietnamese economy.

Through the joint commissions, Vietnam seeks to promote joint ventures with ASEAN states. Within the framework of expanded cooperation between Indonesia and Vietnam, the two countries plan to encourage joint ventures in petroleum, port construction, air transport, tourism, agriculture, forestry, and banking. The Malaysian-Vietnamese discussions have been about petroleum, the rehabilitation of rubber estates, and tourism. Malaysia's state-owned oil company, Petronas, has won two concessions in Vietnam, making Malaysia Vietnam's largest ASEAN investor. Malaysian prime minister Mahathir spent five days in Vietnam in April 1992 to promote increased investment and trade between the two countries. He was accompanied by nearly 200 officials and businessmen. After the signing of a number of agreements on cooperative undertakings, *Nhan Dan* (People's Daily) editorialized that Vietnamese-Malaysian cooperation was "an important factor in building a new Southeast Asia."[33] Thailand sees in joint ventures the possibility of resolving issues in the sensitive jurisdictional areas of maritime space. For example, the Thais have agreed in principle with Vietnam to expand their joint fishing enterprise into broader marine ventures that would include fishing, shipyard, cold storage, processing, fishmeal, canning, and aquaculture.[34] Implementation, however, has been delayed.[35] The Thais have also seriously proposed that the contested areas of the Gulf of Thailand be treated as a "Joint Development Area" for petroleum exploitation explicitly modeled after the Thai-Malaysian "Joint Development Area."[36] The Vietnamese have also proposed to the Thais that the long-dormant Mekong Lower Basin Development Project be reactivated.[37] A concerted effort is being made to establish Bangkok as the financial hub for Indochina.

Singapore's government hung back at first from the ASEAN rush to embrace Vietnam economically, but its posture was ambiguous. On the one hand, it alone of the ASEAN states clung rhetorically to the policy of economic sanctions, but Singapore private businessmen were free to buy and sell. By 1991, two-way trade between Singapore and Vietnam was valued at U.S. $868 million, a nearly eightfold increase from 1989, outstripping Japan's $709 million and making Singapore Vietnam's largest trading partner.[38] Investment remained blocked, however. Prime Minister Lee Kuan Yew, meeting Vietnam's Deputy Prime Minister Vo Van Kiet in Switzerland in February 1990, reiterated that a resumption of cooperation and economic relations was contingent on a settlement of the Cambodian problem.[39] This was made more specific in October 1990, when the Singapore Foreign Ministry stated that in the wake of "significantly improved prospects for a comprehensive political settlement in Cambodia," Singapore would lift the ban on investments in Vietnam and Cambodia once the Cambodian Supreme National Council was represented in the United Nations. The ban was lifted in November 1991, following the signing of the Paris Agreements. In the first six months following the lifting of the restrictions against Singaporean investment, ten projects worth U.S. $30 million were approved by Vietnam.[40] A strong boost to even closer ties between Singapore and Vietnam was given by Senior Minister (former Prime Minister) Lee Kuan Yew's April 1992 visit to Vietnam. During the course of his itinerary, Lee counseled the Vietnamese on economic development strategy and the operation of the market system.[41] Vo Van Kiet claimed that the Lee visit marked a turning point in Singapore–Vietnam relations.[42] The rapidly burgeoning Singapore–Vietnam connection suggests that Thailand will not be exclusive in incorporating Vietnam into *Suwannaphume*.

The increasing levels of ASEAN trade and investment have been important inputs into Vietnam's stuttering economy, particularly while potential major players like Japan, Taiwan, South Korea, and multilateral agencies like the IMF and the ADB deferred to United States sensibilities about sanctions. Moreover, the officially reported ASEAN presence in the Vietnamese economy does not take into account the large illegal trade with Singapore and Thailand that is a key part of the Vietnamese "shadow" economy.[43] But what importance beyond the limited direct economic gains does Vietnam assign to the normalizing of its relations with the ASEAN states? A Hanoi *People's Daily* article at the end of 1990 suggests one spillover: "The improvement of relations between our country and Southeast Asian countries is the most important factor in defeating the hostile blockade policy of the past 10 years against Vietnam."[44] Good relations with ASEAN open the prospects for more diversified economic relations with the Western industrial nations. Trade, aid, and investment from the ASEAN states alone will not be the external stimulus for Vietnamese reconstruction. That will have to come from Japan, the United States, and the EEC. As a senior Vietnamese official indicated to one of Thailand's most respected journalists: "Despite the admiration of ASEAN economic dynamism, the Vietnamese leaders however do not want their country to be the ASEAN's backburner by accepting its second-class technology."[45] If there is to be an external engine of growth for Vietnam it will not be ASEAN, but rather Japan, performing the role for Indochina that it has performed for ASEAN since the Second Indochina War.[46]

Japan's role in Vietnam has been limited by Tokyo's unwillingness to get too far out ahead of the U.S. policy of continued sanctions against Vietnam. The resumption of Official Development Assistance has been on hold waiting for the signal that Washington is satisfied that its conditions for normalization have been met. On the other hand, by spring 1992 it was clear that Japan was becoming impatient and that bilateral aid relations might be established even as Japan continued to hew to the U.S. line in multilateral funding agencies.[47]

A constraint operating to limit economic integration of Vietnam into the ASEAN political economy has to do with structural impediments in Vietnam itself. The ASEAN states, no less than Japan and the EEC, are finding that the infrastructural and regulative deficiencies in Vietnam are major constraints on Vietnam's capability to absorb investment and conduct commercial transactions. This is compounded by Vietnam's domestic political struggle. The proponents of the theory of a rapid ASEANization of Vietnam cannot be heartened by the tension-filled contest in Vietnam over the political requirements for economic reconstruction; that is, the ongoing debate about political liberalization in Vietnam. On the one hand, there are the reformers who argue that economic renovation (*doi moi*) requires greater political pluralism. On the other hand, there is the politically ascendant group that in 1990 through the eighth, ninth, and tenth plenums of the 6th Party Congress insisted on a line that rejects pluralism and adheres to rigid Marxist-Leninist political orthodoxy about the monopolistic role of the Communist party in the state. This is the line that was approved at the June 1991 7th Party Congress.[48] While it may be true, in the words of one analyst, that "there is growing consensus among elite elements in the socialist nations of Indochina that the key to future economic prosperity lies in the further integration of their economies with the Asian 'NICs' and the ASEAN nations (as well as China and Japan),"[49] that consensus obviously does not yet extend to the party leadership.

Vietnam in an Expanded ASEAN?

The bilateral efforts by Vietnam for integration into the regional economy have been symbolically matched by a Vietnamese pre-petition for membership in ASEAN, adding a regional political dimension to the reconciliation process. The presumed Vietnamese requirement for normalized economic relations with the ASEAN nations almost assumes incorporation of Vietnam into the ASEAN corporate structure. Premier Do Muoi's statement, "we wish to join ASEAN very much,"[50] was translated into a more official knock at the ASEAN door in the joint communiqué at the end of Suharto's November Hanoi visit:

> Prompted by the desire to contribute to the consolidation of peace, stability and cooperation in the region, the Vietnamese leaders reiterated Vietnam's wish to accede to ASEAN's Treaty of Amity and Cooperation in Southeast Asia signed in 1976, and at a later stage to join ASEAN.[51]

The prospect of possible future membership in ASEAN has been dangled as a political enticement for a Cambodian settlement for a number of years. It was rejected by a Hanoi leadership that once perceived ASEAN as a tool of Western imperialism and a proto-anti-Vietnamese military alliance. Certainly a case now can be made for an expanded ASEAN as a consultative forum for conflict resolution and economic policy harmonization.[52] But the simple extension of the experience of the ASEAN six to a future ASEAN nine (or even ten, if Burma is included), while seductive, is misleading. As I have written elsewhere,[53] the discussion of Indochina in ASEAN thus far has been centered on the issues clustered around making peace in Cambodia, thus ending Southeast Asia's Cold War. In the longer term, however, it is important to understand that ASEAN is not simply a geographical concept. Its founding was underpinned by certain minimum common values in a well-defined regional political economy. These values are not shared by Burma or the socialist states of Indochina. The fact that the socialist states are making pragmatic adjustments in economic policies has not yet changed the fundamental structure of the state itself, a structure quite unlike those of the ASEAN six. ASEAN unity is going to be difficult enough to maintain among like-minded states without diluting it with membership of non-like-minded states. That would lower the common denominator of consensus decision making to a policy-paralyzing level.

The ASEAN Treaty of Amity and Cooperation

What would be the modalities for the "ASEANizing" of Vietnam? It seems to be generally agreed that the first step would be Vietnam's accession to the Treaty of Amity and Cooperation in Southeast Asia (TAC) signed at the February 1976 Bali ASEAN summit as amended in Manila in December 1987.[54] During Vietnamese premier Vo Van Kiet's travels to Indonesia, Thailand, and Singapore in late October and early November 1991, "significant successes" were achieved in gaining support for Hanoi to sign the TAC, with leaders in the three ASEAN countries welcoming Vietnam's desire to join it.[55] This was seen by Vietnam as a "first step," to be followed by participation in the ASEAN dialogue, and finally, in the "long-term" membership in ASEAN itself.[56]

The terms of the TAC leave it open for accession by other states in Southeast Asia, a deliberate invitation in 1976 to Vietnam to accept true peaceful coexistence. In the treaty, the signatories placed in a binding legal framework the principles of peace and functional cooperation that were already embodied in ASEAN's founding 1967 Bangkok Declaration and the Declaration of ASEAN Concord that was made simultaneously with the TAC. In other words, a state could come within the ASEAN system of cooperation—could become "ASEAN-ized" so to say—without being a member of ASEAN, but a state could not be a member of ASEAN without signing the TAC. Nor is there anything in the treaty that would *ipso facto* guarantee ASEAN membership to a non-ASEAN signatory. The privilege of accession to the TAC was extended to states outside of Southeast Asia in the 1987 protocol amending the treaty (Article l). The case in point was Papua New Guinea, whose accession to the TAC was agreed upon at the July 1987 ASEAN foreign ministers' meeting but whose application for ASEAN membership was declined.[57] What is interesting is the difference in language governing accession by a Southeast Asian state and a state outside of Southeast Asia. The protocol states: "It [the Treaty of Amity and Cooperation] shall be open for accession by other states in Southeast Asia. States outside Southeast Asia may also accede to this Treaty by the consent of all the States in Southeast Asia which are signatories to this Treaty and Brunei Darussalam." Brunei was not an original signatory of the treaty, coming into ASEAN only on January 7, 1984. Brunei's accession to the treaty as a member of ASEAN was part of the "Declaration of Admission of Brunei."[58]

What is consequential about the difference in language between the two clauses is that any member state has a veto over the accession of a state outside of Southeast Asia. This in fact occurred in the run-up to the Fourth Singapore ASEAN Summit in January 1992 when Indonesia objected to a Thai-Singapore proposal to invite the UN Security Council's Permanent Five to accede to the Treaty of Amity and Cooperation,[59] although the Final Declaration sought recognition by the United Nations for the treaty.[60] With respect to Vietnam's accession to the TAC, which some had expected to occur at the summit, the Singapore Declaration simply repeated the earlier language welcoming accession to the TAC by all countries in Southeast Asia. In a press conference following the signing of the summit documents, Indonesian foreign minister Alatas suggested that the ASEAN foreign ministers would meet with their Lao and Vietnamese counterparts to ascertain the latter's intentions regarding accession to TAC.[61] It seems clear that, notwithstanding public official statements, political enthusiasm for Vietnam's early "ASEANization" is not evenly shared among ASEAN's member states. Despite the appearance of an open invitation, ASEAN's regular decision-making process—consultation and consensus—would be required once a formal request for accession to the TAC is received.

Assuming its expected eventual accession to the TAC, just exactly what kind of obligations would Vietnam undertake beyond the endorsement of the general normative values and principles governing relations between friendly peace-loving states? Where the treaty breaks new ground is in its provisions for the pacific settlement of disputes (Chapter IV: Articles 13–17). It introduces a mechanism called the High Council as a continuing body to operate through mediation, inquiry, and conciliation to assist in settling disputes. The High Council does not originate jurisdiction. All parties to a dispute must agree to its intervention. Even if the High Council acts, there are no means of imposing sanctions. In the words of one ASEAN international lawyer, "the voluntary nature of the mechanism is thus based upon compromise rather than binding decision."[62] This less than onerous burden on the signatories is rendered for all intents and purposes nugatory by the fact that the High Council—the "continuing body"—has yet to be constituted after a decade-and-a-half. Furthermore, no ASEAN state has ever applied for relief in a dispute with another ASEAN state to the provisions of the treaty. The problem for the future is not whether Vietnam will abide by the provisions of the Treaty of Amity and Cooperation, but whether it will fit within ASEAN as a security community in the sense that no ASEAN state expects force to be used by another ASEAN state in the pursuit of competitive national interests.

Vietnam in ASEAN: The Economic Dimension

Vietnam's understanding that membership in ASEAN would be a "long-term matter" underlines the fact that, for reasons to be discussed below, there is no sense of urgency felt on either side for the expansion of ASEAN. Both Hanoi and ASEAN seem satisfied with a general notion, as put by the Vietnamese deputy foreign minister in Singapore during Premier Vo Van Kiet's November 1991 visit, that although there has not yet been a formal application, "In the future, I think that probably Vietnam will be a member if other members of ASEAN accept."[63] Assuming, therefore, that eventually the next step in the "ASEANizing" of Vietnam would be formal membership in the grouping, how would that occur?

Although ASEAN has no explicit rules for joining, we should expect that the same procedure used for Brunei in 1984 would be applicable here. Members considered Brunei's application in terms of ASEAN's 1967 declaration, which stated that it was open for participation by all Southeast Asian states subscribing to its aims, principles, and purposes. It was through the unanimous expression of agreement by the ASEAN foreign ministers that Brunei became ASEAN's sixth member; and Brunei through its foreign minister agreed to subscribe or accede as the case might be to all declarations and treaties of ASEAN.[64]

Until the Vietnamese premier's official visit to Singapore in late 1991, Singaporean officials had been the most cautious about Vietnam's membership in ASEAN. Deputy Prime Minister Lee Hsien Loong noted that cooperation between ASEAN and Vietnam is possible, but "cooperation within ASEAN significantly widens the scope of the problem."[65] He pointed out: "Antagonists do not become bosom friends overnight. It is not a matter of lingering doubts but it is a question of some time needed for adjustments for policy shift." In Lee's view, the gap between Vietnam and ASEAN in terms of economic standards, management style, and so forth, will mean great problems of fitting Vietnam into ASEAN. To Lee's caveats we could add a list of other issues that have operated to slow the convergence of Vietnamese and ASEAN interests in a multilateral framework.

There is the problem of Vietnamese refugees scattered in camps throughout Southeast Asia. This "boat people" problem will persist as long as the twin "pull" of better economic conditions and the increasingly distant hope of third-country resettlement motivates people to leave Vietnam. The screening programs put in place in Malaysia, for example, showed that three-quarters of the so-called refugees were economic migrants. The unraveling of the June 1989 Geneva "Comprehensive Plan of Action" on Vietnamese refugees underlines the essential political dimension of what is viewed by many outside of Southeast Asia as a humanitarian and human rights issue. Jurisdictional conflicts in the South China Sea will continue to plague relations between Vietnam and some of the ASEAN states. Malaysia and the Philippines have claimed territorial overlaps with Vietnam in the strategic and potentially energy rich islands, reefs, and waters in the Spratlys. This, of course is complicated by China's claims to the same territory and resources. Intractability on certain issues is illustrated by the fact that despite Indonesia's "dual track" diplomacy and expression of a special relationship with Vietnam, Vietnam's reluctance to negotiate a settlement of its continental shelf dispute with Indonesia to the north of the Natuna Islands has not been overcome.

The lack of a real economic "fit" between Vietnam and ASEAN is another impediment to a rapid integration of Vietnam into the ASEAN political economy. This has become even more apparent since the 1992 Singapore summit decision to establish an ASEAN Free Trade Area (AFTA) utilizing the mechanism of the Common Effective Preferential Tariff (CEPT). ASEAN's new efforts to enhance complementaries heightens the impression that Vietnam is likely to emerge more as a competitor with the ASEAN economies rather than a cooperative partner in a number of ways. In the first place, it will expect in the post-Cambodia order a much larger share of the development assistance pie than it has had in the past. This will come from a shrinking regional assistance pie in a zero-sum competition with the other ASEAN claimants. Of particular significance will be the reallocation of Japanese Official Development Assistance and the investment that follows in its wake. Vietnam will also emerge as a direct competitor in some ASEAN states' traditional export areas. There is also a Vietnamese potential to attract investment that might otherwise go to an ASEAN country. Despite its infrastructure problems, the literate labor force and lower labor costs will become increasingly attractive to low and intermediate technology manufacturing ventures. Tight state control and the absence of "green" NGOs also will make Vietnam a magnet for "dirty" industries, the presence of which is already becoming an irritant in ASEAN. It is not without reason that Singapore's Lee Kuan Yew, who certainly should know the requirements, predicted that Vietnam would become an Asian economic "tiger."[66]

The question to be posed is, what economic advantages would accrue to ASEAN and Vietnam from Vietnamese membership in ASEAN that would not be available in the process of bilateral normalization? From the vantage point of ASEAN's putative underlying economic purposes, we would point out here that up to now there are no demonstrable economic advantages. ASEAN still cannot be shown to have directly contributed to the economic growth of any ASEAN state through its internal economic arrangements. The relationship between

ASEAN and economic development has to be found in its internal political arrangements leading to intra-ASEAN stability and a positive political climate for economic development. Its economic importance is to be found in its external function as the regionalist contact point with the global market economy.

A possible intermediate step in ASEAN–Vietnam reconciliation is to associate the Indochinese states with ASEAN in a less than full membership status. As a prominent Indonesian analyst has suggested: "These countries could be given observer status until their economic development becomes more compatible with the rest of Southeast Asia."[67] I would point out, however, that observer status has yet to lead to membership for Papua New Guinea. The same writer proposes that ASEAN could even adopt a two-track membership scheme: one, the current membership committed to integrative behavior in the ASEAN Free Trade Area; the other, new members who would undertake functional economic cooperation. While taking into account the problem of economic fit, these kinds of schemes beg the question of ASEAN's political dimension and how less than full membership would affect regional harmony and solidarity, the touchstone of the so-called "ASEAN way."

Ironically, Vietnam is turning to ASEAN just as ASEAN itself seeks to restructure its own internal and external economic relationships. The only truly integrative economic activity that is taking place is at the sub-ASEAN levels of cooperation. The most obvious example is the "growth triangle" strategy that is linking Singapore, Indonesia's Riau archipelago, and Malaysia's Johore state. First mooted by Singapore prime minister Goh Chok Tong in December 1989, the concept has been blessed by President Suharto and Prime Minister Mahathir with infrastructure and commercial projects now under way.[68] The "growth triangle" approach has been described as a "mini-ASEAN," much more manageable and workable for real economic cooperation than structures embracing the entire region. A second proposed northern "growth triangle" is the Medan–Penang–Hadyai (South Thailand) region.[69] Intrigued by the idea, even the Philippines has offered a (unspecified) site for a "growth triangle."[70] Although not a "growth triangle" as such, the Thai notion of the *Suwannaphume* consists of subregional economic cooperation and integration, with Thailand as the economic core of a continental Southeast Asian geoeconomy. The Thai vision seems to have Bangkok performing the same economic functions for its neighbors as Singapore does in the southern "triangle." As we have already noted for the Thai-Lao bilateral relationship, this kind of economic "partnership" envisioned may have "neocolonial" overtones.

Above the ASEAN level of economic cooperation, there are strong pressures for larger cooperative structures to perform the tasks that ASEAN does in its six-on-one "dialogues." The Asia-Pacific Economic Cooperation (APEC) scheme launched in November 1989 is the most outstanding example of this.[71] With the inclusion in 1991 of China, Taiwan, and Hong Kong, APEC has become an increasingly inclusive multilateral forum for the developed and developing economies of the Pacific rim region. Less inclusive is the concept of the East Asia Economic Grouping (EAEG), promoted most enthusiastically by Malaysia's Prime Minister Mahathir. The EAEG, which excludes North America, is a reaction to the breakdown of GATT's Uruguay round and moves beyond the idea of cooperative consultation among trading partners in the direction of a defensive trading bloc.[72] Although the scheme has been received coolly by potential members, it is being discussed diplomatically and is officially on ASEAN's agenda.[73] With a name change from "grouping" to "caucus," a formal ASEAN decision on the EAEC was postponed at the Fourth ASEAN Summit. Both APEC and the EAEC were recognized in the Singapore Declaration of the ASEAN heads of government as important concepts in the consultative process on the structuring of regional multilateral organization. Whatever eventually emerges as the appropriate vehicle with respect to Vietnam, we can already say that while there may be a "certain inevitability" to Vietnam's integration into the ASEAN and Asian NIC (newly industrialized country) economic system,[74] it will not necessarily be through the framework of an ASEAN whose economic functions are being superseded at the same time as its political viability is being questioned.

Vietnam in ASEAN: The Political/Security Dimension

Turning to that political dimension of ASEAN, the problem again is "fit." There can be no argument but that Vietnamese membership in ASEAN would add to Vietnam's international rehabilitation, conferring the mantle of ASEAN legitimacy on it. This would be a symbolic gesture for the reunification of the two Southeast Asias. Beyond this, however, would it have functional consequences in the way in which international politics is transacted in Southeast Asia? That is, would Vietnam be brought within an organizationally coherent regional political process? For example, the case can be made that within the ASEAN framework irritations and disputes between Vietnam and other ASEAN states, such as exist in the South China Sea, could be resolved and conflict avoided.

It is generally agreed among analysts both from ASEAN states and outside that ASEAN's identity as a significant Third World grouping is political. More specifically, the ASEAN "success story" is a measure of the six states' political solidarity over more than a decade in maintaining a common front against Vietnam's policy in Cambodia. This is not a particularly original statement. Most analysts would accept that it was the Vietnamese "threat" that animated ASEAN political solidarity.[75] Sheldon Simon has written that the Vietnamese challenge was the "catalyst for ASEAN's newfound political coordination."[76] If it is possible to speak of an ASEAN political community founded on an appreciation of common interest, that interest has to be couched largely in terms of security defined regionally by the perception of a Soviet-backed Vietnamese threat. Intra-ASEAN political harmony and conflict avoidance was a necessary measure to maintain the common front against the external threat. The notion of ASEAN as a "security community," while perhaps accurate, may have been induced by external threat rather than a result of political similarity, culture, ideology, and history. What will be the practical effect on security politics in Southeast Asia when (if) ASEAN and Indochina, the two previously competitive "security communities" in the "Southeast Asian security complex"[77]—to use Barry Buzan's terms—merge? Obviously, the dynamic inspiration of ASEAN—containment of Vietnam—will be transformed. The pertinent question is whether ASEAN as a politically coherent grouping can survive without an external enemy. I would agree with Michael Leiffer that the current ASEAN has not been able to promote regional security to the extent of forging a structure based on common values and interests.[78] It will be even less likely to do so with the incorporation of Vietnam. In the absence of a Vietnam threat, the differing threat perceptions will make community political solidarity more difficult to achieve even if Vietnam were to subscribe to ASEAN's rules of the game. The lack of consensus on alternative U.S. military facilities in Southeast Asia or reactions to the Gulf crisis is indicative of this. A division already exists in the contrasting strategic concerns of the continental as opposed to maritime-oriented ASEAN states. While Thailand continues to be preoccupied with its mainland neighbors, a new "security complex" is developing in the South China Sea. No less a figure than Indonesia's former foreign minister Mochtar Kusumaatmadja has proposed a formal military relationship among Indonesia, Singapore, and Malaysia.[79] Indonesia's Minister for Defense and Security has called for extra efforts to help expand defense ties among the three countries.[80] It is unlikely that any military alliance will develop, but a sub-ASEAN consensus on security cooperation is emerging among the ASEAN states of the South China Sea littoral.[81]

Where would Vietnam fit into a "Vietnam-threatless" ASEAN? It has been suggested that in fact there may be an external threat that would connect Vietnam in a community of interests with the ASEAN six: the People's Republic of China. Certainly part of Indonesia's motivation in pursuing its "dual track" diplomacy was because it saw Vietnam as a potential buffer or ally against China. There is some evidence that this feeling is reciprocated by Vietnam. As a Thai commentator put it, "closer Vietnam–Indonesia ties enable Jakarta to deal with Beijing more confidently. Vietnam sees Indonesia as an ally that shares a common mistrust of China."[82] This shared interest already seems to be at work in the South China Sea conflict zone. Indonesian foreign minister Ali Alatas's proposal for opening a peace process there has been strongly supported by Vietnam.[83] We would caution, however, that Vietnamese orientations toward China are very complex. There are obviously elements of a shared political culture as both leaderships attempt to achieve economic restructuring while leaving the Communist party's authority unchallenged. The November 1991 Sino-Vietnamese summit, which normalized relations between the two states, was driven at least in part by ideology as well as more pragmatic considerations. Certainly in terms of political values, Hanoi and Beijing have much more in common with one another than either does with the ASEAN states.[84]

Until the time is ripe for more ambitious regional security guarantees, and given the diluting impact Indochinese membership in ASEAN will have, it would appear that promotion of security interests in a unified ASEAN–Indochina "security complex" will be a function of the operation of a very traditional balance of power where distribution is independent of ASEAN the collectivity. An important variable, given the absence of the USSR in the configuration of such a balance, will be what role the local actors wish the United States to play. With the termination of the U.S. basing agreement with the Philippines, a continued forward presence of American military forces in Southeast Asia will require some new arrangements. This is obvious with respect to the Straits states where the enhanced U.S. access to facilities in Singapore, granted in 1990, has been symbolically balanced by Malaysia, the most vigorous exponent of ZOPFAN, in its 1992 agreement to expand military cooperation with the United States.[85] The U.S. has explored other points of access as well. Even Indonesia, which criticized the U.S.–Singapore arrangement as opposed to the principles of ZOPFAN, has agreed to some new forms of cooperation with the United States.[86] Although Indonesia now officially at least is unconcerned about the U.S. presence in Singapore, there remains an undercurrent of distrust and suspicion—in the words of the former head of Indonesia's National Defense Institute, "certain secret scheming behind the agreement. . . ."[87]

It is possible to conceive of a Southeast Asian order with Vietnam at a northern continental pole and Indonesia at the southern maritime flank as the major regional actors in a balance of power. Vietnam, resisting both the push of China and the pull of Thailand, its own hegemonial pretensions dashed, would be a link between both the continental and maritime strategic spheres. Any future Indonesian hegemonial ambitions would be harder to achieve in such a balance-of-power system as opposed to the Indonesia-centric ASEAN.

This does not mean that broader concerns about future regional security do not exist. In fact, the predictability of the Cold War balance has been replaced by the uncertainties of the longer-range political and military ambitions and capabilities of other external actors: China, Japan, and even India. There has existed in the past a notional basis for creating a Southeast Asian "security complex." This, of course, is the ZOPFAN. By "subscribing and adhering" to ASEAN, Vietnam would automatically accept the terms of the 1971 Kuala Lumpur Declaration.[88] On the other hand, one can question today the relevance of ZOPFAN, at least in its "Cold War" origins, to the contemporary problems of the distribution of power in Southeast Asia with the disappearance of one of the two superpowers. This seems implied in the Singapore Declaration's statement on ZOPFAN: "ASEAN will seek to realize the Zone of Peace, Freedom and Neutrality (ZOPFAN) and a Southeast Asian Nuclear Weapons Free Zone (SEANWFZ) in consultation with friendly countries, *taking into account changing circumstances*" (emphasis added).

Without going into a discussion of both the normative and practical aspects of a ZOPFAN, it is enough to say that such a zone cannot be implemented without recognition by or support of non-regional actors with security interests in Southeast Asia. This is unlikely to occur outside of a broader, more comprehensive security framework for the East Asian and Pacific region. Note, for example, the Australian and Canadian propositions for a comprehensive security forum similar to the CSCE or even a pan-Asian security organization.[89] It is this kind of pressure that has forced the ASEAN leaderships to address openly the need to discuss common security concerns with interested parties beyond ASEAN circles. While still unwilling to set up a new mechanism to deal with security issues, at the Singapore summit they did agree to intensify their external dialogues in political and security matters through the ASEAN Post-Ministerial Conferences.[90] The addition of China and India as new ASEAN dialogue partners also seems designed to broaden the security dimension of ASEAN's exchanges. Malaysia has offered to host an Asia-Pacific security dialogue as a confidence-building measure, thus maintaining the momentum for the creation of some new framework for the articulation of common regional security interests.[91] The structure most often cited as a possible model is Europe's CSCE. Movement in this direction might be coordinated with an expansion of APEC, taking in not only the three Chinas but also Russia and Indochina. It is even possible that security issues will be included in the discussion of the EAEC in a way that would make more politically palatable in Southeast Asia an enhanced Japanese security role. Until a more comprehensive multilateral security "forum" is established, however, the traditional formats will have to suffice despite the new conditions. These formats, in which bilateralism seems to be ASEAN's preferred approach and the United States is still an important partner, will only slowly be adjusted to accommodate Vietnam.

Conclusion

ASEAN–Indochina reconciliation is a process taking place on two levels: state to state (Vietnam–Indonesia, Vietnam–Thailand, and so forth), and state to the regional grouping (Vietnam–ASEAN). While the former process reinforces the latter, and perhaps is a necessary precondition in the minds of some ASEAN diplomats, progress in state-to-state relations do not automatically mean ASEAN membership for the Indochinese states. Nor is it clear what specific advantages would accrue to Vietnam through membership in ASEAN as long as the Hanoi leadership insists on ideological orthodoxy. Economically, Vietnam's interests will be best served through fuller access to Western markets, capital, and technology. These links will occur independent of ASEAN. Politically, membership in ASEAN would be a symbolic demonstration of the termination of Southeast Asia's own "Cold War." It would not, however, in the absence of new mechanisms for conflict resolution, change the way international politics operates in the region.

The importance attached to Vietnam's membership in ASEAN becomes even more problematical when set in the context of the general evolution of regionalism in East Asia. The APEC, EAEC, and Asian "CSCE" processes seem to be indicators of a broader East Asian political economy in which ASEAN may be subsumed. We can legitimately ask whether ASEAN has outgrown itself. No immediate resolution of the questions raised here should be expected. It is likely that ASEAN's leaders will attack their collective problems in the future as they have in the past, not through strategic planning, but through the work of reactive, ad hoc, incremental decision making.

Notes

1. *Agreement on a Comprehensive Political Settlement of the Cambodia Conflict.* Final Act of the Paris Conference on Cambodia, 23 October 1991. United Nations General Assembly/Security Council, Document A/46/608 S/23177.

2. ASEAN–Indochina relations in the immediate post–Second Indochina War period have been dealt with by the author in "The Emergence of Communist Indochina and Its Impact on the Security of Southeast Asia: Some Preliminary Indicators," in Yung-hwan Jo, ed., *U.S. Foreign Policy in Asia* (Santa Barbara: ABC-Clio, 1978), pp. 123–140; and "U.S. Policy and the Two Southeast Asias," *Asian Survey*, 18:4 (April 1978), pp. 408–421.

3. Detailed reportage of the Suharto state visit to Vietnam is given in Foreign Broadcast Information Service, *Daily Report—East Asia* (hereafter cited as *FBIS-EAS*), numbers 90-223–90-226, 19–23 November 1990 (s.v. "Vietnam").

4. *FBIS-EAS*, 90–226 (23 November 1990), p. 55.

5. Rodney Tasker, "Elusive Peace," *Far Eastern Economic Review*, 31 January 1991, pp. 19–20.

6. *FBIS-EAS*, 87-145 (29 July 1987), p. N–2.

7. The "road map" to American-Vietnamese normalization of relations laid out by Assistant Secretary of State Richard Soloman explicitly states the linkage between peace in Cambodia and relations with Vietnam. "Vietnam: The Road Ahead," statement by Richard Solomon, assistant secretary for East Asian and Pacific Affairs, *U.S. Department of State Dispatch*, 6 May 1991, pp. 330–332.

8. "Mochtar, Thach Get Down to Brass Tacks," *Straits Times*, 24 August 1985.

9. "Joint Communiqué" of the 18th ASEAN Ministerial Meeting, Kuala Lumpur, July 7–9, 1985, paragraph 42.

10. "Sihanouk Suggests 'Cocktail Party' for Warring Groups," *Straits Times*, 7 September 1985.

11. "Just Khmers for Cocktail Party," *Straits Times*, 19 November 1985.

12. The ICK "Declaration on Kampuchea" is reproduced in Donald E. Weatherbee, ed., *Southeast Asia Divided: The ASEAN–Indochina Crisis* (Boulder, CO: Westview Press, 1985), appendix VII, pp.123–124.

13. K. Das, "The Kuantan Principle," *Far Eastern Economic Review*, 4 April 1980, pp. 12–13.

14. The present author was a Senior Fellow at Bangkok's Institute of Security and International Studies, 1988–1989, the first year of Bangkok's opening to the East. See Donald E. Weatherbee, "Thailand in 1989: Democracy Ascendant in the Golden Peninsula," *Southeast Asian Affairs 1990* (Singapore: Institute of Southeast Asian Affairs, 1990), pp. 337–359.

15. Clark Neher, "Change in Thailand," *Current History*, March 1990, p. 102.

16. Paisal Sricharatchanya, "The Golden Land: Ambitious Thinking behind Indochina, Burma Links," *Far Eastern Economic Review*, 23 February 1989, pp. 11–12.

17. "Thai-Vietnam Economic Cooperation to Be Expanded," *Bangkok Post Weekly Review*, 4 October 1991.

18. "VN Premier in Milestone First Visit," *Bangkok Post Weekly Review*, 8 November 1991.

19. Murray Hiebert, "Building a Rapport: Thai-Vietnamese Ties Continue to Grow," *Far Eastern Economic Review*, 30 January 1992, p. 19.

20. "Anti-Suchinda Report in VN Paper Played Down," *Bangkok Post Weekly Review*, 24 April 1992.

21. "Choice of Thai Premier Likely to Upset Khmers," *Bangkok Post Weekly Review*, 17 April 1992.

22. "New FM Hopes to Clear ETO Image in Laos," *Bangkok Post Weekly Review*, 8 May 1992.

23. "Chatichai, Kaysone Hail Growth in Trade," *Bangkok Post Weekly Review*, 16 November 1990.

24. "Laos Berates 'Market' Policy," *Bangkok Post Weekly Review*, 16 July 1989.

25. "Laos to Get Priority in Links with Indochina," *Bangkok Post Weekly Review*, 3 May 1991.

26. "Thailand, Laos Sign Amity, Tourism Pacts," *Bangkok Post Weekly Review*, 28 February 1992.

27. "Three Nations Inaugurate Construction of Bridge," *Bangkok Post Weekly Review*, 6 December 1991.

28. "Jakarta and Hanoi Sign Accords," *Straits Times Weekly Overseas Edition*, 24 November 1990.

29. "Thach Calls for Summit to Boost VN-Thai Relations," *Bangkok Post Weekly Review*, 9 November 1990.

30. *FBIS-EAS*, 91-026, 7 February 1991, p. 30

31. "Malaysia and Hanoi to Expand Economic Ties," *Straits Times Weekly Overseas Edition*, 10 February 1990.

32. Murray Hiebert, "Steps to a Summit: Vietnam, Thailand Prepare for Landmark Agreement," *Far Eastern Economic Review*, 3 October 1991, p. 15.

33. "Malaysians Eye Bigger Vietnam Role," *Far Eastern Economic Review*, 30 April 1992, p. 14; "Malaysian Prime Minister Visits," *Indochina Digest*, 24 April 1992.

34. "Thailand-VN in Joint Fishing Pact," *Bangkok Post Weekly Review*, 7 December 1990.

35. "Vietnam Shelves Fisheries Accord," *Bangkok Post Weekly Review*, 24 January 1992.

36. "Thais Offer VN Deal on Disputed Waters," *Bangkok Post Weekly Review*, 23 November 1990.

37. "Thach Calls for Summit to Boost VN-Thai Relations," *Bangkok Post Weekly Review*, 9 November 1990.

38. Murray Hiebert, "See-saw fortunes: Vietnam Looks to Asia after Soviet Collapse," *Far Eastern Economic Review*, 14 May 1992, p. 56.

39. "Viet Minister Calls on PM Lee in Davos," *Straits Times Weekly Overseas Edition*, 10 February 1990.

40. "Hanoi Approves S'pore Projects Worth [Singapore] $49m," *Straits Times Weekly Overseas Edition*, 2 May 1992.

41. See the reportage on the Lee visit by Han Fook Kwang in *Straits Times Weekly Overseas Edition*, 2 May 1992.

42. "Lee Kuan Yew Warmly Received in Vietnam," *Indochina Digest*, 24 April 1992.

43. Michael Vatikiotis, "The Last Frontier: ASEAN Investment Helps to Buoy Vietnam's Economy," *Far Eastern Economic Review*, 27 June 1991, p. 52.

44. Le Ba Thuyen, "Some Traits in Today's International Situation," *Nhan Dan*, 30 December 14, 1990, as published in *FBIS-EAS*, 90-251, 31 December 1990, p. 72.

45. Kawi Chongkitthawon, "Vietnam's Backdoor to ASEAN," *The Nation*, 24 November 1990.

46. Richard Stubbs, "Geopolitics and the Political Economy of Southeast Asia," *International Journal*, 44:3 (Summer 1989), pp. 551ff.

47. Susumu Awanohara, "Decent Interval: Japan May Pre-empt US on Vietnam Aid," *Far Eastern Economic Review*, 30 April 1992, pp. 12–13.

48. An analysis of the internal debate through the eighth (March 1990) plenum is Charles A. Joiner, "The Vietnamese Communist Party Strives to Remain the 'Only Force,' " *Asian Survey*, 30:11 (November 1990), pp. 1053–1065. For the ninth plenum (August 1990), see Murray Hiebert, "Vietnam: Wasting Assets," *Far Eastern Economic Review*, 13 September 1990, pp. 18–20. For the tenth plenum (November 1990), see Murray Hiebert, "Vietnam: Hard Times," *Far Eastern Economic Review*, 13 December 1990, p. 13. For the 7th Party Congress, see Murray Hiebert, "More of the Same," *Far Eastern Economic Review*, 11 July 1991, pp. 10–11.

49. Charles Burton, "The Role of the NICs in Southeast Asia's Political and Economic Development," *International Journal* 44:3 (Summer 1989), p. 670.

50. As quoted by Murray Hiebert, "Vietnam: Into a Wider World," *Far Eastern Economic Review*, 22 November 1990, p. 17.

51. *FBIS-EAS*, 90–226, 23 November 1990, p. 56

52. Muthiah Alagappa,"Bringing Indochina into ASEAN," *Far Eastern Economic Review*, 29 June 1989, pp. 21–22.

53. Donald E. Weatherbee, "ASEAN—Southeast Asia's New Security Agenda," *Foreign Relations Journal* (Manila) 4:4 (December 1989), p. 14.

54. Texts as given in "Treaty of Amity and Cooperation in Southeast Asia, Bali, 24 February 1976," and "Protocol Amending the Treaty of Amity and Cooperation in Southeast Asia, Manila, 15 December 1987," published in ASEAN Secretariat, *ASEAN Documents Series 1967–1988*, pp. 39–44.

55. "VN Premier in Milestone First Visit," *Bangkok Post Weekly Review*, 8 November 1991; "S'pore Welcomes Viet Desire to Sign S-E Asian Amity Pact," *Straits Times Weekly Overseas Edition*, 2 November 1991; Murray Hiebert and Michael Vatikiotis, "ASEAN's Embrace: Vietnam Premier's Trip Leads to Improving Ties," *Far Eastern Economic Review*, 14 November 1991, p. 19.

56. News conference in Jakarta by Vietnamese deputy foreign minister Vu Khoan, "Hanoi to Open New Era of Co-operation," *Straits Times Weekly Overseas Edition*, 2 November 1991.

57. Yaw Saffu, "Papua New Guinea in 1987," *Asian Survey*, 28:2 (February 1988), p. 250; Donald E. Weatherbee, "Indonesia's Foreign Policy: The Maturation of Regional Power," paper prepared for Southeast Conference Association for Asian Studies, January 1988, pp. 23–24.

58. "Declaration of the Admission of Brunei Darussalam into the Association of Southeast Asian Nations, Jakarta, 7 January 1984," as given in ASEAN Secretariat, *ASEAN Documents Series 1967–1988*, p. 45

59. "Jakarta Blocks ASEAN Amity Move," *FBIS-EAS*, 92-016, 24 January 1992, p. 4.

60. "Singapore Declaration of 1992," text as published in *Thailand Foreign Affairs Newsletter*, 2/92.

61. "Alatas: Indonesia Satisfied with Summit Results," *FBIS-EAS*, 92-019, 29 January 1992, p. 5.

62. Vitit Muntarbhorn, *The Challenge of Law: Legal Cooperation among ASEAN Countries* (Bangkok: Institute of Security and International Studies, 1987), p. 19. See also the discussion of the conflict resolution provisions of the treaty in Purificacion V. Quisumbing, "Problems and Prospects of ASEAN Law: Towards a Legal Framework for Regional Dispute Settlement," in R.P. Anand and Purificacion V. Quisumbing, eds., *ASEAN: Identity, Development and Culture* (Manila: University of the Philippines Law Center, 1981), pp. 300–318.

63. "Vietnam Interested in Joining Regional Groups," *Straits Times Weekly Overseas Edition*, 15 November 1991.

64. "Declaration of the Admission of Brunei."

65. "Deputy Premier Lee Views Possible ASEAN Entry," *Straits Times*, 13 December 1990.

66. "Lee Kuan Yew Predicts Next 'Asian Tiger,' " *Indochina Digest*, 1 May 1992.

67. Jusuf Wanandi, "Looming Challenge for ASEAN," *Far Eastern Economic Review*, 23 January 1992, p. 15.

68. Pushpa Thambipillai, "The ASEAN Growth Triangle: The Convergence of National and Sub-National Interests," *Contemporary Southeast Asia*, 13:3 (December 1991), pp. 299–314.

69. "Growth Triangle 'Indicates What ASEAN Can Do,' " *Straits Times Weekly Overseas Edition*, 8 September 1990; N. Balakrishnan, "Logical Linkage," *Far Eastern Economic Review*, 3 Janauary 1991, pp. 38–39.

70. "Aquino Seeks Another Economic 'Growth Triangle,' " 92-017, 27 January 1992, p. 7.

71. Nusara Thaitawat, "APEC Becoming 'Economcally' Desirable," *Bangkok Post Weekly Review*, 2 February 1990; Shim Jae Hoon, "Growing-up Pains: Formalisation of APEC Grouping to Loom Large at Talks," *Far Eastern Economic Review*, 14 November 1991, p. 27.

72. Nigel Holloway, Anthony Rowley, Shada Islam, and Michael Vatikiotis, "An Insurance Policy: East Asian Trade Grouping at Top of Region's Agenda," *Far Eastern Economic Review*, 25 July 1991, pp. 52–56.

73. Pichai Chuensuksawadi, "Mahathir's Proposal for Asian Grouping Finds Little Backing," *Bangkok Post Weekly Review*, 22 March 1991; Anthony Rowley, "In The Bloc-Hole: Kaifu to Stall on East Asian Trade Group Plan," *Far Eastern Economic Review*, 17 January 1991, pp. 11–12.

74. Burton, "The Role of the NIC's in Souteast Asia's Political and Economic Development" p. 675.

75. For example, Michael Antolik, *ASEAN and the Diplomacy of Accommodation* (New York: M.E. Sharpe, 1990); Michael Leiffer, *ASEAN and the Security of South East Asia* (London: Routledge, Kegan Paul, 1987).

76. Sheldon W. Simon, *The ASEAN States and Regional Security* (Stanford, CA: Hoover Institution Press, 1982), p. 92.

77. Barry Buzan, "The Southeast Asian Security Complex," *Contemporary Southeast Asia*, 10:1 (June 1988), pp. 1–16. By "security complex" Buzan means "durable, and relatively self-contained patterns of security relations generated by the local states themselves."

78. Leiffer, *ASEAN and the Security of Southeast Asia*, p. 157.

79. Mochtar Kusuma-Atmadja, "Some Thoughts on ASEAN Security Cooperation: An Indonesian Perspective," *Contemporary Southeast Asia*, 12:3 (December 1990), pp. 161–171.

80. "Murdani: Let's Boost 3-way Defence Ties," *Straits Times Weekly Overseas Edition*, 10 August 1991.

81. Amitav Acharya, "The Association of Southeast Asian Nations: 'Security Community' or 'Defence Community'?" *Pacific Affairs*, 64 (Summer 1991), pp. 73–93; K.U. Menon, "An ASEAN Defence Community: Real or Imagined?" *Asia-Pacific Defence Reporter*, April 1991, pp. 28–30.

82. Kawi Chongkitthawon, "Vietnam's Backdoor to ASEAN."

83. "Spratly Islands: Jakarta's Next Target for Peace," *Straits Times Weekly Overseas Edition*, 12 January 1991.

84. Lincoln Kaye and Murray Hiebert, "A Lesson in Ideology: China, Vietnam Sign Trade and Border Pacts at Summit," *Far Eastern Economic Review*, 21 November 1991, pp. 10–11.

85. "Malaysia and US to Raise Status of Joint Exercises," *Straits Times Weekly Overseas Edition*, 13 February 1992; "KL to Expand Military Co-operation with US," *Straits Times Weekly Overseas Edition*, 11 April 1992.

86. "Permanent Bases Less Crucial Now, Says Cheney," *Straits Times Weekly Overseas Edition*, 2 May 1992.

87. Gen. Sayidiman Suryohadiprojo as quoted in "Move Should Not Cause Concern, Jakarta Reiterates," *Straits Times Weekly Overseas Edition*, 11 January 1992.

88. Text as given in *ASEAN Documents Series*, pp. 34–35.

89. "The New Disorder," *Far Eastern Economic Review*, 13 December 1990, p. 25.

90. *Singapore Declaration*.

91. Michael Vatikiotis, "Helsinki, Asian Style," *Far Eastern Economic Review*, 14 May 1992, p. 20.

Index